LEAVING WOODS CREEK

ONE MAN'S DISCOVERY OF "THE VOICE" OF GOD

LEAVING WOODS CREEK
BY JOHNNY MAYS

Is a publication of

NationaLight Ministries International Inc.

PO BOX 5 Thorp, Washington 98946

http://www.nationalight.net

TABLE OF CONTENTS

FORWARD

"The things that have always been important: to be a good man, to try to live my life the way God would have me, to turn it over to Him that His will might be worked in my life, to do my work without looking back, to give it all I've got, and to take pride in my work as an honest performer."

- Johnny Cash

What you're about to read, I've experienced almost entirely firsthand. I had a front row seat to a young man who had just realized his faith. I understood this very young. I was fortunate to witness that faith grow, be tested and tried, be stretched and be attained through the life of a good father. A father who was a fighter and an outlaw in some ways.

He had to function outside the laws of mediocrity and mainstream, having to think outside the box and was an example of true grit and ingenuity.

Much like a cowboy in a western, he made his way through life on a wing and a prayer, and then, in search of "The Voice of God", he would come to hear that voice and the wing, and a prayer turned to sheer faith, stepping out in trust, that the promises of God are true and able to support us.

This life spanning seventy-four years is a testament to how we are born with individual gifts and callings. We are meant to have a relationship with our heavenly father that ebbs and flows from our earthly bodies and minds to His super-natural purpose and plan.

This life experience is lived out in the successes and failures of our life's attempts. We are meant to go after our dreams and reach them. We are meant to love and lose, and win and achieve. And the life of my father is a full spectrum of the life the Lord is calling us to. The search for His Voice and finding His Heart.

The things that are important to my Dad have grown out of a full life of amazing places, people and the witness of God's moving hand. And like Mr. Cash, my father's desire is to see the will of God worked out in His life. The search for finding the Voice of God, began with, "Leaving Woods Creek".

Libby Star Mays

PREFACE

"Lord, remind me how brief my time on earth will be.

Remind me that my days are numbered—how fleeting my life is.

You have made my life no longer than the width of my hand.

My entire lifetime is just a moment to you; at best, each of us is but a breath."

We are merely moving shadows, and all our busy rushing ends in nothing.

We heap up wealth, not knowing who will spend it.

And so, Lord, where do I put my hope?

My only hope is in you. Psalms 39:4-7

Think of life as a mountain, a mountain that we all must climb. At the beginning of our assent each of us will leave the base of the mountain with a different perspective of what the mountain means to you. Each of us are incomparable. We think differently, most often because of the people who were around us at the beginning of our lives. The influences of these people will have helped to shape your thinking. We will eventually come to realize that some of those influences made the journey more arduous than it had to be. On the other hand, we also learn, it was only by their support that you survived the climb.

"No man is an Island, entire of itself; every man is a piece of the Continent, a part of the main". This expression is a quotation from John Donne's Devotions.

Based on the reality that we are all part of the human root. Your story and my story make our story. We are connected in some form or fashion. Every individual tributary, is a stream which flows to a larger stream or other body contributing to the history which we are all writing.

My beginning was a place affectionately known as Woods Creek. This is where my life entered the world and where the seedbed of my personality was dug. In my book you will hear the many stories of this gestation from the womb to now. Many of these tales will be very familiar to you. Some of them maybe news to you. After all, are we not all still learning from each other.

I have always referred to my mountain as "Truth". I didn't start out looking for the truth, I wasn't that smart. My only purpose at the start was one of satisfying my longings and my curiosities. It wasn't until I became famished for the need to know and the want for understanding, that my climb became a pursuit for truth. On my climb the truth I was seeking came to me, incarnated in the person of the Lord Jesus Christ. When I learn to discern "The Voice" of God, I was then able to understand what The Lord spoke when He said;

"I am the way, the truth and the life. No one comes to the Father but by me."

In a world where politically, correctness is tolerance and reasonableness, this world negates the truth of Jesus as unacceptable. The world prefers the vain idea that, "As long as I try to be a good person, it's not important how or what I believe, it just doesn't matter."

"The world believes there are different paths up the same mountain, but they all lead to the peak." But the world is wrong!

I truly believe as you read the testimonies of the miracles and my discovery of the Amazing Grace of God, which I share in the pages of my book. I believe my witness to the truth will enhance your faith and be a benefit to you as you make your climb with success. I challenge you to follow me up my mountain and discover "The Voice".

"My sheep hear my voice, and I know them, and they follow me. I give them eternal life, and they will never perish, and no one will snatch them out of my hand. My Father, who has given them to me, a is greater than all, and no one is able to snatch them out of the Father's hand. I and the Father are one." John 10:27-30

One of the purposes of God giving us the Holy Spirit is so that we can accomplish this purpose. It is through the exercise of our pursuit of God's Truth, that we can worship and know whom we worship, that we meet the Father and receive the blessings that come from His hand.

But without faith it is impossible to please Him

for he who comes to God must believe that He is,

and that He is a rewarder of those who diligently seek Him.

Hebrews 11:6

DEDICATION

Definition of legacy: "a gift by will, especially of money or other personal property: something transmitted by or received from an ancestor or predecessor".

To all my family by the flesh and by the Spirit I give to you my legacy. From the words of the Apostle Peter;

"Silver and gold, I have not; but what I have, this give I to thee: In the name of Jesus Christ rise up and walk".

Acts 3:6

I dedicate to you all, my story. The testimony I have chronicled on these pages define the scope of this legacy which I offer to you. These stories are the summation of my wealth. My treasures are found in the gifts of God's Grace given to me. I am a man who had been disgraced by his sin and shame, but found redemption in the pages of God's Word. I give all the glory to God who lifted me out of a horrible pit. He put a new song in my heart and established my path. He gave me ears to know and understand "The Voice" of my Heavenly Father. My dearly beloved, if you will heed these truths I have written concerning the Lord Jesus, and if you pursue His wealth, you will find the priceless treasure that we have as an inheritance. Don't wait to seek Him, but seek Him now, while He may be found.

"an inheritance that is kept in heaven for you, pure and undefiled, beyond the reach of change and decay. And through your faith, God is protecting you by his power until you receive this salvation, which is ready to be revealed on the last day for all to see. So be truly glad. There is wonderful joy ahead"1 Peter 1:4-5

Chapter 1

I love a rainy night. It always brings back wonderful memories. I love rain especially when it comes suddenly, unexpectedly, it makes me smile. As a boy from Alabama one of the memories that remains with me still, is listening to the rain falling on our corrugated galvanized tin roof top. It was best when the rain came at night while I lay buried in grandma's feather bed, pinned down by layers of quilts. The sounds of the rain would be amplified by the stillness of the southern night. It was musical. It was nature's lullaby composed by the gentle rhythm and the soothing pitter-pattering of raindrops. Quieted by its song, the rain made me feel safe. It made me feel like I belonged to something good. Soon I would be sleeping.

My grandparent's old house was divided by a long hall that went from the front door to the back door. Pa, my grand-father called it the dog run. Down the dog run to the rear of the house was my room which was directly across the hall from the kitchen.

My Dad and my younger brother Gary slept in a bedroom at the front of the house across the hall from where Pa and Mama Mays slept. Even though their bed was setup in there, my grandparents called this their living room. They probably placed their bed in there, because here is where the fireplace was.

Also in the living room were two rocking chairs, a couple of straw bottom straight back chairs, my grandmother's mirrored dresser and one very old table where Pa kept his tobacco box and his Bible. My favorite thing in the living room was the radio, a Zenith Model "cube" radio.

When radios were first starting to be retailed, radios were not cheap. During the Great Depression, the average price of a radio sold in the United States had dropped down to about forty-seven dollars. According to one survey in 1950, before they got a television, people listened to radio an average of nearly five hours a day. At Pa's house, there was no television because there were no stations that he could receive. That was okay by me because I have always loved radio. Some of my favorite broadcasts back then were...

The Shadow, "What evil lurks in the hearts of man?"

The Fat Man, "He Steps on the scale, his weight, 380 lbs."

Then of course America was laughing out loud with the Amos & Andy Show, you could hear Kingfish telling Andy; "I say...I say Andy, ooh Sapphire she gonna kill me". And how about the crime stopper shows like "Gangbusters", which I always pantomimed shooting my imaginary tommy gun when the broadcast opened with machine gun sounds. My Dad's favorite, "The Lone Ranger", remember Tonto saying to the masked man, "What we do now Kemosabe."

For chills and thrills and the fear factor, you had the "Inner Sanctum", which sent us all diving under the covers with the sound of a squeaky door opening at the top of the broadcast. It was great entertainment and great fun.[i]

As the morning dawned the rain had stopped. I awoke to my bedroom chilled by the departing night. This indeed was a new day, the day The Lord had made.

Waking up in that house after a rainy autumn night was amazing. The aromas and sounds floating through the chilled air were a colorful mixture of the wet red clay just

11

outside the back door, the glimmering dampness of old wood needing paint, and the brilliant clatters of grandma's kitchen.

As I dug myself out from my bed I hit the cold hardwood floor full speed, leaping across the dog run, and through the kitchen door, squeezing past the wood box which I had filled with pine kindling and split oak the night before. Stealth like I slipped behind the wood burning cook stove which would be my front row seat to a culinary concert.

Everyone called her Ma, that is everybody but me. For some reason and I don't know why I called her Mama Mays. She would hardly notice I was there. I guessed it was because she expected my coming. Nothing was said, no need too. Just be still, watch, and listen, while my appetite grew.

There, on the stove top, black coffee was brewing, and crackling in the pan, home cured bacon. The real stuff. Not something stripped from a plastic wrapper, but thick and tasty, fried crisp, a little salty, perfectly butchered by Pa himself with the help of our neighbors at hog killing time. There too, were fluffy yellow eggs scrambled in the iron skillet and brown gravy being poured in a bowl, she called it her sawmill gravy.

I watched her peeking into the oven as the second batch of biscuits were near baked, wiping her hands on her apron made from printed flour sacks, which she wore like a uniform.

She turned to stare at her first batch piled high in a basket in the middle of the long dining table crafted by Pa's two hands.

The kitchen was her domain and the table she prized was covered by a freshly ironed checkered table cloth. Accompanying the table was a full-length bench on the wall-side where I would sit to Pa's left and my brother Gary to the left of me. On the other side and at the ends, were more of those straw bottom high back chairs. Mama Mays would when it was time, sit across from me and to her husband's right, my Dad always sat at the opposite end, down table from Pa.

With the finishing touches to her masterpiece, I watched her, my mouth watering for those warm golden-brown nuggets stacked in the basket, just waiting to be spread with her homemade butter, jams, jellies or applesauce. She nodded her head in self approval, as she made her final inspection, "perfect", she whispered. I agreed, it was perfect, everything was perfect.

Saying nothing to me till the time was right, she spoke, "Better get your britches on boy, and them hands, give them a good washing, and get your brother too, cause your Pa and Daddy will be a coming in from doing their chores in a minute. "So…Shoo…Go on now."

Leaving on her command I moved from my happy place, dashing across the dog run, quickly dressing, stopping only briefly at the red trimmed enamel wash pan. Drenching my face and hands in the cold water which had been drawn by her earlier from our well located just out the back door, it was invigorating. Grabbing my brother, I quickly gave him the once over and then we were off to a feast.

I loved her quietly. I suppose because she wasn't one for talking, she was more about the doing. My grand-mother Jetty Naomi Mills was twenty years younger than

13

Pa, and was his second wife. Pa's first wife Nancy died some time before, leaving him alone with a bunch of kids. Pa had children nearly as old as Jetty, which I learned about after I was much older.

Pa was a grand fellow. Everyone called him Pa, or Bud. His real name was John Alvin, my Daddy's name was John Oliver, and I was named John William, after Pa and my grandfather William David Pope. For some reason, they all called me Billy. Maybe it was easier for everybody. I didn't know for sure, but I didn't mind either.

Pa was getting too old now to do much of the farm work, so that's why Dad was here, to help Pa with the place. Pa wasn't only a farmer. He had been a teacher in a community they called Poplar Log. At one time, he was also the postmaster. As the story goes, Pa owned his own post office which was lost in a fire.

Many years later my brother Ken became the mayor of Hamilton Alabama, he would discover in the city archives that John "Bud" Mays had been the first Alderman of the city.

You would never know it by looking at him, but Pa was well off. He probably had more land than money. He owned land as far as you could see, several acres around the old house and much more down the road and across "Woods Creek" and all the way to the Highway 278. His properties were mostly forests for timber. There was farm land for growing cotton and corn, and some pastures for the mules and cows.

Pa was a noble and handsome man, and was known all around the area, Woods Creek, Pea Ridge, Bull Mountain, and Buzzards Roost, wherever the old Buttatchee River flowed people knew Pa. He had a reputation of being a man of integrity, honest as the day is long. Folks said, "that when Bud Mays gave you his word it was good as gold, it was his bond."

"A good name is to be chosen over great wealth; favor is better than silver and gold". Proverbs 22:1

You may be thinking by now, Billy, where is your mother during all this time? Well my mom was working in Michigan and keeping my baby brother Kenneth which we expected to see them both sometime around Christmas. My mother more than once told me the story of how Michigan would become a big part of our lives, and how it came about that she happened to go there the first time.

She said, "I guess I was sixteen going on seventeen, when one day while my brother George and I were finishing up with the sugar cane patch. "We had stopped to rest for a bit and I said to George,"

"I need some money!"

"What do you need money for", George said sarcastically.

"I'm going to go to Michigan and get me a job."

"Why, you're so backward you wouldn't ask for a job if you went there", he said half-jokingly but with a serious tone.

"I need some money George", Mother implored.

So, in response to her request, the next day George came to her, "Here's twenty dollars, I borrowed it on your mule, so sign the note."

Then with twenty bucks she bought a bus ticket, a suitcase, a few clothes, and off she went. She told me with her first paycheck she sent back the twenty dollars to Uncle George to pay the loan on the mule.

Shortly after her first trip, Mother would return to Alabama to marry my Dad on February 20, 1943. Then, just little over a year later I was born in February 21, 1944. In that same year Dad joined the Navy. With Dad gone, Mother would return to Michigan with me and her mother accompanying her to help her on the journey.

Her mother's maiden name was, "Phoebe Bede Cardilla Sullins-Pope". She was of Irish descent and quarter Native American, which tribe, no one has ever known. The most striking feature of my grandmother was her beautiful long red hair which she usually wore braided up in a bun. I called her Grandma. I can still see her sitting in one of those straw bottom high back chairs pulling a hairbrush through her red hair, making it to curl softly around her shoulders, and flow in beautiful waves sedately to the floor.

Mom told me, "it was hectic for them at that time traveling on the Greyhound Bus, because on the bus there was standing room only and every bus stop would be crowded with soldiers and sailors coming and going because of the war. Then too, there were hundreds if not thousands of others like ourselves traveling north to work in the factories."

She told me, "when they stopped in Louisville to change buses; they would not have been able to board their bus to continue their trip, had it not been for one of the soldiers insisting that they be allowed back on the bus".

She said, she really believed the bus driver consented only because he thought we were with that soldier, by the grace of God we made it safe and sound".

Chapter 2

It was early on Sunday when the labor pangs first began...it was also their one-year anniversary, February 20, 1944. This is a leap year and the expecting mother will celebrate her twentieth birthday just ten days later March 1. On June 2, her husband will also turn twenty. What they didn't know, that before this day is over, these two young marrieds will make one of the biggest decisions of their young lives.

Back in July, when they first learned they were going to have a baby, they made their decision the baby would be born, in Pa and Mama Mays old house. When the doctor arrives, he prepares the house and his patient for a routine delivery. There were no reasons to expect any problems and why should there be. After all, the old doctor has lost count of how many times he's brought a baby into this world.

But unexpectedly the doctor stops his examinations. Peering over his spectacles, he looks up, his face strained with concern, and taking a long look at my Dad, he says;

"John...I am so sorry to tell you this, but there's a problem, your baby is just too big and there's nothing I can do. I can't save them both. It's impossible. You will have to make a choice, either your wife or the baby."

Can you imagine, here you are, not even twenty years old, and you've just been told that you must choose, who will live or who will die. Just think about that for a minute. How can a person at that age, or for that matter any age, find the courage to make such a life changing decision? There is only one place where that kind of courage can come, by the grace of God through prayer and faith.

I can't tell you how many times I've told this story just as it had been told me, literally dozens of times. Still, the more I tell it the more convinced I am that The Lord was there that day; His Presence was with my parents, grandparents and with the doctor. I have always believed, God heard their prayers and I am awestruck when I think of what they were going through that day, and the decision they came to, when they both agreed..."Dr. Burleson, there has to be a way...some other way... something else we can do"

You know, when I think of my Dad... I am satisfied that there is no one... not a single person, who would have blamed him if he had said, "Doc, you have to save my wife."

It would have been the right choice to make. Both common sense and logic dictates it. "Let her live...we can have another baby...she's too young to die and too much life ahead of her. Sure... we will weep, and we will mourn, but we will get through this".

You know, I have learned as Christians, when we are going through tough times, we always have other options that the world doesn't offer. We have the option to believe for a miracle. The option to ask God for what seems impossible. The option to trust in the Creator of All Life. And for sure... that kind of faith... the kind of faith to make those choices, can only come by the grace of a loving and caring God.

As everyone waits you can see the doctor pulling at his chin as he studies the faces of his old friends Bud and Jetty, two people he deeply admires.

With deep compassion and empathy, he looks at the worried face of their son, my Dad, as he watches him comforting his suffering wife, my Mother.

It will seem like an eternity for everyone at the old house that day before the answer finally comes. As the doctor reaches for his handkerchief, he wipes the perspiration from his brow, there's a pause, and he takes a deep breath and says;

"Okay.... "There might be a chance, howbeit a small one… and only if we can get them to the hospital in Russellville in sufficient time."

With caution so as not to add to their distress, he warns them, "but listen kids, even if we can do this...you have to know there's no guarantee."

All my life God has intervened for me, and now here, before I was born, His divine providence and grace are playing a part in a miracle.

As history would have it, shortly after the War of 1812, the U.S. government funded the building of a road from Nashville to New Orleans. It was named after Andrew Jackson and called Jackson's Military Road.[ii]

This road will pass right through what will become Russellville, Alabama and the future sites of Pikeville, the first permanent county seat of Marion County and the now present county seat...Hamilton...our home town. Without this historical road, there is no city of Russellville. Without the city of Russellville there is no hospital, and without the hospital there is no chance for us. This is the road which will take us to "Our Miracle".

Think about this scene. Here you have a woman in labor and a frantic father in a 1941 Ford sedan. It's anybody's guess as to how many miles the old doctor has put on the motor and tires...and by the way...those are country miles.

For the first eight miles, you will be speeding down a very bumpy, dusty gravel road and that's just to get you to the main road, the historical Jackson Military Road. The trip will take almost two hours covering forty grueling miles as the crow flies, filled with dangerous curves and plenty of steep hills. You make the entire journey with desperate hope, you leave Pa's old house in fear and in prayer. It will be a difficult trip, especially for my Mother.

Exhausted, the expecting parents arrive at the emergency entrance and just in time. In very little time a son is born, the mother is safe and well, the father is filled with gratitude, and the old doctor is relieved and happy it's successfully over.

So, there's really no need for me to go into all the details of what happens at the hospital, for the outcome is obvious, I am here telling you their story as it was told to me. On Monday February 21, 1944, I entered this world by the grace of God, and with the faith and courage of two wonderful parents and the expertise and wisdom of an old country doctor.

Remember when the doctor said, the baby is too big, well he nailed it. I weighed in at eleven pounds and twelve ounces, a heavyweight, a real roly poly. From the time, I was two years old I can recall my Daddy singing to me that old Bob Wills song, "Roly Poly, daddy's little fatty, bet he's gonna be a man someday."[iii]

That thought always brings back memories of our evenings at Pa's old house which were always a large wonderful part of our family life. We all looked forward to Saturday nights listening to the Grand Ole Opry on Pa's old tube radio coming to us in real time from the Ryman Auditorium in Nashville, Tennessee on WSM 650AM on the radio dial, sponsored by Martha White self-rising flour.

George Hay the founder of the Opry and who billed himself as the "Solemn Old Judge", when he was the host would open the broadcast after first blowing his steamboat whistle and then saying, 'Let her go boys'.

During my time, there were multiple hosts of the Grand Ole Opry...like Hank Snow, Ernest Tubb, and Mom's favorite Little Jimmy Dickens or "Tater", as Hank Williams called him which was inspired by Little Jimmy's song "Take an Old Cold Tater and Wait". The music at the Opry was great and for hours we all tapped our toes, clapped our hands and sang along.[iv]

Most evenings however...my ears would be glued to my folk's storytelling. They would talk, and I would listen, as we all basked in the cozy warmth of the fireplace, watching the wood burning as the plots and descriptions of their tales thickened.

While they talked, our fire would begin to cool to a somber glow. When that happened, either Dad or Pa would lean out of their chairs to poke the fire with a wrought iron poker which always stood in its place nearby. They would poke and turn the black smoldering wood, until the red, yellow and blue flames were resurrected and begin their ascent up the old stone chimney.

Watching them stoke the fire, poking and turning the wood, I imagined the fire was fighting back, with leaping embers and snap crackling noises, as if to say, "what more do you want from me."

Those evenings in the old house reminds me of a Norman Rockwell picture. There was Pa and Mama Mays in their rocking chairs moving in perfect syncopation. Dad joining the chorus line as he rocked leaning on the back legs of his straw bottom high back chair with his store-bought cigarette hanging from the corner of his mouth. Pa would have his evening smoke from his very own home-grown tobacco. Mama Mays never sat down empty handed. She always had knitting or crocheting going on as she chewed on her sweet gum toothbrush loaded with Garrett snuff.

Mama Mays, like many of the women folk in those days dipped snuff on sweet gum twigs. They prepared the twigs by chewing one end softly until it formed a small brush which conveyed the dark brown snuff.

Back then smoking and dipping snuff appealed to both men and women. Most snuff came in five or 10-cent cans, bottles or glasses.

The Mays' ladies favored the Levi Garrett brand which sold for 35 cents. Garrett snuff came in a brown bottle with "bubbles or notches" imprinted around the bottom of the container. On each bottle, there were one to four of these notches.

My mother who would say, "You can have your Abe Lincoln and George Washington, but that Levi Garrett was nobody's fool."

You see Mom thought the more notches the stronger the tobacco – one notch being the weakest and four notches being the strongest. My Mother would settle for nothing less than four notches. You know...I never had the heart to tell her the truth...that the bubbles or notches had nothing to do with the flavor or strength of the snuff, but indicated the location of where the bottle was made.

Long before the Surgeon General warned us of the dangers of tobacco, tobacco was very popular. In fact, our government included cigarettes in the "C" rations given to our soldiers which they often used as a form of currency, trading them for other needed things.

Back in those days about the only packaged cigarettes you could buy were Camel, Chesterfield, Lucky Strike, Old Gold and Wings. For only fifteen cents you could get a pack, and if you had to pinch your pennies, the cheaper "Wings" brand could be purchased for a dime.

The "Bull Durham" brand was a loose smoking tobacco, sold in small cotton bags with a drawstring. I can still see the old men sitting in their bib overalls around the old potbellied stove at the country store, with their "Dr. Peppers" in one hand and their rolled Bull Durham smokes pinched between tobaccos stained fingers on the other hand. And what was hanging from the bib pocket of those overalls...a drawstring from a Bull Durham bag. All of us kids could find lots of uses for them empty tobacco bags, like holding your prized marbles and such.

At times when money was short, Dad would smoke "Prince Albert" tobacco which came loose in a tin and with cigarette papers, so you could "roll your own."[v]

Just down the road from us lived one of Dad's friends. A farmer like us...but when he farmed he had to do it all with one arm. With his one arm he'd plow his mules, chop his firewood, milk his cows, doing it all with one arm. Some folks say he lost his arm in a sawmill accident, others say it was a gunshot wound. Whichever it was and I'm not sure, but I was always amazed how he could roll his own smokes with one arm.

How did he do it? Well he usually wore a long sleeve denim shirt. He would lift the stub arm, and then make a cradle for the paper in the denim cloth right where the elbow bent. Then laying the paper in the wrinkle he would pour the Prince Albert tobacco in.

Now...here's the amazing part. With just one hand he would gather the tobacco filled paper...roll it... then licking the papers edge wet to seal it... then...he was ready to smoke.

Speaking of smoke...as I watched the flames dancing in the fireplace, all that tobacco smoke filled the room of the old house. I would have struggled to breathe. Smoke never agreed with me, but "stupid is as stupid does", and like other boys I would eventually give it a try.

In Alabama and all over the Deep South there are two kinds of weeds that grow everywhere. Rabbit Tobacco and Kudzu.[vi]

Most folks speak evil of Kudzu. They say it's a destroyer of the environment. In Alabama, it's everywhere...like a giant green net, trapping the roadside ditches, power poles, fences and trees. I'm weird I guess, because I must admit, I sort of liked its artistic presence, and the way it seemed to caress everything it touched.

25

Now... If there is any one plant that represents the meadows and hillsides of Alabama, it is "Rabbit Tobacco". It's hard to miss the silvery-green leaves of this plant dotting the landscape of the Deep South. Some folks say the leaves are full of energy and power like some magic herb.

I remember the day when Pa caught my brother and I red-handed smoking that rabbit tobacco, rolled in paper we ripped from an old edition of the Sears and Roebuck catalog which was kept in the outhouse. So... to teach us a lesson against the woes of smoking, Pa made us both, inhale his strong homegrown until we both turned green as lizards.

But...despite Pa's best efforts to discourage us, we would eventually fall into temptation again... and from about sixteen till I was twenty-nine I would indulge in the habit, which I am happy to say the Lord delivered me from, which came unsolicited in October 1973.

One evening that year, while sitting in my apartment a musician I had known from my playing days in the honky tonks came to see me. His name, Joe Blassingame. Joe and his brothers, Earl and Ray had a country band, fittingly named, The Blassingame Brothers.

As people will say... Joe had gotten religion. I would later learn that all those boys were raised in church by a godly mother whom everyone called Sister Blassingame. Back in those days...a lot of musicians I had worked with, had a story or two about church which they would talk about. I too... had a church story I can tell.

My story begins with "Sweet Linda". A neighbor girl who lived about a half mile down the road from me. We were sixteen at the time and kind of sweet on each other.

We rode the same school bus and would always save a seat for each other, so we could hold hands. The truth was... holding her hand pretty much sized up our courtship. Then too, the only other place we could court besides bus or school was in the front room of her house which placed us in earshot of her parents' bedroom. So, I can tell you for sure not much going to happen there.

On occasions though, when I saw the opportunity and I felt lucky and brave enough to try, I would steal a kiss from "Sweet Linda", which I did with great fear, and I'll tell you why. I was more than convinced that both her Pappy and her dimwitted younger brother were about half crazy.

In fact, and it's the God's honest truth...one night... after our courting was done and as I left her house stepping into the cool night air, I was surprised when I found the night sky fluorescent with light from a full moon. In the silver glow of the moonlight I could even see the porch light of my house down the gravel road shining like a beacon. So... still thinking about the last kiss I had just stolen, I started home.

As I walked the path from Sweet Linda's house down to the road, I had no sooner stepped onto it when the first gunshot rang out. The sound of the gun blast shattered the stillness of the night, and with a swishing noise the bullet flew past my ear, hitting the ground in front of me.

Startled...I looked back toward their house silhouetted on the hillside, then I looked over to the old dairy barn shadowed by the moon. Crack... another shot came, the second bullet exploded in front of me causing the gravel from the road near my feet to ricochet in every direction, I was completely paralyzed. I thought, "My God, who's shooting." As I came to my senses, with a panicked reflex,

27

I dove from the road, into the ditch…rolling down the Kudzu covered ditch bank.

Fortunately for me, in Alabama we have great ditches, deep and wide ditches, and when I hit the bottom of that ditch I started running. Hunched over and low to the ground, my head bent so to stay beneath the line of fire, I ran. I ran like the devil himself was after me.

My Dad always teased me about my running, saying, "Son you can run pretty fast, the problem is, you just run too long in one place."

Well…I can tell you right now, on this night, Dad would have been proud… because I ran like a scalded cat. As I ran, I stumbled, and I crawled my way down that ditch, I could picture in my mind Sweet Linda's crazy dim-witted brother.

I thought, "Had that fool been lurking in the shadows of the old dairy barn with rifle in hand waiting for me to head home?" And like I said, "I wouldn't put it past his crazy daddy to put him up to it".

But taking no chances, I didn't come out of that ditch till I got to the creek, then easing out and over the bridge I dashed home, thinking to myself, "what the heck was all that about."

I never told my folks about the shooting incident because I knew it would upset my Mother and I wasn't too sure what Dad would have done had he found out about it. So, you can imagine how surprised I was, when just an evening or so later, Sweet Linda and her family came driving up to the house to ask my brother and me to go to church with them.

Okay, so I guess we are all a little crazy at times, for like a complete idiot I went with them. The truth was...I just couldn't resist Sweet Linda. So, for a week of nights, all of us kids rode in the back of their old truck which was loaded with fresh picked cotton to the Baptist church.

It was weird, being in the same space with that crazy brother. Every time I looked at him with that wry, evil smile of his, I wanted to throw him out of the truck and watch him bounce all over the black top. I could just picture his goofy face, hair, teeth and eyeballs scattered all over the highway. But... I let it go...after all...it was revival time.

Every night the little church house was filled with church folks and sinners. I remember sitting by Sweet Linda holding her hand beneath the song books, while picking cotton lint off my trousers which I got from the truck ride. As all those Baptists sang "I'll Fly Away", and rocked to "The Rock of Ages" I sat on the church bench, pretending I was listening to the young evangelist.

Wait just a minute; let me clarify something for you. It wasn't that I couldn't hear him... Man... I couldn't help but hear him, because as soon as he started his preaching he started his yelling. He yelled about how we were all sinners. He yelled about how we were all going to hell if we didn't get saved and baptized. He yelled especially at the young folks, for our sinful ways, for our cussing and smoking and playing those rock and roll records.

"You are all lost and going to hell you are," he would yell. I watched that preacher night after night, as he yelled, spit, and ran the isles with his face beet red from all his hard preaching.

29

The last night of the revival finally came and by then all my friends including Sweet Linda, had responded to the invitation, claiming to be saved, of which I knew better.

Now...listen.... just in case you don't know...the thing they call the invitation is that part of the service when you are coerced again and again by the preacher to come forward to the altar and confess you're a sinner. And accompanying the invitation is the church organist, playing the old hymn "Just as I Am" over and over.

So here I am... the last night of the revival and it seems that the only people left in the church who are still hell bent is my brother Gary and me, and for sure that crazy brother of Sweet Linda's and more than likely her crazy daddy too.

"This is no good" I thought, "You don't want all your buddies in heaven while you're in hell dancing with the devil... and after all, how long can a fellow resist... really...after the thirty ninth time you hear."

"Just as I am, without one plea

But that thy blood was shed for me,

And that thou bidst me come to thee,

O Lamb of God, I come, I come.[vii]

It was more than I could bear. As the church organist played one more verse, I looked down at my knuckles turning white from gripping the back of that pine knotted pew, and I thought, "I got to go." So out of the pew I flew...but instead of heading to the altar... I made a mad scramble to the front door. Out the door I stumbled gasping to breathe again, sucking in the cold night air as I bent over coughing and grabbing my knees.

As I slowly straightened up I noticed the night was lit by a
solitary light which hung like a street lamp over the door of
the church. Some older folks were leaving, backing quietly
away in their trucks and cars... and all you could hear was
the gravel crunching under their wheels. Just over there,
half in the light and half in the dark was a group of men
standing huddled and leaning against the bed of an old
truck telling jokes and smoking, there may have been a
bottle of lightning tucked away among them as well.

As my breathing started to slow back to normal, my mind
was still racing. I kept rehearsing the last thing the preacher
had been yelling, "Tonight is your night to get saved."

I thought to myself, "maybe I should go back in there and
join my friends and of course Sweet Linda too, she would
be happy to see me." Just as I turned to go back,
surprisingly and to my dismay, appearing under the light at
the church front door, was the evangelist.

His white shirt illuminated by the light of the outdoor lamp
hanging over his head, drenched with perspiration his
shirt became transparent and beneath it you could see his
undershirt. He had his thin black tie loosened at the collar
and tossed over his shoulder.

My heart leaped as I thought, "Is he coming after me." I
watched the preacher his eyes panning the parking lot,
pausing to study the huddle of men who quieted at his
appearing. "Nice evening," he said, stepping out of the door
yet still in the light. He hesitated for only a moment to look
at me, and then he made his move.

Into his front pocket his hand went as he lifted the pack of
Pall Mall cigarettes. The red package covered with
cellophane glistened in the church light.

31

He then tapped the pack of cigarettes in the palm of his other hand, as one cigarette seemed to magically levitate from the pack.

Then he gracefully lifted the pack to his mouth retrieving the factory rolled smoke with his lips while his face glows yellow from the flame of his Zippo lighter while he lit the cigarette. With a deep breath, he lifted his head toward the stars as he takes a drag on his smoke...while he walks by me moving toward the huddle of men...he exhaled.

Like the air escaping from his lungs, so went my thoughts of everything I had been feeling. My want of salvation faded as quickly as the preacher's smoke in the cold damp night air. It would be thirteen years later before I would decide for Christ. And oh...by the way... I never courted Sweet Linda again. I guess my soul wasn't the only thing I lost at the church that night.

Now... let me get back to my deliverance story and to godly Sister Blassingame. If you can remember my friend Joe had stopped by my place and he told me his mother is having religious services. He said... "My mother would like you to come with us and play your guitar at a special service she is having tonight."

For my first thought, I wasn't interested, so I resisted kindly to Joe's invitation. He persisted, "Johnny my mother would sure appreciate if you and Judy would come." With mixed feelings...again I gave him the excuse that I didn't know the songs. But he insisted and assured me I wouldn't have any problem with the music.

You know when I think about it, my not being able to say no in certain situations, has always been a big problem for me... and here again...even though I didn't want to go, reluctantly I agreed. With my guitar in one hand and my wife Judy holding the other we rode away in Joe's car.

Let me pause here. I just realized that I haven't formally introduced you to Judith Arlene Mays, my second wife. At the time of this writing we've been married for 47 years, but if you just hold on, I will get to talk more about this special woman.

By now we had driven some distance, and I was starting to wonder if we were ever going to get wherever we were going. I was relieved when Joe started slowing the car, letting it coast to a stop. As we were all getting out of the vehicle, I am looking, but I don't see a church. What I saw was a house...just as Joe says, "it's a commune."

We had arrived at a commune...a hippy commune. Back in the late sixties and the early seventies California had a number of these kinds of communities. This one however was different...it was a Jesus commune.[viii]

Now trust me this service was nothing like the revival service I just described at the little country Baptist church when I was a teenager. These folks were, or had been, and I am sure some still are, pot toking, acid dropping, wine drinking, California, stone cold hippies. But tonight, well... tonight they were praising Jesus.

As Joe and I played, I watched, my Judy watched, it was all so new to us. Then Sister Blassingame stood and makes an announcement "we are going to pray."

Next thing I know Judy and I are standing in a circle, our hands joined and people praying. Loud praying, some in English and others in what I would later learn they called unknown tongues.

Then like a Texas tornado, without a warning, I am waking up flat on my back on the floor, with this Pentecostal grandmother straddling me and looking me straight into my eyes, telling me, "son you will never be the same again." The next person I noticed was my wife looking over the shoulder of Sister Blassingame with her eyes big as saucers, telling me, "get up John, get up."

Trust me there was nothing more I wanted than to get up, while at the same time I am thinking how in the world did I get down here in the first place, laying out like I'd been hit by a bolt of lightning.

Well I must tell you, the remainder of the evening was a total blur, until finally Joe is dropping us off at our apartment. Judy walks quickly ahead of me, my mind still spinning from this evening's experience and I think it was the same for Judy. Still, the words of Sister Blassingame kept echoing through my mind, "son you will never be the same again."

As I climbed the stairs to our second-floor apartment walking the balcony toward our door, I noticed the pack of Tiparillo cigars in my shirt pocket. Do you remember those, the little cigars with the plastic tip? I had been smoking those things without inhaling in effort to quit smoking, if that makes any sense. Well as I lifted them from my pocket a familiar voice from within me spoke, "you will never need to smoke again."

With those words I tossed the cigars, and like a whirly bird they flew from my hand down, down and to my surprise into the swimming pool in the middle of the court beneath our second-floor balcony. From that very day forward, I never smoked again. Thank you, Jesus.

Chapter 3

The old house Pa had built was on a hillside and so to bring it to level the builders placed the front of the house on stone pillars. Because of this there were several steps going up to the front door that open to the dog run. From this vantage point you could see either kinfolk or strangers coming up the gravel road for more than a mile off.

As you stood there absorbing the view...panning the countryside, your thoughts were, "it is all so magnificent". The surrounding hills were filled with soft and hardwoods, oak and pine...redwood and dogwood, breathtakingly beautiful. It appears the hills tenderly touched each other lifting themselves to the heavens, as the valley flowed softly towards my beloved "Woods Creek". As your eyes swept over terraced fields of fluffy white cotton, the lyrics of the song came to mind;

"I wish I was in the land of cotton,

Old times there are not forgotten;

Look away! Look away! Look away! Dixie Land.

In Dixie Land where I was born,

Early on one frosty morn"

Look away! Look away! Look away! Dixie Land.[ix]

Just to the left of the old house like a sentinel keeping watch "stood the old oak tree that we use to play on". To the right of the old house were tall Junipers stretching themselves and pointing toward the sky. Then beneath the shadow of the Junipers, standing alone and sedate, opened like a bamboo umbrella, is the Formosa tree with its fragile gentle branches.

Across the road securely framed and protected behind a tall chicken wire fence was the garden of gardens. Going into that garden was like entering "The Garden of Eden". Growing there in the warm rich earth was every imaginable vegetable you could desire.

Large purple eggplant and green crisp celery, tomato plants loaded with vine ripe red juicy tomatoes. Bunches of orange carrots and long neck yellow squashes. Large and delicious cabbages from which we made our sauerkraut and coleslaw, and lots of leafy iceberg lettuce.

There were peppers of every color and kind...red, green, and yellow, both hot and sweet. A necessity for every southern table were the red, white and yellow onions and growing nearby, a row or two of friendly green scallions.

Beans you bet, we have them… Lima beans, butter beans, pinto beans, string beans, beans galore. How about corn? You can't have a garden without table corn. Our tall sweet corn skirted the north side of the garden. Did you ever think about how many ways you can use corn?

Well...there's steamed corn, creamed corn, and corn on the cob. You can grill corn or boil corn. You can add corn into your soups or jambalaya. There's corn salsa, corn salad, scalloped corn and corn chowder. Cornpone, corn cakes all hot from the oven covered with sweet cream butter, skillets of golden cornbread always good in milk. And finishing out with one of my favorites...home style grits with thick black molasses stirred in them... now, that makes a real hillbilly breakfast.

There nested in the corner of the garden, is Mama Mays' favorites herbs. Sage, sage is a great herb for cooking. Parsley, has so many uses in the kitchen! ... Oregano.... Mint. ... Coriander. ... Rosemary. ... Basil. ... Chives. Knowing how to use these is where the real art of country cooking comes from, and no-one was better than our women folk.

Next to the garden was the orchard. Pa's trees gave us several varieties of apples. I always looked forward to when they dried the apples to make those wonderful apple turnovers. And as I mentioned before, Mama Mays always served apple jelly, apple sauce and apple butter at her table.

As the Tom T. Hall song goes, "Ain't but three things in this world that's worth a solitary dime, but old dogs and children and watermelon wine".[x]

Well I can't speak much about watermelon wine, but I can tell you this, around our house we loved the melon patch, which had both red and golden meat watermelons, and growing there too were the big round cantaloupes, and muskmelons.

Nearby the melon patch was the peanut patch. We ate the peanuts roasted or raw, plain or salted. I love my mother's homemade peanut brittle it's the best. Many people don't know this, but peanuts are a legume and grow under the ground.

When it came to potatoes, there were mounds and mounds of potatoes. I love those Irish spuds baked in the oven covered with homemade sour cream, or peeled, boiled and mashed smothered with chicken gravy and fried in grease with skins and all.

And fit for any Thanksgiving table were the delicious baked sweet-potatoes and yams...deliciously good when candied with those little marshmallows melted on top.

One of the main staples for any dinner table in Alabama is black eyed peas or purple hulled peas. Dad and Pa always planted dozens of rows of peas which after were picked by the bushels.

When the picking was done, the work was just beginning. We would spend hours sitting together, adults and children on the front porch shelling them peas all the while laughing and singing and telling stories. Everything gathered from the garden, the patches and the orchards were either used right away in the kitchen, or canned.

Now it was always a puzzle to me, why they called it canning, because we didn't use cans, we used glass jars, Mason jars. The Mason jar had been around since the late 1800's... invented by a Philadelphia tinsmith, Mr. John Landis Mason. Some folks call them Ball jars after the Ball Corporation, who was an early manufacturer of the jars.[xi]

One of the chores I had at canning time was to draw water from our well and fill the thirty gallons, black cast iron kettle, which sat by the wood pile close to the rose garden. Dad would build a fire under the kettle, so the water would be brought to a boil… then the Mason jars were sterilized by submerging them into the hot water, and only then were they ready for use.

Because the jars were clear glass, once they were filled you could see the contents and knew exactly what you had. Thank God for Mr. Mason and Mama Mays, because of their partnership we would have plenty of food for the winter.

Oh...for sure I loved the apples from the orchard. But my real fondness I found in the orchard was much more than the apples...it was the birds.

In Alabama, we have beautiful birds and we have lots of them. I remember reading somewhere, that there are over four hundred different kinds of birds in Alabama. Some of the birds make Alabama their home and then other birds just like to stop by every now and then for a visit when they're flying by.[xii]

In Pa's orchard, I would see the; Sparrow and Bluebird, Robins and Red Birds, Thrushes and the singing Mockingbird and sometimes the Thrashers. The cutest were the busy little Hummingbird suspended in flight removing nectar from the blossoms with their thin long beaks. Then those rascals, the blue feathered bandits, the Blue Jays and then the knock, knock, knocking of our neighborhood Woodpecker. But then of course the pride of Alabama our State Bird... "The Yellowhammer".

I hate to tell this story, but I once shot one of those Yellowhammer. I had just got my first Daisy "Red Ryder" BB gun and I couldn't wait to have my first kill. There in the orchard sitting on the fence was my victim. Proudly I ran to the old house to present my trophy to Mama Mays, only to regret it later. I never saw her so angry with me. "You know you killed our State bird".

When she saw how disturbed I was of my crime...she comforted me by saying. "Son if you want to shoot something that we can cook, you got to get yourself a Quail." She told me, "Take your hunting down in the old cornfield". So, off I went still red faced from crying, but comforted now that I had her blessings.

40

The old cornfield had not been planted for a while because of a creek that ran through it over the past few years had flooded it, so now it was grown over with saplings and tall sedge grass...a perfect habitat for Quail. So here I go on my adventure, creeping through grass taller than me, with my Red Ryder BB rifle cocked and loaded.

Abruptly and with the deafening sound of a thousand thunder rolls, rising in perfect unison, a covey of Quail right in front of my eyes. I was so startled I nearly wet my pants as I fumbled to shoot but to no avail, for as suddenly as they appeared they disappeared to safety. I didn't know it then, but that day would be the last hunt I would ever make.

One Alabama bird I remember the most was the whippoorwill. I learned to whistle their calls while lying in my bed. At night, you could hear them calling to each other from tree to tree, over the hillsides and down the valley. Their mournful laments always reminded me of the lines from one of Hank Williams great songs, who by the way was another good old boy from Alabama.[xiii]

Hank was born in Mount Olive, down in Butler County, he is a legend in country music and as Alabamians we were all proud of Hanks rags to riches story. Unfortunately, the prolific singer/songwriter died young, not yet thirty ...on January 1, 1953. The newspapers said his funeral was the largest cvent ever held in Montgomery. The tears still come to my eyes when I hear those evocative lyrics;

"Hear that lonesome whippoorwill,

he sounds too blue to fly,"

"Did you ever see a robin weep,

when leaves begin to die?

That means he's lost the will to live,

I'm so lonesome I could cry.... "[xiv]

Walking out the back door of the old house, you wouldn't walk no more than twenty feet till you were headed straight up a hill and right into the woods. We didn't have any plumbing in the old house...but if you looked just to your left as you went out the back door, there was the well. We drew the water up with a bucket and thank goodness it was a shallow well, so it was no chore to draw water.

Mama Mays always wanted her water bucket full. She kept the bucket sitting at the end of the dog run near the kitchen door. When you wanted water from the bucket you could always find the white and red enamel dipper, hanging on a nail over the matching white and red enamel wash pan.

The water from our well was the sweetest water ever and always cold no matter the season. Mama Mays not only liked her water bucket full, but she kept her tea kettle full too, sitting on the wood stove so you'd have hot water in just a minute for a cup of tea along with one of her leftover biscuits that she kept covered sitting on her table. On occasion, if you were lucky, there might even be a bit of that bacon left from breakfast for you to squeeze into a biscuit.

In Alabama, there are many natural springs, cold creeks and rivers. One of the cleverest uses of a natural spring came from Dad's cousin by marriage, Mr. Demp Marcum. Demp was married to the daughter of my Dad's half-sister from Pa's first marriage who everyone called Aunt Nettie. Aunt Nettie lived on a narrow lane. As you past by her house the narrow lane dead-ended at Mr. Marcum's front yard.

Mr. Marcum was a genius of sorts, at least I thought so. He was ahead of his time. Before anyone else around, he had water plumbed into his house while everyone around him was still drawing water from their wells.

He accomplished this in a very innovative way. Up the hill, above his house was a natural spring shooting right out of the side of the hill. Mr. Marcum built a concrete pool in front of that spring, so he could catch the water. Then he would open the valve allowing the water to flow by gravity into and through a big pipe, then by reducing the pipe size, he'd get all the water pressure he wanted right in his house.

To help control the water pressure the water exited out of the house traveling up and through a pipe attached to a very high pole, then the water would free fall to the ground and flow down the natural creek bed away from the house into a pond where he'd water his animals.

Now, in my way of thinking, this goes to show you that just because someone is from the south doesn't mean they're backward. In Alabama we have our legends and heroes, and I'll just name you a few.

To start with there's Helen Keller, born in Tuscumbia. She was the first deaf blind person to earn a Bachelor of Arts degree.

How about the smooth voice of Nat King Cole, an American singer and musician, born in Montgomery? From the big band era, Alabama gave you Lionel Hampton, jazz musician, born in Birmingham.

Then the "Real Deal", Evander Holyfield, former World Heavyweight Championship boxer, born in Atmore.

The one-time wife of George Jones, Tammy Wynette, country singer and member of the Country Music Hall of fame, was born in Red Bay.

Baseball Hall of Famers, "Hammering" Hank Aaron, born in Mobile, "The Say Hey Kid" Willie Mays, born in Birmingham and "The Wizard of OZ" Ozzie Smith, born in Mobil.

Then the first principal and president of the Tuskegee Institute, George Washington Carver a scientist, though believed to have been born into slavery in Missouri was adopted as a son of Alabama and we are all proud of him. Martin Luther King was born in Georgia, but in our heart of hearts we feel he's ours.

The Alabama Hall of Fame is long with scores of actors, musicians, athletes, politicians and on and on it goes.[xv]

As we left Aunt Nettie's heading back to the old house, often we would stop along the way, to pay our respects to our kinfolk, buried at Moses Graveyard in the woods on the top of the hill. Generations of Mays folk are buried there, Pa and Mama Mays, some of Pa's children and alongside them my great grandparents Aaron M. Mays and Martha Jane Glascock.

A few years back I did a genealogy study of Martha Jane Glascock and discovered she was a descendant of royalty. Her grandfather just a few generations before her was James Stewart I, King of Scotland whose wife was, Queen Joan Beaufort Stewart. The queen was a great, great granddaughter of a fellow called John of Gaunt, Duke of Lancaster, who was the third son of Edward III King of England.

My research showed me that John of Gaunt, Duke of Lancaster had fathered five children outside marriage, one early in life by a lady-in-waiting and four surnamed "Beaufort "by Katherine Swynford. Katherine was Gaunt's long-term mistress and third wife. The Beaufort children were three sons and a daughter. The daughter was the great-great grandmother of Queen Joan Beaufort Stewart.[xvi]

So here we are in Alabama just a stone's throw from Woods Creek, standing in Moses Graveyard in front of my great grandmothers' headstone, who was ten generations removed from Joan Beaufort, Queen of Scots, from whom are descended, beginning in 1437, all subsequent sovereigns of Scotland, and successively, from 1603 on, the sovereigns of England, of Great Britain and Ireland, and of the United Kingdom to the present day.

Northern Alabama was settled by the descendants of aristocratic English families, German farmers, Scots-Irish textile workers, and other European immigrants who lived along the East Coast. When land on the coast became scarce, "Alabama Fever" struck thousands of farmers, who headed to newly opened lands in Alabama to grow cotton.

45

Years of depression eventually caused cotton prices to plummet. Some farmers left for Texas, Oklahoma, and Arkansas, while others found jobs in newly industrialized cities like Birmingham and Atlanta. Ancestry[xvii]

Now as interesting as this is what I am going to share now is awesome. I continued my search on the Mormon owned website and the genealogy stream I was following would bring me to a fellow named Rhesa Ben Zerubbabel. However, this is where my search online dried up.[xviii]

Knowing that Rhesa Ben Zerubbabel was a Bible character, I hoped that I might get more information about him from the scriptures, and sure enough there he was in the Gospel of Luke chapter three.

Starting with verse 23 the verse begins with Jesus... *"Now Jesus Himself began His ministry at about thirty years of age, being (as was supposed) the son of Joseph, the son of Heli,"*

Counting forward from there fifteen generations I found Rhesa in Luke 3:27…. *"The son of Rhesa, the son of Zerubbabel"* …. There he was in the genealogy of Jesus.

Though my research online had dropped off, the stream continued in the Bible, straight ahead fifty-two generations to the fountainhead verse in Luke 3:38, *"the son of Enosh, the son of Seth, the son of Adam, the son of God."*

So, there you have it and they said it couldn't be true. But it is as I have always believed, when you are in Alabama living on Woods Creek you are as about as close to The Garden of Eden as you will ever get and within reach of The Lord God Almighty. AMEN

Chapter 4

Autumn is my favorite time of the year on Woods Creek.
Everyone at the old house are celebrating because the
harvests are finished; the cotton is picked, the corn is
pulled, the hay is put into the loft of the old barn, and all
the canning is in the pantry. The results once again
prove that faith, hard work and persistence pays off. This
season of the year reminds me of the passage in God's
Word;

*"Whatever you do, work at it with all your heart, as though
you were working for the Lord and not for
people". Colossians 3:23;*

This principle guarantees your hard work to be blessed with
success and the testimony which follows will bring glory
and honor to our Savior.

Thanksgiving Day, Christmas and the New
Year are seasons, of gratitude, joy and hope. This
Christmas at the old house will be very special. As I hoped,
my Mother and little brother Kenny have come home from
Michigan after several months. No one could be more
excited than my Dad, who will finally have his family
all together again.

My Mother came bearing gifts for everyone, and the gift
she gave to me would be life changing...my very own Jerry
Mahoney ventriloquist dummy. You know what I mean.
You pull the string, the dummy's lips move, and when you
throw your voice without moving your lips, it leaves the
impression that the dummy is talking.

My dummy was a duplicate of "The Jerry Mahoney"
dummy, a creation of the American ventriloquist, Paul

Winchell.[xix] Back in the early fifties Winchell had his own television show. My mother knew that his program was one of my favorites, so giving me this gift was perfect. I would name my dummy "Jimmy".

This is the truth, though I hide it pretty good today, ever since my youth I have been a shy and reticent person. I have always been a person who was more focused on my internal feelings rather than on external things. I guess you could say I am an introvert. I've read that Psychology says introverts and extroverts are often viewed in terms of two extreme opposites, but the truth is that most people lie somewhere in the middle. As a child unless I was spoken to...I really wouldn't have much to say. Since I was usually quiet some folks thought of me as shy or even a bit backward. The truth... I was deeply submerged within my own world. Mother knew this and understood there was nothing to worry about. She had no hidden agenda as a reason for giving me Jimmy, you know, somehow hoping that he would bring me out of my shell. No, not at all, my Mother doesn't think like that.[xx]

But nevertheless, Jimmy did unlock something within me. With Jimmy on my lap I found it easier for me to express myself in ways I was never able to do before. With this new freedom of expression, I found that people would listen to me while we performed our act. I must admit, I enjoyed being the center of attention. By our making them laugh I felt acceptance and acceptance is what I needed. Like a cool drink of water on a hot day, getting the people's applause quenched my internal thirst.

Hamilton, Alabama our hometown, is in the foothills of the Appalachian Mountains and is the county seat of Marion County. The county courthouse square is the centerpiece of our town. Our town is a crossroads so at any time, you will see travelers and long-haul truckers, driving through on their way to Memphis by way of Tupelo Mississippi, the birthplace of... "Elvis Presley the King of Rock N Roll", or maybe going to and from Chicago, Nashville, Atlanta. As a young boy I believed that from Hamilton I could go anywhere in the world and I couldn't hardly wait to get started.

There's more than travelers going in and out of town. There were farmers bringing wagons of cotton or corn to the cotton gin or corn sheller. On school days, big yellow school busses were lining up to drop the kids off at either Hamilton Elementary or Hamilton High School, the home of the "Aggie Bulldogs", which originated in 1895 as West Alabama Agricultural School, hence the name "Aggies".

Saturdays in Hamilton was the busiest day of the week. The town would be bustling with men and women in their best hats or bonnets congregating in all the shops around the court square.

The only other shopping we got to do at the old house was when the peddler would come by, which was about twice a month. He would drive up in an old Ford farm truck which he had built a large van box on the rear of it, with side doors. When I stood by the truck it was taller than me, so the peddler would lift me up and let me walk around inside. One could buy "everything from soup to nuts", even live chickens which were in cages on the back of the truck. Mama Mays would let me save out a few eggs from our weekly collection to trade to the peddler for candy. As much as I enjoyed the peddler, going to town on Saturday was an adventure.

Surrounding the court square stood a concrete wall about three feet in height. It was on this wall that men folks visited with friends and neighbors arguing politics, talking about farming or just catching up on the local news, while their women folk would do the shopping. Of course, the ladies too would be sure to catch up on the latest gossip as they busied about complaining with the store clerks about the prices. Here are some fun facts you might find interesting; The average price of new house in 1953 was a whopping $9550, while a working man could earn on average about $4,000 a year. These numbers were even smaller in Alabama. Nevertheless, with all that money you could afford twenty cents a gallon, so you could drive the new car you bought for just under two thousand dollars. Like they say, "the rich get richer and the poor get poorer".[xxi]

It was at that court square where I was introduced to segregation. You see, on one fourth of the four walls is where the black folks sat, while the other three sides of the square only the white folk sat. Outside the courthouse were posted signs, at drinking fountains and on toilet doors. "White Only", "Colored only". As a boy, I never understood why it was this way. I would think, "What could be so wrong with these colored folks." I didn't have an answer, but I was sure it was wrong...because in my heart I felt hurt, even anger, it just didn't feel right. You know what grownups seem to find normal and acceptable, will very often feel wrong to a child. Back there on that court square everyone regardless of where you sat on the wall couldn't have possibly believed that this could be okay. I believe that every person who will be honest must admit that treating people with such distain is unacceptable. Fortunately, in just a few years on a certain day in Montgomery, one very tired, very brave black lady,

"Rosa Parks", would refuse to sit in the back of the bus and because of her determination all this wrong would start to change. The fact is, change would soon come to the wall around the courthouse. It turns out that when the new courthouse was built on the same location the old wall was not put back. I think it was because the wall was a reminder of a time when things were wrong, and folks didn't want to be reminded of that time anymore.[xxii]

The New Year started off with an unexpected announcement. My Dad had gone to the town of Hamilton and when he returned he told Mother he had sold the corn crop and with the money he bought the Lion Oil service station.

In the mid-1950s, the Lion Oil service stations were a common feature along the roadsides of Alabama. In the South there were more than 2,000 Lion service stations. The founder of the company Thomas Barton decided to call his company "Lion Oil" because of his fondness for wordplay. Lion Oil is a palindrome, spelled the same forward and backward. I always loved the Lion sign at Dad's station. It was cool. I'm not the only one who thought it was cool, the 1960s gave rise to the popular "Beauregard Lion" mascot of Lion advertisements and the sign became very collectable.[xxiii]

Dad's Lion station was quaint with a great location, at the intersection of Highways 278 and "The Old Jackson Military Highway." It was a two-pump station, with an area where Dad could repair flats.

Outside the front door was a coin operated box cooler. When you lifted the top of the cooler it exposed soda pop bottles hanging on a rack dangling and submerged in cold water. There in the cooler was Coke, Dr. Pepper, Nehi Grapette and Orange and finally RC Cola. To retrieve your soda, you put a dime in the slot, slid the soda down the rack and lifted it out. The "Drink Coke" bottle opener was attached to the side of the cooler, so you could pry the top off.

Next to the soda cooler were the oil rack and a stack of used tires. When you came inside the station, you stepped onto an oil stained plank floor and with every step the planks responded with a quiet groan. Lingering in the air was a sweet-smelling mixture of gas, oil, and tobacco smoke.

Once inside you could purchase oil filters, radiator hoses, fan belts, spark plugs and general automotive merchandise. Behind the counter there's a cigarette rack and shelfs of assorted tobaccos and snuffs.

Perched on top of the glass display case was a large selection of your favorite snacks still in their boxes. Candy bars of every kind, lots of Wrigley's chewing gum, penny candies and treats like Tom's Peanuts a nickel a bag. Perhaps the first grab it and go combination which was sometimes called "the working man's lunch", was an RC Cola and a Moon Pie…which probably became popular with 1950's Big Bill Lister song, "Giv'me an RC Cola and a Moon Pie."

"Give me an RC Cola and a Moon Pie

I'm playin' Maple on the hill

I'll catch that freight train on the blind

Leave my corn down at the mill.

Cause I sold my calf for a dollar and a half,

So, Brother, I can pay the bill.

Give me an RC Cola and a Moon Pie

I'm playin' Maple on the hill"[xxiv]

My Dad's station was dimly lit by a single light bulb hanging from the ceiling, an old potbellied coal stove in the middle of the floor heated the place. Encircled around the stove was about a half dozen straw bottom high back chairs like those at the old house. And sitting in those chairs like knights at King Arthur's round table, the wisdom of generations past, in their bib overalls, with their smokes pinched between their tobaccos stained fingers. They would laugh at their own jokes...jokes that they couldn't tell at home and then they would argue politics or Bible doctrines, like, "once saved always saved".

In 1953 the subject of the day was America's newly inaugurated president, Dwight D. (Ike) Eisenhower. I remember during the campaign, the slogan "I Like Ike" could be seen everywhere, on coat lapels, roadside billboards, power poles and such. The campaign badges and buttons from that era are still prized collectibles today. If my memory serves me well I think there was an, "I Like Ike" poster still hanging in the station.

Ike was an American hero. It had been just ten years before his election, that President Roosevelt decided that Eisenhower would be Supreme Allied Commander in Europe, and a year later he was promoted to General of the Army. This high command allowed the General to demonstrate to all Americans his great talents for leadership and diplomacy.

One of my greatest accomplishments as a kid during those days was winning my Dad's admiration for my talent of ventriloquism. With the script Mom had written, Dad would proudly bring me and Jimmy to the Lion Station and tell all the men sitting around the potbellied stove to listen to his boy and his dummy. I would perform for the old timers and they in turn would give me nickels and by me cokes which I would fill with Tom's peanuts.

So, the Lion service station became my debut stage to what later would be more than six decades of being in front of folks, first as an entertainer and then as a minister. The Lion Station gig would also prepare me for the big time, beginning with my third-grade teacher asking me to perform in the High School talent show held in the auditorium.

For a third grader, this was the big time. However, the size of the stage, the brightness of the lights and along with the fact that I couldn't see a soul in the audience made our performance you might say, a little lackluster. I placed second in the contest based on the "cuteness factor", behind a very gifted high school senior, doing his imitation of "Al Jolson, in blackface, singing "Mammy". It was however my introduction to show business.

Spending Christmas at the old house with the whole family was wonderful. Sadly, I was unaware this would be my last Christmas on "Woods Creek". In September 1953, Pa would go into heaven. Pa always said concerning his faith, "I can't tell you the time, but I can take you to the place, where The Lord saved me, by His wonderful grace." Pa's funeral would be conducted at our home church, the Pleasant Grove Baptist Church.

After Pa died, we all naturally assumed my father would inherit the old house and the land. It didn't happen. I learned much later that whatever happened to my Dad's inheritance it left a bitter taste in my father's mouth which is why he would leave "Woods Creek" for a season.

Dad sold his Lion service station, packed up everything, and off we went back to Adrian Michigan. Sadly, my alter ego Jimmy, got lost on the way, with my interest as a ventriloquist gone too. Leaving Woods Creek was sad...however it is the genesis of what my life was to become, and the old house would always be in my heart. As they say, "you can take the boy out of the country, but you can't take the country out of the boy." Thirteen years later I would return.

Chapter 5

My story of Adrian, Michigan began, if you remember, way back when Mother, Grandma and I came north in 1944, and later in 1945 my Dad would follow us there. My earliest memories were the Housing Projects on Beecher Street. They were long single-story buildings made of concrete blocks painted white and separated into four apartments, with front doors painted Hunter Green. Each apartment had a front room, two bedrooms, bathroom and kitchen with stove and icebox.

The apartments back doors opened to an alley with a coal bin for each residence. It was also at the back door where the milkman would deliver our milk and the ice man would deliver our ice.

With big tongs, the ice man would grab a block of ice from his truck...hoist the block of ice to his shoulder which was draped and protected by a leather pad, from there the ice would rest as he brought it into the kitchen and placed it into the freezer compartment of the ice box.

I felt fortunate that the green door on our apartment faced Beecher Street which had a big yard going from the door to the sidewalk. It was in that big yard where most of the kids in the projects would come to play and ride their bicycles.

While living in Adrian my brothers Gary, Kenny and Joe would be born. While we lived on Beecher Street, Gary would be hospitalized with his first bout of rheumatic fever which would affect him the rest of his life. There too, Gary and I both started kindergarten at the Lincoln Elementary School on Division Street then onto the first grade at Garfield Elementary School on Cross Street.

It happened one day as we were walking home from school that Gary began crying and complaining that his legs were hurting. After a long painful struggle to walk we arrived home. Soon the family doctor would come and then just as quickly my Dad, Mother and Gary left. I really didn't understand what was happening, but later my parents would explain that my brother was very ill, and he was going to be in the hospital a long time. I thought about him every day and I wondered if I would ever see him again. He was my best friend and I missed him so much. I can still recall the day he came home and even though he still had to stay in bed, doctors' orders, we both were happy to be together again. I loved that boy.

It's funny but I still remember the names of my first teachers, White and Brown. My first-grade teacher Mrs. White and older woman with hair as white as snow. My second-grade teacher Miss Brown was my first love, until one day as she was writing on the blackboard, she …passed… gas! I was stunned...I couldn't believe it...she had been so perfect...how is this possible. The girls giggled, my buddies laughed out loud and I was embarrassed for her as she looked back over her shoulder as if nothing had happened. My infatuation for her was lost that day and from that moment forward she was just teacher. I would spend my third grade at Hamilton Elementary back in Alabama, but after our return to Michigan again, I will spend the remainder of my elementary education right there at good old Garfield.

Just across Beecher Street from the projects was "The Big Elm" grocery store. The store got its name from the big Elm tree stump in front of it. It was a mom and pop size store owned by a Jewish man who gave my Dad a running tab which he paid every payday. When I found out about it I would sometimes sneak over and get something sweet and put it on the tab. Dad never made a fuss about it. The store had a penny gum ball machine that had special yellow with blue stripes gum balls. If you were lucky after putting your penny in the coin slot, if one of those prized balls fell into your hand you could trade it for a nickel candy bar, and my favorite has always been "Snickers".

The big yard was also home to a very special event that happened almost every Saturday. Ladies from the Salvation Army in their long black dresses and small black hats would come there. They would gather all the project kids and there were a lot of them...all of us just about the same age...having been born during WWII. Strategically the ladies would give us all big jaw breakers, which when placed in our mouths made it almost impossible for us to talk.

Once we were corralled and quieted, they would then place on their green flannel board, paper characters of people, animals, and buildings as they told us Bible stories. We enjoyed the tales of the shepherd boy named David who would slay a Giant and be crowned a king. The story of the flood and Noah's Ark was one the kids really loved. My favorite was Joseph's coat of many colors and of course the most important story of all...the baby born in a manger, which became a man and died on a cross for our sins.

After the stories, they would have us bow our heads, close our eyes and invite Jesus into our hearts. With our jaw breakers now in our hands, we would open our hearts door to which they said Jesus was knocking, and then we would ask Jesus to come in. The Salvation Army ladies left a tremendous impression on me and I hoped that Jesus was in my heart.

I have always loved southern Michigan, but being back here this time was bittersweet. Though several months have gone by since the passing of Pa, my thoughts of him, the old house and Woods Creek would always sadden me.

Adrian, was referred to by the local folks as "the Maple City" due in part to the many sugar maples and other maple species found throughout the neighborhoods.

In the month of March 1954, my brother Bobby Joe was born. Having a little baby filled our springtime with joy and laughter. I was really looking forward to playing baseball in the park and swimming at the school pool that summer. However, my summer plans would be interrupted with Dad telling us that we would all be traveling with him because of his new job.

My Dad was working with a construction crew building Quonset grain elevators. The company had contracts all over the Midwest. We all packed up and joined the company caravan like a band of gypsies traveling from construction site to construction site. For Dad, it was all about the work, for us kids, it was more like a vacation. Staying in motels, having picnics at roadside rest areas, going places, we had never gone before, it was all so exciting and so much better than what I had planned.

Our last stop on the tour was Garrison, North Dakota. At the time we arrived in Garrison the great Garrison Dam, an earth filled embankment built on the Missouri River, was just finishing up. The work on the dam created a housing shortage and the only house Mom and Dad could find was a two-room house owned by a very elderly German couple.

Can you imagine six people in one bedroom? It didn't bother us too much for it was still like camping.

I have always felt the reason Dad was restless and moved about so much was because he never felt he belonged anywhere on earth but "Woods Creek". The summer job finally played out and this would end our adventure, so back to Adrian and our house on State Street.

Returning home, we were met by the Autumn of the year. The leaves of the sugar maple can form a complete color wheel throughout the year, turning several shades of green, then from yellow to orange, and finally to red in the fall. Like grandma's quilt they covered the streets and yards and their quiet slumber brought a peaceful relief to my aching heart for Pa and Mama Mays and the old house.

Winter came. When I was young I loved the snows of Michigan, the winter that year was exceptional, beautiful.

We couldn't have known that before and after the summer tour, my Dad was just trying to survive financially and keep his family fed. The times were difficult for him. My brother Gary was still struggling with his physical challenges, and Dad couldn't find any work. My Mother told me once that she begged Dad to ask for help during those days. Feeling like a failure and humiliated by the thought of it, he went with my Mother to the welfare office.

Soon Christmas came, and my mind swirled with longings for "Woods Creek". As the Christmas morning dawned a huge surprise awaited the whole family. I would have never known this either had Mother not told me the story years later. Some people from the welfare office came to our house early on that morning with bags of groceries, including toys for the little children and for Gary and me, brand new bicycles. Mother told me, she wept with joy as she and Dad placed all the presents around our Christmas Tree. As far as we children were concerned, Santa had come to our house. My brother and I were so excited, the only thing we were thinking about was riding, riding, riding everywhere on our new Western Auto Flyers. Western Flyer was an American private label brand of bicycles, tricycles, scooters, play wagons, pedal cars, tractors, and roller skates, sold by Western Auto stores.[xxv]

There was a time in Adrian, when my brother and I, probably knew just about every street in the city, not only because every time we moved back we lived in a new neighborhood, but now with our trusty Western Flyers... we scouted out every street and alley.

There are six streets in "The Maple City", which are very important to my story, East Beecher Street, State Street, South Winter Street, Cross Street, South Main Street and James Street.

My first story starts one day as I was riding home from school for lunch. When I turned on to State Street. "The Voice", spoke to me once again. The first time I ever heard "The Voice", I thought it was my imagination. It was an internal voice, soft as a whisper. But today it was different. Today for the first time "The Voice" was loud, distinct, like someone was right there talking to me. Before it was a quiet inward nudge, directing me or correcting me. But today "The Voice" is boldly pronouncing, "Your wife's name is Judy from Sacramento, California".

This was crazy...befuddled at the thought, "what the heck does this mean."

Now this is hard to believe but it's true and even more amazing, I didn't know a single person named Judy. I had never spoke the name Sacramento unless it may have been in a geography class. Without a doubt I was perplexed.

For years after my experience with "The Voice", I pondered this mystery. I knew "The Voice" was real and I knew the message was something special. Yet, the first time I found myself standing at an altar in the wedding chapel in Sacramento, getting married to my first wife Marion Lee Camp... just before I was to say I do, the thought came to me, "her...name is not Judy." It didn't seem right that day and it would prove to be true. "The Voice", continued speaking to me all my life. Yet I would continue to usually ignore it, accept on one very important day to which was to come.

I have already told you a little of Beecher Street and State Street, now let me tell you my story of South Winter Street. Starting at East U.S. Highway 223, South Winter ran north, beyond East Beecher Street, crossing over the Adrian and Blissfield railroad tracks, then continuing past Cross Street, it intersected with South Main Street.

The Adrian and Blissfield Railroad Company was originally built in 1834 by the Erie and Kalamazoo Railroad and is still one of the oldest operating railroads in the United States. My brother, cousin and friends would spend hours playing beside those tracks. We would build forts in the ditches beside them. We would lay pennies on the rails and let the train flatten them when it came by. It was great fun.[xxvi]

Just over those tracks and to the second house on the left was the big Victorian style house which would be our home for the next few years. The owner had made it into a duplex, so when we first moved there we lived in the smaller side of the duplex. Living in the larger side was my Dad's sister Ruth, her husband Curtis and my cousins Annette and Doyle.

Eventually Aunt Ruth's family moved away, and we moved into the larger side of the house, while at the same time my Grandma Phoebe, my mother's widowed sister Leota, and her two boys Mike and Charles, moved into the smaller side. Aunt Leota's husband Arnold had been killed in an accident while driving a lumber truck back in Alabama.

The backyard of the big house had a large standalone garage and an orchard of apples, pears, cherries and a garden spot. The fence at the end of the garden separated our place from the Garfield Elementary School playground which made it convenient for us...we would simply climb the fence and...there was our own personal playground. We could swing, slide the slides, climb on the monkey bars, play tennis, have a game of football or baseball. On Saturday's the school promoted a play time in the gym where we played dodge ball.

There was one house that stood between us and the railroad tracks. The McNichols. The McNichols kids were Shirley, Sandy and Gary. Most evenings all the kids would play until after dark. We would chase fireflies, sit on the porch and talk or play hide-n-seek. I would always try to hide with Sandy, so I could sneak a kiss without anybody knowing, though I think most did...but it was ok...we were the same age and in the same class.

Very often during the week Gary and I would go about town with our wagon searching and collecting soda bottles. For every bottle we found and depending on the size, we could get two or three cents per bottle from Mr. Jenkins at the Bill Jenkins Sinclair Station. We usually would cash in between twenty to fifty cents. Just enough to go to the movie house on Saturday.

The Family Theatre was located at 136 South Main Street and we were there every Saturday and all-day long. For just ten cents we could see a double feature, cartoons, a newsreel and a serial. Our favorites were the cowboys. We knew them all and we knew the names of all their horses. For us, the two greatest of all time, were Roy Rogers and Gene Autry.

Roy Rogers, "The King of the Cowboys" and his Golden Palomino Trigger. I learned that Roy's real name was Leonard Franklin Slye, born in Ohio, he first came to California as a singer and was one of the founders of The Sons of The Pioneers. With his trademark horse Trigger, they appeared together in nearly one hundred films, not to mention the television show.[xxvii]

Gene Autry the Singing Cowboy, and Champion, the "Wonder Horse of the West". Gene was country music's first "multi-media" star, with nine gold records and one platinum album, and at the same time, an audience favorite in movies, on radio, and on television.[xxviii]

There were many other big silver screen heroes, Alan Ladd, William Boyd, also known as Hop-along Cassidy, Bob Steele, Johnny Mack Brown, The Durango Kid, and Lash LaRue. Then too, their comical sidekicks like

George 'Gabby' Hayes and Smiley Burnett, just to name two, always kept us laughing.[xxix]

The weekly serial was a story that played on installments. Capturing our imaginations, the serials Rocket Man or Flash Gordon brought us back week after week to see who would save the day and rescue the girl who was about to be sawed in half or run over by the train. All of this for just a dime and boy we were hooked.

By the time I was in the sixth grade the era of Rock N Roll was in full swing. Though one could say, the seed of rock n roll, had been around for years when first conceived in the juke joints of St. Louis, the cotton fields of the Mississippi delta and the streets of Chicago and New York. The musical gestation of rock n roll would culminate in the womb of rhythm and blues all nurtured by studios like Chess, Decca and RCA. With bluesmen such as Muddy Waters, Howling Wolf, Little Walter, Willie Dixon, this music would be delivered home by none other than Chuck Berry.[xxx]

Meanwhile, down on the corner of Union and Marshall at Sam Phillips' Sun Records studio, the boys from Memphis, Elvis, Jerry Lee Lewis, Carl Perkins, Johnny Cash and Roy Orbison, were bringing the genre to its adolescence, merging the blues with rock and country licks...calling it Rockabilly. "Great balls of fire, rock n roll was shaking our nerves and rattling our brains".[xxxi]

Most everyone has heard the Elvis story, but did you know that Sam Phillips sold Elvis' contract to RCA Victor Records for a paltry sum of $35,000. In 1955 that sounded like a lot of money, and to Sam it was. He needed that money to relieve his financial difficulties which his label

65

Sun Records was going through. Elvis would become RCA's biggest selling recording artist and take the throne as the "King of Rock N Roll".[xxxii]

At the epicenter of this phenomenon exploding around the world was science. In the laboratories America's brightest minds had developed what they called the "transistor." With the development of the transistor in 1953, the transistor radio would become the most popular electronic device in history. Now the young people of the world with their portable radios and record players in their hands, could have this new music with them everywhere they went. Rock N Roll was alive and going global.[xxxiii]

I must tell you the music of these "cool cats" got into me and birthed in me a passion for playing music as much as my ventriloquist dummy Jimmy had released in me the desire to be an entertainer.

My musical quest would start in the sixth grade at the Garfield Elementary with my music teacher announcing that any sixth grader interested in being in the Junior High Band should come to a special class after school in the music room. This class would be directed by the conductor of the High School band. Well you better believe I was there. It was hard for me to contain my excitement. This teacher wasn't just any teacher, she was from the band at the High School...I mean how big is this!

As she passed out the music books she also gave us a musical instrument, a plastic flute. She continued by giving us our first lessons; on how to hold it, how to blow it, and the fingering positions so we could play the scale.

My first assignment was to practice the scale and learn the first song in the book, "Twinkle, Twinkle Little Star".

Well by the time I could get home to tell my Mother the news, I had already mastered the first song. I didn't put that flute down the whole weekend. Over and over I played. Not just the first song, but every song in the book, even the last one, The Marines Hymn. The Marines Hymn is the most recognizable military hymn and the oldest official song in the U.S. Armed Forces. The Marines Hymn is a reminder of the sacrifice and courage that Marines have shown on the battlefield.

"From the Halls of Montezuma,

to the shores of Tripoli;

We fight our country's battles,

in the air, on land, and sea;

First to fight for right and freedom,

and to keep our honor clean;

We are proud to claim the title

of the United States Marine."

I could hardly wait for the next class where we're all going to be asked to play the song, Twinkle, Twinkle. During the class, every kid stood with their music on the music-stand, playing the assignment on their flutes. By the time it gets to me I am totally bored with Twinkle, Twinkle. Then at the very last moment I decided I was going to play... "The Marines Hymn". What happens next would make a deep wound in me for many years to come. Before I could get to the part, "we fight our country's battles", the battle was on.

Suddenly the band teacher jumps from her chair and with a swinging blow knocks my music book from its stand. She was obviously livid, she yells "you sit down mister". I was mortified, ...stunned...I couldn't move. I saw the horror and the shock in the faces of my classmates.

"Sit down", she barked again, "and you better learn to stay with the class."

I was numbed, I couldn't speak. I couldn't think. I couldn't feel...just numb. I know she continued to speak to the class and she spoke to me as I left the room, yet I never heard a word...I had gone deaf and mute. I didn't speak to a soul as we left the music room. When I got home, I couldn't tell Mother. I just never spoke about the music, the band or anything else. My Mother did casually ask about it once, but I just mumbled something and never really confided with her about my devastating experience.

For some reason, right after I started the seventh grade we left South Winter Street and moved to James Street. On James Street, my love for Rock N Roll was growing. Every day I would rush home from school to play my radio or records and watch Dick Clark and American Bandstand. I would dance along with the rhythm and sound of "At the Hop", with Danny and the Juniors" and I played my air guitar on numbers like "Johnny B. Good "and "Blue Suede Shoes". The truth be told, Rock n Roll was more than the music. I was really digging the cool fashions that came with the music. During this time, the latest fads were black leather jackets, ducktail hairdos, Levi's jeans and converse sneakers. My hair was so greased with Royal Crown Pomade, that when I left for school on those snowy cold winter morning, the snow would freeze to my hair, as I would settle into the classroom my hair seems to melt, it was gross.

Other than that, the year would have been uneventful except for Johnny Garcia. Johnny and I had most of our classes together. I think it was the way I dressed that caught Johnny's attention, because he dressed the same way, but even cooler, because he had sideburns and he was also known to be a tough guy. The fact that he was all of that would turn out to be a tremendous benefit for me, because, before the school year was over Johnny would come to my rescue more than once.

The first time was swim night at the school swimming pool. All the guys were playing tag at the pool, running all around, jumping into the pool to escape a tag from whoever was, "It". I wasn't a very strong swimmer and I don't know if my friends ever noticed...but I never got into the deep end of the pool where the water would be over my head. But it did happen. Not realizing my location near the deep end of the pool, I dove to escape a tag and down I went...all the way to the bottom...into the deepest part of the pool, way over my head. As I was sinking, I knew immediately I was in trouble.

When I hit the bottom, I found my footing and pushed as hard as I could, backup to the surface. I was in a panic mode, gasping for air. I frantically fought...but I sank to the bottom again. With strength leaving my body, I pushed again, this time only barely making it to the surface. I tried to scream but no sound would leave my throat, and down I would go again. Then suddenly, I felt my body lifting...lifting...as strong arms pulled me up to the surface and to the edge of the pool.

My eyes were burning with pool water and in panic...I was clinging to the pool side...trying to catch my breath. As the image started coming into focus through water filled eyes, it was my rescuer, Johnny Garcia. He smiled with concern, "You alright man"? Thoroughly embarrassed by the entire incident, I shook my head yes. I was extremely thankful. I did finally learn to swim.

The next time trouble showed up came when this bully in my shop class called me out because of how I dressed and said he was going to kick my butt. I really wasn't too worried about this guy, so I told him I would meet him after school. I showed up, then he showed, and showing up with him were a half dozen of his buddies.

I knew I was in trouble, so I prepared myself mentally to get a real beating. Then curiously, they all began to slowly backup...then turning...they ran. The bully being the first to go. In stunned wonder, I turn to look over my shoulder and who was there, Johnny Garcia, coming to my rescue again. I don't know if he had somehow heard about what was going to happen to me after school and, so he planned to be there, or that he just happened by. Johnny was my friend, he would invite me into his home where I got a taste of real Mexican food for the first time. I think about him often and I pray he had a good life. This era was what I called "The Leave it to Beaver" era. It was the best time in America. I wish that America was still here for my children, my grandchildren and now my great grandchildren. My family left Michigan in 1958. I would return twice, once in 1961 and then again in 1968 to Cross Street.

Chapter 6

So here we are leaving Adrian again heading back to Alabama and the reason is simple, Dad is out of work. The Michigan auto industry back in 1957 had fallen off by a third, making the year 1958 the worst auto production year since the war. This downturn created a ripple effect of unemployment starting in Detroit with about twenty percent of the work force out of jobs.

Then to add to the woes of working folks, was yet another self-inflicted wound crippling the American economy. It seems that we Americans can't resist the cheap foreign products. So as imports increased to feed our consumer frenzy, the American raw materials trade decreased severely, particularly in Europe thus creating an economic anomaly. Rather than prices falling as it would be in a normal recession, prices across the board rose by close to three percent. So not only were there less jobs, but prices in the marketplace were higher. This left economist scratching their head, and my Dad is feeling the itch too.

Here we are, back to the red clay dirt and the rolling hills. However, this time there will not be an old house to return to. After my grandfather's death, his old home place and the house had been sold, so for now we haven't a house, so we are houseless. I use the term houseless to describe folks like us who have family to turn to, but presently they don't have a house to call their own. I believe when a person has family ready to help them that person can never be homeless, because families are home.

Jesus tells the parable of "The Prodigal Son". The story is about a father who has two sons. The younger son asks for his inheritance and after wasting his fortune becomes destitute. Now, realizing that he is houseless and in financial ruin, he remembers his home and his father. He returns home to his father who is relieved that his boy is alive and welcomes him back with open arms.

This story illustrates my point. When a person has a family waiting for your call, you are never homeless. The homeless of America if the truth be known, are those individuals who have abandoned their families. They have estranged themselves to the degree that they no longer have a family to turn to. You've heard this said, "home is where the heart is.

On our arrival we are invited to stay with my Uncle Bernard and Aunt Ruby whom graciously opened their house to us. Uncle Bernard is my Dad's older brother, a very stoic individual, somewhat of an intellectual, and a tremendous help to my Dad. My Aunt Ruby was a kind woman. She had a tiny thin body and her voice was very high pitched. She was always fluttering about like a busy bee. The two never had children, but to their credit they lovingly took all six of us into their house. They were very loving to us, and for that I was grateful.

Unfortunately jobs in Alabama were no less sparse. When you live in an agricultural community if there is any work it will be in the fields or something related. With the help of Uncle Bernard, Dad went to work with James Ray the owner of the cotton gin. Dad also found some construction work, helping to build the old folks home and tearing down the old Marion County courthouse. We were settling in with our kinfolk as time came to start school.

I would soon discover the campus of Hamilton High was conservatively different and perhaps even a bit behind the times compared to my experience in Michigan. No black leather jackets here and only a few guys had ducktails, a hairstyle made popular by Elvis and James Dean. No not here, not in hick-town USA. To add to the strain of my adjusting to these new surroundings, I learned firsthand from these farm boys they didn't really cotton to this Yankee intruder. The student body at Hamilton High was largely farm kids with a slight sprinkling of town kids. Unlike Adrian which was substantially integrated, this campus was not. There wasn't one single kid in that school who was not white. That's right, no blacks, no Hispanic, nor any other sort of ethnicity could be found. I wouldn't describe them as "White Anglo-Saxon Protestant" for WASP refers to an elite social class of powerful white Americans of British Protestant ancestry. I can say for sure that elite or powerful doesn't fit, only white country boys and girls from the Appalachian foothills, traditional southern Christians, Baptists, Methodist and Pentecostals are dominating this Bible Belt community. Every social activity here centers around three things, farming, football and church.[xxxiv]

The school-year in Hamilton begins early in August but as soon as the fall harvest starts, school is dismissed for the season, so the farm kids can help their families with the work.

On Friday nights it's all football. At home games you could see the lights at Sargent Field illuminating the sky heralding call that the Aggie Bulldogs were in the house. Every football player was treated like gods and the cheerleaders were thought of as prima donnas.

Until now the only time I was ever in this high school building was the time I won second place in the talent show as a third-grade kid. It's been six years since then and now as a freshman I'm entering the hallways of the old school once again. I wouldn't know it on that day, but this would be the last year I or anyone else would be educated in that old building.

No one ever seemed to know how the fire started in the school, though most everyone you heard talk had tales of arson. There was a bit of scuttlebutt around town about the fire, which raised suspicions rested on the facts that when the voluntary firemen get to the firehouse to get the equipment, the firehouse lock on the door had been jammed. So, by the time the door was pried open the school was lost.

Trying to assimilate into the school socially was as I have mentioned, tough. Luckily for me I had played a lot of baseball in Michigan. Not that I am bragging, but I was a pretty good player and a good catcher too. So here I am in the ninth grade, in a new school and the game of baseball will prove to be my way of gaining acceptance with my peers.

It all started with a game of catch. One of the varsity players a pretty good pitcher somehow learned that I played the position of catcher. He's throwing the ball hard and I am having no problem receiving it. What we hadn't realized is that we had drawn a crowd of onlookers. In the crowd was Coach Bobby Lott. The Coach interrupted our play and ask me how I had learned to catch so well.

I told him my cousin's husband Clint had taught me and that I played in a youth league in Michigan. You might say I scored a home run that day, for soon I was the talk of the campus even though I did have a Yankee accent.

When baseball season opened, I was riding the bench behind the team's starting catcher Willard Frye. A big fellow and a very good player. My lucky break and Willard's bad break came during one of our first games. The play happened at second base when Willard came sliding into the bag. After the dust settled there lay Willard, clutching his right hand...he had broken his thumb. Since this was his senior year he would never play baseball again for the Hamilton Aggies. I played out the remainder of that season which proved to be my one and only season. I did receive an athletic letter for baseball which I wore proudly on my school sweater. I kept that sweater with me for years, but like so many things in my life, it too has been left behind.

The greatest blessing that year was the birth of a baby sister. Peggy Ann was born on February 2, 1959. She would be my Mother's last child, after four boys, she finally has her girl. We all adored her and still do.

For my poor Dad, life was not getting any easier. Finding work was still almost impossible, however Dad made a deal to try his hand as a sharecropper. What's a sharecropper? A sharecropper is a person who works on another man's land and in return the cropper gives the owner of the land a share of the crops produced usually on 50/50 basis. The owner provides land, the equipment and half of the seed money. The share cropper provides his half of the seed money and does all the work. There is usually housing provided and space for a garden, maybe some chickens, pigs and a cow thrown into the deal. There are benefits and costs for both the owners and the croppers. For the owner the deal encourages the cropper to remain on the land throughout the harvest season to cultivate the crop and bring in the harvest. When it came to the risks, both the landowners and sharecroppers shared, whether the harvests being large or small or the crop prices being high or low.xxxv

My Dad's first attempt as a sharecropper was a tragic failure, not for the lack of his trying but because of things not in his control. Back in those days all farming in Alabama was dry farming, which means you had to hope for rain. Unfortunately for Dad the rains came alright, rain, rain and more rain, too much rain. The tragic results were, we couldn't keep the Boll-weevil and the Johnson grass out of the fields. The crops were all but lost.

If that wasn't bad enough, to add to my parents' misery they suffered the news that a tragic accident had happened. While at the babysitter, baby sister Peggy Ann was severely burned by electrocution. It occurred while crawling on the floor she contacted an exposed wire of an electrical cord from an oscillating fan. It was frightening news, but by the grace of God she survived, howbeit our precious little girl would be scarred for life. That never stopped Peggy she grew to be a tremendous person. Beautiful both inside and out. She was smart and very popular in school. During football season, she was a cheerleader. During basketball season, she was chosen as an All-American high school athlete. In fact, she was the most notable athlete in our family, the first woman inducted into the Marion County Athletic Hall of Fame. I loved that girl.

Sometimes one begins to wonder if the troubles will never end, if the dark cloud will never lift. It's like the old Ray Charles song;

"My bills are all due and the babies need shoes,

But I'm Busted

Cotton's gone down to a quarter a pound

And I'm Busted

"I got a cow that's gone dry

And a hen that won't lay

A big stack of bills

Getting bigger each day

The county's gonna haul my belongings away,

But I'm Busted"[xxxvi]

One thing I can say about my family, they have learned how to take a punch. We all said good bye to the first farming partnership Dad had made, for he made a new sharecropper deal on a farm in Detroit. No not Michigan, but Detroit, Alabama, a wide spot in the road just seventeen miles from Hamilton. Though it was outside the school district, it was close enough that I could drive myself to school in my Dad's 1950 Plymouth.

The new farm and a second chance at being shar croppers became with different feelings. I guess because we were all so grateful that little sister Peggy was doing well. Despite the financial setbacks we were making a strong comeback.

Our new house was very small, but I think the smallness helped to bring us closer together. It was here where I received the gift of my first guitar.

Just down the lane from our little house lived a kind old lady. She often came up to visit Mother and would always have something special to give to our family. It might be vegetables, fruit or something sweet like cookies or a pie. She often hired my brother Gary and me to do chores for her around her house. I don't think I ever mentioned anything to her about my wanting a guitar while I was working for her. I don't know how she knew, perhaps from my Mother, but she discovered that I loved to sing, and I wanted a guitar. It happened on one of her visits. I was sitting on the porch the day I saw her come walking up to our little house with a Stella guitar in her hand. She said, "this guitar belonged to my son, but he never learned to play it, he didn't seem to care for it". Then she gave it to me. "It's for you", she said with a gentle smile. My jaws dropped, and I swear my heart leapt. It was the most awesome gift I had ever received. I could have kissed her, but, I couldn't... well...she was a lady.

My Dad had learned to play guitar when he was a young man and, so he taught me my first three chords, C, F and G. You know, you can play hundreds of songs with just three chords. I couldn't put it down. With every spare moment, I played, and you could hear me playing my guitar everywhere. Besides getting my guitar, the two most memorable events in Detroit were the day I out ran the law in Daddy's old Plymouth and the day I was introduced to the holy rollers.

As I mentioned I was driving to school in Hamilton about seventeen miles one way. The first half of the drive was all dirt roads. From the little house to the main road was a narrow country lane connecting to a larger two-lane gravel road, which would merge on to the black top highway. It happened more than once as I would come onto the gravel road driving too fast, the town constable would appear out of nowhere and then the chase was on. It was like a "Wile E. Coyote and the Road Runner" cartoon chase. My Dad's old Plymouth would be kicking up a dusty contrail swallowing the Constable's forty-nine Ford. He never caught me... well... never may be a bit exaggerated. I guess you could say I was caught and didn't know it.

One day returning home, as I approached our little house, what did I see, but the Constable's old Ford sitting in the driveway. There was the lawman himself talking to my Dad and you can be sure, they were not discussing the weather.

I nodded to both as I walked hurriedly past trying not to have any eye contact. Soon the law would leave in his old Ford, but now I must face Dad, my judge and jury who was still sitting on the front porch. Finally, … I was summoned to appear. "So, the old Plymouth outrun that Ford", my Dad asked, half smiling. I nodded to affirm my answer as I said, "yes Sir". That was it, that was all that was said, case closed. I had found mercy. Still for the next week I didn't drive to school, Dad drove me. I don't think my Dad was happy with my speeding, but still kind of proud that his Plymouth was faster than the Ford.

Being young is an awesome time of life. But being a teen-ager during the late fifties was even more exciting. It was one of the most amazing times in America. For me it was easy to understand what Winston Churchill meant when he said, "America at this moment stands at the summit of the world". I for one felt that way. I felt I was on top of the world, even though life seems to always be trying to knock you down.[xxxvii]

Not only was America strong militarily, after all we had been victorious in war, but now our economy was beginning to win too, and despite the difficulties some of us were facing we were all beginning to feel like winners. The nation's population was growing at a rate of more than four million babies a year, that alone should say something about the love that was being shared. The Veterans were buying houses on their GI Bill and the government was spending money on new highways and roads. It was now 1960 and I was awakening to the wonderful world for the sweet sixteen. The music, the girls and a new realization of what I wanted me to be.

While in Detroit I made a new friend. Just down the road from me there lived a young man named Royce. I will never forget how he looked. He was as we would say back then a cool cat. He wore clothes like Elvis and all those Memphis Cool-Cats. Royce was a straight guy, though he loved wearing pink. He had a pink shirt, a white belt, and pink socks. No blue jeans for Royce, black slacks, with white patent leather shoes was his style. His hair was a pompadour, long, black and wavy, combed in ducktails. Believe me this dude was a chick magnet. Not only the way he looked was cool, but his car was awesome and loud, a black fifty-five Pontiac. This Daddy-O personified cool. Looking at him you would never be aware of his challenge. Royce was deaf. He could talk, but only the way a person talks who can't hear themselves. But, I think that too was another aspect of his cool mystique.

Another cool thing about Royce, he was a Christian. I remember the first time I was invited into his house. As we walked into the front room I noticed that on the television screen, was Oral Roberts.

Evangelist Oral Roberts was one of the most controversial preachers of the day and one of the first televangelist at that time. Oral was noted for his short sermons but long prayer lines. After he preached he practiced the doctrine of the laying on of hands. While people passed by him, he sat in a chair on the stage under his big tent, as the TV cameras captured the sights and sounds of his healing and deliverance service. At the end of his television program he would ask his television audience to place their hand on their TV screen and touch his hand and believe for their miracle.[xxxviii]

The day I walked into Royce's house there was his mother on her knees with her hand on the screen. As we walked by her she never looked up but continued as if in a trance watching the TV preacher. Royce simply said, "She's praying, she prays a lot".

Royce and his mother attended a Pentecostal church. I remember my first introduction to their church. Royce came by with his mother and drove us to the meeting. It was revival time. The church was packed and with pretty girls attending. They all flocked around Royce, I just watched him in total astonishment. Soon the service would begin. The music was exciting, guitars, tambourines, bass, piano and everyone singing to the top of their voices.

When the preacher started it was an explosion of emotion and enthusiasm, preaching about the power of God and how nothing was impossible if you believe.

He spoke of how God was a healer, a deliverer and the Savior of all who would believe. He preached from behind the pulpit, on the altar benches, standing on the pews everywhere, his choreography was hypnotic.

It was summertime and the church were packed, so to cool the place every window in the church was open. You could hear outside everything that was going on inside. The preacher ran from one side of the church to the other side, often pausing in front of a window to preach to the crowd outside. As I watched I thought, "wouldn't it be funny if he dove out the window", and sure enough, no sooner than the thought crossed my mind out the window he flew.

"No way"! I jumped up from the back pew where I was sitting dumbfounded and began my exit out the door and who should I meet coming through the door, the preacher, still preaching at the top of his lungs saying something about Jesus coming soon.

With his entrance into the church many of the men began to follow his lead, jumping, waving their arms and shouting, "thank you Jesus"! The women too began to dance and shout, while shaking their heads ecstatically causing their long hair which had been wrapped in a tall fashioned hairdo to fall to their shoulders. Then the strange language of unknown tongues began to manifest. It was more than I was ready for, but still very exciting. I spent the remainder of the service outside wondering about what I had witnessed.

Dad finally tired of sharecropping after that season, which made me happy, so we moved back to Hamilton. I always liked Hamilton, but I was beginning to be bored. For the next year I struggled to be motivated in school.

I would day dream and wonder about the world that I so desperately wanted to see.

During that time, I was having problems with my feelings toward Dad. It's as if I had lost confidence in him. Rebellious, I didn't think of myself that way. I loved my Dad, but I hated what we had become, poor, and I blamed him. My grades in school started failing. This was difficult for me because I had always been a good student. When the school year ended I would be held back. The next year wasn't any better and I just knew I had to get away. I ask Dad to let me join the Navy, I was seventeen now. He said maybe if I would try harder. However, he never gave me permission. Knowing I didn't have his support made me more determined than ever to get away and I was looking for any chance to leave.

Then I met Joe. Joe was just a year or so older than me. He was already out of high school and was attending classes at Itawamba Junior College, over in Fulton, Mississippi. Joe also played the guitar, so music sealed our friendship. We would trade songs and guitar licks. Then we started singing together. We discovered that our voices harmonized well. With lots of practice we built a strong repertoire of songs and we tried to emulate the styling of The Everly Brothers who were an American country-influenced Rock N Roll duo, known for steel-string acoustic guitar playing and close harmony singing. That described Joe and me perfectly. Every opportunity we could find or create we would perform.

During this time, I would often watch Channel 4 TV from Columbus, Mississippi which had a country western band that performed every week. I decided that we had to give it a shot. Without telling Joe the whole truth, I talked him into

83

going to Mississippi and performing. To convince him, I told him I had talked to the folks at the station, which was a little white lie, I had only written to them about our coming and to which they never gave me a response. I will never forget as we turned onto the road which led to the station my nerves got the best of me. I quickly confessed that no one knew we were coming. To say that Joe was perturbed would be an understatement. He was angry. As we entered the station, seeing all the cameras, the lights, the sets, it was everything I had imagined. Someone noticed our guitars in hand, and ask us about our being there. "We're here to sing on the show". After a bit of confusion, they consented to give us an audition and unbelievably, they let us do the show.

We were intoxicated with excitement as we drove away from the station back to Alabama. I knew I had found what was missing in my life. The music made me feel like I belonged to something, it gave me a sense of identity. I wanted this. I wanted to perform in front of people more than anything in the world and I was ready for whatever it took to fulfill my dream. That night launched us. We would continue playing for school dances, at concerts on the back of flatbed trucks and on the local radio. My Mother was a strong supporter; unfortunately, my enthusiasm wasn't well received by my Dad. I finally resolved there was nothing left for me to do, I had to leave home.

Joe had an older brother which was on leave from the Navy. One night while we were practicing, I overheard him say he was driving some folks to Adrian. I couldn't believe my ears; this will be my ticket out of here. I pleaded with him to let me ride along.

I told him I had an Uncle, Aunt and grandmother living there. He said okay, although I sensed reluctance in his voice. I hurried home to get some of my things and to tell Mother of my plans. When I got home to my surprise my Dad was there. I had hoped to miss him, so I knew when I saw him this wasn't going to be easy. When I broke the news, all hell broke loose. Dad said, "You're not going anywhere". In fear and trembling I insisted that I was, and about that time Dad's belt left his waist, "I'll beat the hell out of you boy".

I couldn't believe my own voice when I heard me say, "You have used that on me for the last time." No sooner than the words left my mouth that I felt the power of his right fist hitting the right side of my chest and down I went. In that same moment came Mother to the rescue, she stepped in between us, while I tried to get to my feet. She looked sternly at my Dad and said almost yelling, "John, stop this right now. This house has gotten too small for the both of you; one of you has to go". Dad walked away, I got up and apologized to the family then said goodbye to them. I was seventeen and I would never live at home again, although I would try too on a couple of occasions. I was off to see the world and I was going to somehow make some music along the way.

Chapter 7

It's now 1962 and I am back in Adrian thanks to my good buddy Joe and his brother. I'm also here with the blessings of my Mother. When I got here last year my Uncle Olin and Aunt Lois let me stay with them. Even though they had a big family of five kids and they were also taking care of my grandmother Phoebe, they made room for me. To help pay my own way I went to work with my Uncle on his beer truck. He delivered Carling's Black Label beer and Frankenmuth Ale both in bottles and kegs brewed in America's Oldest Microbrewery and Michigan's Original Craft Brewery dating back to 1862![xxxix]

Today is March 20th and I've been waiting for the mailman to bring me a letter from home. In February I turned eighteen, so I wrote my Mom and ask her to send my birth certificate. Today it came. For more than a year I've been contemplating this day. During supper tonight, I'll tell the family of my plans and let Uncle know it's going to be a short day at work for me tomorrow. Supper time finally came.

"Uncle Olin, I'm going to need to be off by noon tomorrow, because I'm going to see the recruiter about joining the Navy." "Are you sure about this" he asks. "Yes, I am", I said, it's all I've been thinking about for some time and now the opportunity has come for me to try".

Aunt Lois and Grandma were sad at the hearing of my news. My little cousins on the other hand got real excited and began to beg their parents if they could go too. "Don't be silly", laughed Grandma.

"Y'all might get yourself shot". We all laughed at their excitement and the idea of them going. For the rest of the evening they all played soldiers and war.

The next day at lunch time Uncle Olin dropped me off downtown near the hotel where all the recruiters had their offices. We said our goodbyes; he wished me luck as we shook hands. As he drove away I watched the Carling's Beer logo on the rear of the beer truck disappear as he made the turn at the end of the block.

Inside the hotel the lobby smelled of smoke and dust. Dark wood paneling covered the walls of the foyer; a worn and frayed carpet runner led me to the front desk where stood an old fellow in a dingy white shirt with tattered collars supporting a wrinkled paisley tie. Looking up and over his spectacles he asks in a frail gravelly voice, "you need a room sonny"? "No Sir, I'm looking for the recruiter's office". "Joining the army are ye", No Sir, I'm going to be a sailor". With that he pointed down the hall with his crooked little finger, "just down yonder young feller". I turned in the direction he had pointed and found a large door hid in the dark panels with an opaque glass window with black painted letters. "UNITED STATES ARMED FORCES".

As I opened the door the hinges made a painful screeching sound. Once inside I noticed the room had a high ceiling with dusty fans hanging like they had been lynched. On the plastered wall to the right of the door was a display of posters neatly framed from the war era. Two of them jumped out at me; the poster of a sailor in the dark navy-blue uniform with a duffle bag thrown over his shoulder walking up the gang plank boarding his ship with the caption, "FIGHT" … in very large red letters.

Beneath this is a medium red cursive font with the words, "let's go" … and at the very bottom in bold black letters the words, "join the fight".

Hanging in the very center of the half dozen or so posters, was the iconic, "I Want You" poster, with the stern-faced Uncle Sam pointing outward with his right index finger, his eyes glaring at you no matter where you stood, he's seemingly shouting "I WANT YOU", in bold red and blue capital letters.[xl]

In the center of the quaint office I spotted a lone recruiter his head nodding as if he were half awake and half sleeping with his chin resting in his hand. He was sitting behind one of three heavy looking mahogany desks.

"Where's Your Navy Recruiter", I heard my voice shouting, as it also echoed under the high ceiling of the office.

Startled the recruiter came to attention in a panic, his face blushing, he begins shuffling papers on his desk as if he had lost something.

When his eyes stop, he looks up and says, "uh...uh...yes..., O no, no he's not here right now...he's gone to lunch...is there something I can do for you...something that I can help you with"?

"You sure can", I said grumpy like, "I came to join the Navy, so if you can get me in the Navy and get me out of town, you can help me, that's what I want".

The recruiter looked at me with a smile, followed by a slight yawn, "Well, I can't get you into the Navy". He pauses as he continues to move things around on his desk.

His answer causes my heart to sink a bit, "but I can get you into the Air Force and I can sure enough get you out of town."

"How long before the Navy guy is back?", as I'm looking around hoping to find a Navy man standing in a corner somewhere.

Before I could say anything else he says, "Let me ask you, "Why you so gung-ho about joining the Navy anyway"? I became a bit irritated at his remark, and though I didn't feel it was any of his business as to why I wanted to be in the Navy, I answered. "Well to be honest, my Dad was in the Navy during the war, and I've just always wanted to be a sailor."

The recruiter said, "why don't you try the Air Force, don't you like flying? I thought how did he know I loved flying. "Listen… all you have to do is pass a test and you'll be in Texas before you can say long live Davy Crockett. That's where you'll get your basic training, San Antonio, home of the Alamo, don't you want to see the Alamo? Well if you pass my test and our physical, you'll be on your way".

"Flying, Texas and the Alamo", as I seriously consider this possibility, I began to daydream of how I might look in the blue Air Force uniform, with a few stripes on my sleeve and some medals on my chest like his. "Okay...What do you think"? His question snapped me back to the present moment.

I answered, "Okay, why not, let's do it".

I filled out an application, signed some papers of intent, and step one was done. He then gave me instructions about the time and place I should meet him to leave for Detroit

89

for the testing and my physical. I had just enough time if I hurried to get from the hotel back to the house and say goodbye to Grandma and Aunt Lois. With tears in my Grandmother's eyes I said my farewells. That evening I joined the recruiter along with a couple of other guys. We boarded a small military bus and we soon arrived in Fort Wayne, Detroit, Michigan.

On March 22, 1962, I passed the test and the physical exam and the next thing I know I was lifting my right hand,

"I John Mays, do solemnly swear that I will support and defend the Constitution of the United States against all enemies, foreign and domestic; that I will bear true faith and allegiance to the same; and that I will obey the orders of the President of the United States and the orders of the officers appointed over me, according to regulations and the Uniform Code of Military Justice. So, help me God."

I have thought about that oath and that day many times over the years and in retrospect I'm sure glad the recruiter sold me on the Air Force, because I would later discover on a fishing boat in the East China Sea, that me, boats and oceans don't do well together, I get deathly seasick.

In 2016 on the 22nd of March all day that day I was haunted by the recurring thought that there was something special about that day or there was something I was supposed to be doing. It finally dawned on me that it had been fifty-four years since I took that oath, and as far as I know I have never been released from that promise. I'm still under oath and don't be mistaken, it means the same to me today as it did then.

The following day I was on a chartered plane, to San Antonio, Texas and Lackland Air Force Base. As we deplaned we boarded a blue military bus to our next stop where I would meet and be introduced to by far the meanest mannered and the most vulgar talking man, I have ever known. There is no better way to describe him. This D.I. "drill instructor", for all you non-vets, cursed at us from the moment we stepped off the plane until the day we left Texas almost two months later.

I decided right then and there, that the only way to get through this was for me to stay in the shadows, out of sight, under the radar, and volunteer for nothing. There was one bit of information he did spew out of his vile mouth on that first day which caught me by surprise, for I hadn't really thought about it. "Now hear this all of you, sorry pieces of humanity", he shouted, "you are going to be mine for next two months and my beloved Air Force for the next four years".

"Four years"! I thought to myself, "I had it in my mind that the enlistment I signed up for was only two years. Oh well, I sighed, two years, four, it doesn't really matter. I have nothing better to do at least for a while." I just never thought about it again, except that…." who else but me would be that stupid".

My plan to stay anonymous worked, except for one time. Just before we were to graduate and leave Texas and go on to my next assignment, I had to pull an eighteen hour stretch of guard duty from noon till 6am the next day. Unknown to me at the time, the rest of the guys had marched all day practicing for this graduation parade scheduled the next day. The script was that all the squads would pass and review before the base Commander, his officers, dignitaries and a few visitors. Guess what, I couldn't believe it when the D.I. said I had to march and I better not mess it up. So here I go into that parade totally unprepared without any practice and was unfortunate enough to be placed on the perimeter of the column, the side facing the viewing stand.

Oh, my goodness, did I ever mess it up. When the column came to the place where we are to make the final turn to pass and review, it all fell apart, because my entire file was supposed to line up on me to make the turn. I however got too far behind the file in front of us and we were completely out of sync, marching behind the cadence. It was an absolute mess and I knew right then I was in some deep trouble. After we got back to barracks the D.I. called me into his office, closed the door, cussing me, calling me names I had never heard before. Then when he tired of that, he began to punch me everywhere but my face and said, "Mays, you better be glad you're getting out of here". He didn't realize what an understatement he was making, because I couldn't hardly wait to put this vile man in my rearview mirror.

Just before I left Lackland Air Force Base, the squadron was called before the Commander. He gave us a little farewell speech and told us how proud he was for our graduation. Then it was the First Sergeant's turn. Echoing the Commander with his congratulations, the Sergeant then asks if any of us had any complaints. I looked around and caught the eyes of my D.I. glaring at me. I gave him a little taste of my indignation as I mouthed without making a sound of course, "later dude". I thought to myself, "I could really bust you right now mister", it goes without saying I didn't like that man, but...I opened not my mouth.

We were done with Texas and now for a relaxing bus ride to Biloxi, Mississippi for our technical training which awaited me at Keesler Air Force Base.

It is summertime on the Gulf Coast of Mississippi and man it is hot and humid. A few things I don't have to worry about anymore is marching, running the obstacle course, doing jumping jacks, judo squats, push-up's, sit-up's or going to the firing range. Which the truth was, I never really minded those things, in fact I rather enjoyed them. But that was all behind me now; well that is everything but, K.P., kitchen police.

After getting to the base, I was anxious to begin my technical training, but I discovered that every new class must first perform two weeks of K.P.

Keesler Air Force Base in the early days was called Keesler Army Airfield and it has been around since 1942, named in honor of 2nd Lieutenant Samuel Reeves Keesler, Jr., a Mississippi native and distinguished aerial observer, killed in action in France during the First World War. In 1947, the Radar School arrived on Keesler and that's why I'm here.[xli]

By 1962 the base is showing a bit of wear. The chow hall was setup in an old WWII Quonset style building. A in a Quonset is a structure of corrugated galvanized steel built semicircular cross-section configuration. I'm sure you've seen them before, they're still around.

Nevertheless, old military style Quonset huts are not all Mississippi has, in fact the one thing they've got plenty of, are bugs... insects of all kinds. The truth is the cock-roaches I found in the base chow hall were monstrous in size and these giants owned the chow hall at Keesler.

I will never forget the morning I was on the service line spooning SOS, while standing right next to the civilian cook who is frying eggs any way you like them on his hot griddle. SOS, for your information is a chipped beef white gravy typically served on toast, better known by the troops as (s--t on a shingle).

Now you really must try to picture this. Not only is it hotter than blazes in Mississippi and the humidity is almost as high as the temperature, but while standing by that griddle you can add another ten degrees at least. The civilian cook is a huge black man, weighing in at over three hundred pounds, with huge rolls of fat making his jowls so enormous that his neck has disappeared. Wrapped around the area where his neck should be, is a towel, strategically placed there to catch the sweat pouring off his face and jowls. Yet despite the effort, every now and then you could hear the hissing sound of perspiration hitting the hot griddle, psst, psst, psst.

Now to add to this scene, you've got to understand something, this man has been flipping eggs for so many years that his whole routine has become robotic. "How Y'all won't yo eggs", as he flipped and fried eggs turning them with this Goliath size spatula which is held in his catcher's mitt sized hand, the only words I've ever heard him say for the past two weeks is, "How Y'all won't yo eggs", in his deep Mississippi Delta drawl and he is totally uninterested in who responds, for he never looks up from the griddle. "Over hard, over easy, scrambled, came each request".

Today I was assigned by the Cook Sergeant again to be responsible for spooning up the S.O.S. which I had acquired a taste for, especially if you loaded it with ketchup. In fact, I've learned in my travels I can eat about anything if there is ketchup around.

In any case, on this morning things will get a little exciting when someone hollers, "what the heck…. look at the size of that roach". Sure enough, crawling along the splatter board of the grill about half way up, a three-inch roach monster moving cautiously along, trying to go unnoticed. The next thing I heard was, "How Y'all won't yo eggs", followed by a loud splat of the Goliath sized spatula followed by a sickening crunching sound of a smashed cockroach struck by the weapon of choice in the hands of a three hundred-pound, black robot. The cook never breaks meter as he scrapes the remains of the roach off his spatula on the side of his griddle while all the troops who witnessed the killing passed by, without their eggs on their trays. I thought I would literally die laughing.

I enjoyed the radar school but was glad when graduation day came. I didn't get to leave right away as first scheduled because I had some dental work the Air Force said had to be done before going overseas. I guess they seem to think there were no dentists in Okinawa. But in about a week I was on my way home to Alabama for my first leave, and then I would be headed to Travis Air Force Base, California to get my plane to Okinawa, my first duty station.

While I had been gone from Alabama for nearly a year now, my Dad had taken a job in Birmingham, so there's where I would meet them. I was very happy to see everyone but was more anxious to get on with my life, besides to be honest with you, I felt out of place there. I have learned this lesson in life, when you go back to something, you will find that things are never the same as you left it. Soon I would be leaving as I hugged my Mother, shook hands with my Dad f and waved farewell from the window of the Greyhound Bus pulling out of Birmingham.

For the next three days and nights I would enjoy discovering the scenery of the west as we traveled across America on Route 66 which we got onto in Memphis. Wow, it was exciting; I was really on my way, going somewhere I've never been. I can still smell the diesel exhaust of the bus as we boarded the express to California. Like it was yesterday, I can still hear the voice of the Memphis Bus Station public address announcer ringing from the loud speakers directing that all westbound passengers should get aboard.

"All aboard please, all westbound out of door number three; for Little Rock, Oklahoma City, Amarillo, Albuquerque, Flagstaff, Barstow, San Bernardino, all points west, all aboard please".

It recalls the lyrics to the song Route 66 written by Bob Troup and sung by Nat King Cole.[xlii]

"If you ever plan to motor west, travel my way, take the highway that's best.

Get your kicks on Route sixty-six.

It winds from Chicago to LA, more than two thousand miles all the way.

Get your kicks on Route sixty-six.

Now you go through Saint Louis, Joplin, Missouri, and Oklahoma City is mighty pretty.

"You'll see Amarillo, Gallup, New Mexico, Flagstaff, Arizona.

Don't forget Winona, Kingman, Barstow, San Bernardino.

Won't you get hip to this timely tip: When you make that California trip

Get your kicks on Route sixty-six."

California here I come! When the Greyhound crossed the California state line, I felt something move deep within me. It was close to that feeling you get sometimes when you feel like you've been there before. What's it called? Déjà vu, the phenomenon of having the feeling that you're experiencing something that you've already experienced. It's hard to explain but entering California I had the feeling I had been here before and now I have come back to where I belong…it was love at first sight.

In all my life's travels, I've circled the globe more than once. I've travelled to over four continents, all fifty states, and thirty nations, but when I'm back to the Golden State, it's homecoming for me. California is where I feel I've always belonged. In 1962, I knew I wouldn't be here on this first visit long, but I knew in my heart, I would be back.

Upon my arrival, I checked in at headquarters Travis. I was given a bunk in the transient quarters and in less than twenty-four hours I was boarding my flight to Okinawa. I would be riding in the Boeing 707 four-engine jet airliner commonly called the "seven o seven". It was the greatest aerial experience up to then that I had ever had.

It wasn't my first plane ride of course, remember I had flown to Texas. But even before Texas. As a high school kid back in Hamilton, I would often cut school and hang out at our little airport. The man who ran the airfield also had a crop dusting business. I would help him from time to time, in exchange he would take me up in his Cessna 172 Skyhawk. Man, I love to fly, and nobody expresses the euphoria of flying any better than John Gillespie Magee, Jr. in his sonnet;

"HIGH FLIGHT"

"Oh, I have slipped the surly bonds of earth, and danced the skies on laughter-silvered wings

Sunward I've climbed and joined the tumbling mirth of sun-split clouds - and done a hundred things you have not dreamed of - wheeled and soared and swung high in the sunlit silence.

Hovering there I've chased the shouting wind along and flung my eager craft through footless halls of air. "Up, up the long delirious burning blue I've topped the wind-swept heights with easy grace, where never lark, or even eagle, flew; and, while with silent, lifting mind I've trod the high un-trespassed sanctity of space, put out my hand and touched the face of God." [xliii]

In the early eighties, I took flying lessons too. I did take offs, landings and had most of my class room work finished. I was just within reach of my dream with enough hours to go solo, but something happened before I could get my pilot's license...so going solo is still on my bucket list.

Today though I am on board this "707", adventure bound, with my first stop on the tiny Pacific island called Wake. Here is a little history of the island if you're not familiar with it.

Just days after the attack on Pearl Harbor on December 11, 1941, Wake Island came under attack by the Japanese Navy. Because of the courage of some U.S. Marines, along with some naval personnel, and civilians, these brave Americans fought back the attempted invasion by sinking two Japanese destroyers and a Japanese transport. Unfortunately, the island of Wake would finally fall to the enemy just twelve days later in a second attack with the support from a Japanese carrier-based aircraft returning from the attack on Pearl Harbor. Wake Island would remain occupied by the Japanese forces until after the Japanese surrender, and then the US Air Force would take it over.[xliv]

From my window seat, I watched our approach and descent to the runway on the tiny island. I thought to myself, "I hope there's enough runway for this big bird". It was no problem, we touched the ground like a falling feather. In just hours, the aircraft was refueled, all of us were back in our seats and on to our next stop, Okinawa.

My tour in Okinawa was for eighteen months. My duty station was located on the south end of the island at a place called Yoza Dake Air Station. It was considered a remote radar site resting atop the Yoza Dake plateau, five hundred feet above the East China Sea on the west and the Philippine Sea to the east.

One thing I can tell you about my stay in the South Pacific, it made a man of the world out of an ignorant kid. Not proud of that, just saying.

When I left home, I was wet behind the ears, a seventeen-old virgin, fresh off the farm and dumber than a stump. I really had no idea what sin was, but I would soon fall into the devil's snare. In fact, my education was not unlike the movie script from the Marlon Brando film:

"The Teahouse of the August Moon"
Example:

In Okinawa, no locks on doors.

Bad manners not to trust neighbors.

In America, lock and key big industry.

Conclusion:

Bad manners, good business.

Another example:

In Okinawa,

wash self in public bath with nude lady quite proper...

but a picture of nude lady in private home quite improper.

In America, statue of nude lady in park win prize...

but nude lady in flesh in park win a penalty.

Conclusion:

Pornography, question of geography.

'But Okinawa most eager to be educated by conquerors.

Not easy to learn. Sometimes very painful.

But pain make man think.

Thought make man wise.

And wisdom make life endurable."[xlv]

The one positive thing that I did take away from Okinawa was a love and appreciation for the Asian people. These folks are wonderful; they are warm, hospitable and kind. The women...Oh those Japanese women, enchanting, seductive, with a rare and pure beauty. "Not easy to learn".

November 23rd, 1963 about two o'clock in the morning I awoke to the base siren blaring down the halls and into my room. As I awoke my first thought was, "seriously, a drill now... at night, I should say morning". When suddenly I heard someone running down the hall shouting in terrified panic, "the President's been shot, they've killed the President". My first thought was, "What in the world... shut up...that isn't funny". I hurried out before I was half dressed, I left the dorm running as fast as I could.

Once outside I could feel the cool night air brush across my face. I noticed on the lighted flag pole, that "Old Glory" was moving about by a slight breeze. I could feel my body heating up as I ran up the hill toward the "block-house". That's what we called the building which housed our radar equipment and offices. As I approached the gate the Air Police was waving the people through who were just ahead of me. By the time I got to the front of the block house the others had disappeared behind the door. I keyed the code to the door lock and as it opened I pushed through running down the hall, pass the break room, the radio room and into the dark room.

The darkroom is a large cavernous room filled with electronic gear, radar and radios. The only lights in there are small desk lights dimly lit, glowing radar screens and a very large illuminated Plexiglas display board with a map of our surrounding area printed on it.

It was also marked out with concentric circles and azimuth lines marking degrees of the compass.

Behind the Plexiglas were airmen whom we called plotters wearing headsets with microphones plotting data which they were receiving from the radar operators. On the plotters side of the board everything the plotter wrote had to be written backwards so it could be read by those facing the board and analyzing the data. Ever plot, all the data, along with associated symbols identifying every airborne aircraft in the area, complete with its direction and altitude, had to be plotted accurately and current. No mistakes were permitted.

As I entered the room the first thing I noticed was the readiness alert status light attached to the wall. It's like a traffic signal light with different colors, a red light meant battle station conditions, we are at the highest alert of readiness, or in other words we are at war.

The amber color would be the next highest state of readiness; at this level pilots are sitting in their cockpits ready for takeoff. The readiness light showing when I entered the darkroom was a terrifying amber. "My God" I thought, as I saw the amber light and the Plexiglass board filled with data of many aircraft already aloft all over the island. Obviously, many of our fighters had been scrambled. When I thought of China being just a stone's throw away from us, my eyes were immediately drawn to that portion of the map.

I took a deep sigh of relief as I straddled my chair behind my radar console and I was happy to see there was no activity on the coast of China. The mike chatter was suddenly broken when the Captain began speaking through our headsets. The overwhelming news was heart wrenching as the Captain confirmed that our Commander and Chief, President John F. Kennedy had been killed. Every man in the room was devastated. Men were weeping, others were cursing, we just couldn't believe it.

The Air Station at Yoza Dake remained under amber status for a couple of more days. Only the married fellows who lived off base were dismissed to leave the site just long enough to get a little sleep and shower. Honestly though, no one was in the mood for being anywhere else. For the first time since I had left California, America, now seemed a long way away. My family seemed out of my reach. I felt as though all I had in the world were the people here on this rock out in the middle of the Seas which surrounded it.

As we all experience in our lives, time has a way of slipping by us. I truly hadn't realized that I had lost touch with my family, until the day I was called into Major Rings office. "Mays, I've got a letter here from the American Red Cross, it seems your mother has contacted them and is concerned about your whereabouts." "Seriously", I thought, "Surely that can't be".

The Major; "You know what you're going to do right now before you leave this office? You are going to write your mother and I'm going to mail it for you, and listen mister this better be the last time I see you in here, that's an order". Well needless to say Mother got her letter in just a matter of days.

Before I left Okinawa one of my pals told me he was going to take the G.E.D. test. When I ask him what that was all about, he said, "you take a test and if you pass it's the same as graduating from high school, anyone can take it". I went with him. I think this was one of my proudest moments at that time of my life, when I finally got the results back and I had passed. This made me feel good about myself again. I had been so disappointed for quitting school and leaving home the way I did. This success motivated me to want to do better.

The timing for all this couldn't have been any better. Not only do I have my G.E.D. diploma, I've been given a promotion in rank to Airman 2nd class. I have also received my new orders. I am being assigned to an airborne squadron in the states at McClellan Air Force Base in Sacramento, California. California, here I come, and I will be flying.

Life's great, things are starting to come around and I can hardly wait to get started. But first things first. Before I can leave this island, I have some loose ends to tie up. Which means all my debts must be paid and I have a few. Nothing big, but I owe the base store some money, my drinking buddies some money and a few poker debts. By the time I shelled out my money to my debtors and one more bon voyage celebration in the village.... well let me put it this way, when I landed in Travis, I had a whopping $2.10 to my name....and the sad part of this story, I had a thirty-day leave. I could have gone anywhere I wanted to go, back to Alabama perhaps or maybe Adrian, but not now, no way, not on two bucks. My only choice was to get to Sacramento, get to the base and get myself checked in.

I found out there was a Greyhound bus leaving from Travis to Sacramento and the price, can you believe it, two dollars. That's right when I get to the bus station in Sacramento I had ten cents left, just enough maybe to make a local phone call or then maybe not.

The Greyhound bus station was in the middle of downtown Sacramento. I inquired with the bus driver as to how I could get to McClellan. He told me it was quite far from here. He suggested I take a taxi or city transit. I was too embarrassed to tell him I only had a dime. As I left the station I ask a stranger and I told him I had no money and I needed to get to McClellan. "Get over to 16th Street, he said, "stick out your thumb and hope for a ride". He did remind me that with me in my uniform I shouldn't have any problem getting someone to give me a lift and you know that's exactly what happened. Another Air Force guy came by and took me straight to the front door of my new squadron building.

As we drove I was taking in the sights and sounds of California. I must tell you even though it was February, (which reminded me I would soon have my twentieth birthday) the sun was shining, the sky was blue, the Palm trees were swaying in the gentle breeze, and the girls, were drop dead gorgeous.

In 1965 The Beach Boys would release one of my favorite songs that really said what I was feeling.

"Well East coast girls are hip,

I really dig those styles they wear

And the Southern girls with the way they talk,

they knock me out when I'm down there.

105

The Midwest farmer's daughters

really make you feel alright

And the Northern girls with the way they kiss,

they keep their boyfriends warm at night.

I wish they all could be California,

I wish they all could be California,

I wish they all could be California girls"[xlvi]

Upon our arrival, I thanked the driver for the ride and the conversation, grabbed my gear and walked up to the building. The sign over the door read "965th AEW&C headquarters. Just inside the door was the front desk and behind the desk was the acting CQ. "Charge of quarters". I would find out later as I explored the facility that on the first floor were living quarters, laundry room and the mail room. The second floor housed the Flight Commander, the First Sergeant, the Adjutant offices and the day room. The third floor was all living quarters.

"I'm here to check in", I told the CQ as I handed him my orders and ID.

CQ: "I can't seem to find you here in our incoming for February".

"You're right you won't find me there, you see I'm not supposed to be here until next month. I'm supposed to be on leave in Birmingham, Alabama that's what I told the clerk who checked me out in Okinawa".

CQ: "So you're not taking your leave".

No, I'm here to go to work".

The CQ found my orders in the March incoming files, gave me the key to my first-floor room, then told me to see the First Sergeant the first thing Monday. I had forgotten today was Saturday. I tossed my gear on the bed and crashed for a while, then got up and changed into some civilian clothes and ask the first person I met, "excuse me, can you tell me, when do they feed around here"? He said, "About 1600" hours", and he offered to show me the way when it was time. That was good news because you can't eat on a dime and I was starving.

Chapter 8

So here I am, it's Monday morning in California and I feel like a lottery winner. I couldn't be any happier. It's like the first day of the rest of my life. I am now a proud member of the 552nd Airborne Early Warning and Control Wing at McClellan Air Force Base, California and the 965th Airborne Early Warning and Control Squadron.

As the CQ had instructed me I got up early and checked in with the First Sergeant. The old Sergeant got me sorted out, with the finance officer so I could get paid; my new pay scale was being raised. Because I'm now an Airman 2nd Class, my base pay went up to $123.00, plus I get a personal allowance of $55.20, and now there will be an extra $50 a month in my check for flight pay, which starts as soon as I graduate flight school and get at least one flight a month. In 1964, I was making a grand total of a whopping $228.20 before taxes, but of course that included free room and board.

The postal clerk gave me a mail box and combination, the supply clerk issued my new flight uniforms, which included a flight jacket, a couple of orange flight suits (which are like pullovers), my new crew member wings and new boots. The First Sergeant enrolled me into Flight School, which will be a month-long course training me on the equipment I will be operating aboard my new work-place, the EC121D Aircraft.[xlvii]

Now, I'm well fixed and in my place, and I could hardly wait for school to begin which won't happen for a couple of weeks. No problem though, because technically I am still on leave. My room was designed for two occupants but for the time being it was just me. I shared the latrine and shower which was built between my room and the room next door. After I drew my pay, which included some travel pay, more than I would normally get, I did a little decorating by putting a nice beige paint on the walls and hung a couple of modern prints of musical instruments. I also bought a new Gibson acoustic guitar at the Sherman Clay music store. There was also ample shopping within walking distance just outside gate "A". There was an "all night cafe, on "A" Street where many of the base personnel hung out. It was one of my favorite places. This area was a suburb of Sacramento called North Highlands.

Just up Watt Avenue was the original "Tower of Power record store." The store carried records of every imaginable genre of music you could ever want. You didn't have to really buy any records, because they had sound proof booths and you could sit in there and listen to all the music you wanted, not to mention the view, because lots of girls hung around the place.

Soon Flight School would begin and with a brand-new feeling in the air, I decided this was my opportunity to get a fresh start, so I had determined to take this time seriously. No more excessive drinking, which by the way here in California I had to be twenty-one to legally purchase alcohol and consumption of alcohol was prohibited in the rooms, by orders of the Squadron Commander. I was going to try to stay out of the poker games as well, so I could save some money for my leave when I could get it. From the first day of my enlistment I have had eighteen dollars a month, the price of a twenty-five-dollar US savings bond automatically deducted from my check, which was sent directly to my Mother.

So that's it, it's time to buckle down and study hard. My hard work started paying off right away, for I had a near perfect grade point average, top of the class when, "the letter" from home came. The news in the letter gave me a feeling of uncertainty concerning my future at McClellan.

Mom had mailed me this letter and enclosed was a telegram which came from the USAF. The Air Force was thinking I was home on leave and had tried to contact me there via a telegram. The telegram informed me that I was not to report to McClellan but to go to Norton Air Force Base which was just east of San Bernardino, California.

I thought to myself, "no way, this can't be happening. I'm already plugged in here". Nervously I took the letter upstairs to the First Sergeant; he read it and said, "Hold on Mays let me see what the Colonel has to say about this." I sat there still thinking "this can't be happening"! "Mays...Mays, come on in here man the Colonel wants to talk to you."

The Colonel's office was just across the hall, yet I thought my legs would collapse before I got to him, I was so nervous. Not that I was worried to see the Colonel, but afraid there was nothing he could do to help me, and I was going to have to leave.

"At ease Airmen. I see you have a problem here", said the Colonel. "The Sergeant tells me you're already in school and at the top of your class, is that right"?

"Yes Sir, Sir... I've been trying really hard Colonel Sir, I'm not going to have to leave am I"?

"Well that's up to you, you've got orders here, so you could go if you want to, or I could probably get this sorted out, so

110

you could stay". I turned to look at the Sergeant, as if to ask, "what should I do", all he did was nod with his eyes and directed me back to the Colonel.

"Well Sir, if it's alright with you, I'd just as soon stay." "Alright then Mays get out of here and keep up the good work, I'll take care of this".

I snapped to attention, saluted the Colonel, did an about face. I had to restrain myself from shouting as I glanced at the Sergeant and gave him a smile with a nod of appreciation...he smiled back. As I left the Colonel's office my heart was overflowing with gratitude.

"My goodness", I thought, "I was just at the proverbial fork in the road for sure". This would not be my last time that I would come to a fork in the road. This journey called life continues to bring us to places of decision. The place where you must choose. Do I go to the right or do I go to the left, do I stay, or do I go? Like the lyrics from "The Gambler";

"You've got to know when to hold 'em,

know when to fold 'em,

know when to walk away, know when to run.

You never count your money

when you're sittin' at the table;

there'll be time enough for countin'

when the dealin's done". [xlviii]

I have often thought about my visit in the Colonel's office.

If I had chosen to leave that day my life would probably have been completely different. You know some folks have the belief that whatever will be, will be. I'm not one of those people. I believe in personal choices. I believe the decisions we make on life's road sets our course. Now that doesn't mean that every direction we take in our lives originates within us. Sometimes we must make decisions because of uninvited circumstances which change our path of life extremely. However, as a Christian I've determined to commit my way unto The Lord, and He helps me to make the choice of taking His directions and choosing His will for my life. Like one of my favorite passages in scripture says;

"Trust in the LORD with all your heart; do not depend on your own understanding. Seek His will in all you do, and He will show you which path to take." Proverbs 3:5, 6

Of course, you must remember I didn't know this awesome spiritual wisdom in 1962. Yet, I must be honest and say that even after I became a Christian, there would be more times than I care to remember that I would ignore The Lord's leading and make the mistake of a bad decision. But I've also learned that where sin abounds, grace much more abounds and the promises in God's Word never fail, for as it is written;

"And we know that God causes everything to work together for the good of those who love God and are called according to his purpose for them." Romans 8:38.

Sure, different paths can make for a plethora of choices and each path has its own story. My life is exactly like that, a bunch of little stories, when combined reveal who I have been and who I am today.

"What about the future", you ask. For me, all I know for sure about tomorrow is what God has promised and what God said He will do. As the song "It Is No Secret" written by Stuart Hamblen says;

"It is no secret what God can do.

What He's done for others He'll do for you.

With arms wide open He'll pardon you.

It is no secret what God can do.

There is no night for in His light,

you'll never walk alone.

Always feel at home, wherever you may roam.

There is no power can conquer you,

while God is on your side."[xlix]

Hamblen was one of radio's first "singing cowboys." As a preacher's kid from Texas he didn't handle his fame very well. His friends would describe him as a drunkard and a brawler which "landed him in jail "many times." This all changed for Stewart in 1949 after meeting the evangelist Billy Graham. The result of this new friendship changed his ways. One of Stewart Hamblen's closest friends would ask him how he'd changed his ways, how did he get sober. He told the friend that it was no secret what God had done for him and what God could do for his friend too. The friend told Hamblen "you should turn those lines into a song"; that friend's name was John Wayne, the movie icon.[l]

I can only imagine that if I had left McClellan and gone to Norton Air Force Base, I would probably have never met my first wife Marion, we would have not been married, and our son John Oliver would have never been born. I also would never have met my second wife Judy, and would not have the beautiful family that I have today. Regardless of which fork in the road I took, it would still be me and the history of my life up to this point would still be my story. But I know without the life I have lived thus far, the other road would probably have made a different me, maybe better, maybe worse, I will never know, because it's not a story a could tell you. But the stories I am telling you happened, they are true.

Soon I would graduate at the top of my class and I would start earning my permanent wings. I loved our flying missions. In the radar field, they say that a Radar Operators life is hours of boredom, and then moments of stark terror. I can't tell you how many times we were in an emergency. Once while flying back to base from the Aleutian Islands, the Captain tells us he has shut down one of our engines.

"The EC121 has four 18-cylinder Rolls-Royce engines it's a great flying airplane. Yet with that said you can't imagine how eerie it feels when you look out the porthole and the prop which is supposed to be spinning is standing still, lifeless. The military term for this is," the engine is off, and the propeller is feathered". This isn't the first time one of our crews had to hobble home on three motors, even though this situation wasn't welcomed, I felt confident it was doable. That is until the announcement you never want to hear, "suit up boys, we may shut number two down as well". Trust me, that'll get your heart pumping double time.

"Alright you heard him, yelled the crew chief, get with it". Suiting up means wetsuits, wetsuits mean water and by water I'm talking the Pacific Ocean. Back in-Flight School we've been trained for these kinds emergencies and we all know the drill, but still, as I waited, every moment felt like we were in suspended animation. After a long twenty minutes, the Captain spoke again,

"Okay, you can relax boys, looks like we got it under control; it seems to be working again…. but...keep your fingers crossed". We landed in one piece, safe and sound.

By the time spring rolled around new orders came down from HQ, that we would be going TDY. "Temporary duty". In the Air Force, TDY refers to a travel assignment at a location other than your permanent duty station; it's usually a relatively short duration, typically from two days to 179 days in length.

This TDY would be McCoy Air Force Base, Orlando, Florida and the assignment is to fly off the coast of Cuba at some very low altitudes making sure there are no attempts by the Russians to interfere with our surveillance aircraft or our fighters.

My first duty assignment at McCoy was that as CQ of the Airmen's quarters. Besides security, as CQ your eyes and ears are listening and looking for any kind of emergency that might occur in the night after lights go out. Also, CQ has the added responsibility to wake the troops whom have asked for a wakeup call. Well, when morning came guess who needed a wakeup call, that's right, big dummy. I had slept through the morning, so by the time I awoke, several of the men were going out the door cussing me for falling asleep and failing to wake them and now due to my negligence they were going to have to explain why they were all late for work.

I thought to myself, "Son of a gun", and out the door I flew to the squadron office.

Almost fainting from running and out of breath, I say to the Airman at the front desk, "I got to see the First Sergeant". "Go ahead" he says, "he's right in there, but I have to warn you he's on the warpath this morning". Looking in the direction he pointed I could see a man. CMS McFarland, the First Sergeant.

He was about 6'3", 225lbs, shoulders the width of a refrigerator. Chief Master Sergeant is the highest, enlisted rank in the U.S. Air Force, and his official term First Sergeant is not a rank, but a special duty held by a senior enlisted member of a military unit who reports directly to the unit commander and is denoted on the rank insignia by a lozenge (known colloquially as a "diamond"). He is often referred to as the "first shirt", or "shirt".[li]

Again, I thought, "My butt is grass and this guy's the lawnmower."

"Excuse me Chief", I said, with my hat in my hand and my butt in my throat.

Chief: "What did you do Airmen, spit it out"

I confessed my negligence to him of how I had failed to get the men up in time. I didn't tell him it was because I had fallen asleep. He interrupted me about have way through my confession.

Chief: "This is just what's wrong with today's Air Force, we mollycoddle these youngsters to dang much. Get on outta here son and don't worry about those lazy no accounts, they need to grow up...what the heck is going on, now get outta here and don't worry about it". I nodded with an expression of thanks, then taking his advice I got outta there. Most of my duty at McCoy was lightweight, just an occasional flight.

We didn't do much flying for reasons I could never figure out, and made me wonder what we were doing here in the first place. But as my Dad use to say, "yours is not the reason why, yours is but to do or die". One good thing about this assignment, was my aircraft commander, a full bird colonel whom I admired, impressive and a great guy. He would later become our squadron commander back in McClellan and guess who will be our new First Sergeant, that's right, McFarland.

With so much time on my hands I decide to go into Orlando and check it out. While hitchhiking into town, a sleek fire engine red Plymouth Barracuda pulls over. The driver was a local Airmen and ask, "where are you going".

Over the rumble of the exhaust I said, "I thought I would check out Orlando". As we rode I told him my story about what I was doing here, and he said he'd be glad to show me around. I really enjoyed touring about in this chick magnet of a car, trolling the streets for any sightings of girls. He said he knew a place where there were lots of girls. As we drove up to the building, I noticed that we were parking in front of a nursing school and man was he right; there were girls everywhere, beautiful girls in their pristine white nursing uniforms. "Eureka", I thought, as we parked and then strolled around the campus.

"Hey ladies…, you want to meet a guy from California" spoke my driver.

"California", what so special about California"? "I saw that car Y'all are driving, are you a wannabe movie stars from

California or a just a couple of short haired Air force guys from McCoy."

Man, this little dark-haired beauty had our number. "I'm stationed in California, I answered, and I'm here temporarily on a special mission". "Special mission", she looked over her shoulder unimpressed as she walked by me then she chuckled, "well now maybe we should go get some lunch and talk about this special mission". I looked at my driver as she took the arm of one of her girlfriends, "come on girl, let's let these soldiers buy us lunch".

At lunch, I reminded her that we're not Army, but Air Force. She looked over the top of her coke as she sipped her straw then gave me the cutest smile from the most beautiful scarlet red lips. Then she agreed. "I know honey, I know a flyboy when I see one… I was just playing with Y'all". We ate, we talked, we laughed, and as we walked, we talked about California, about music, about upstate New York where she was originally from, but had lived in Florida most of her life. "There's no place like Florida she argued", I just let her talk.

It was getting late; the night was falling, and the girls had a curfew. We hurried back, not realizing how far we had walked, so we barely made it just in time before the school doors would be locked. Before they left us my driver and I arranged to meet them later in the week and go for a ride in the Barracuda.

As it turned out I spent all my personal time away from the base with Linda, and even though she lived in the dorm, which I found out was required by the nursing school, her family lived in town. Nice folks they were too, very down-home sort of people.

When it was time to leave McCoy, and get back to McClellan, I promised her I would write and call.

Through the rest of 1964, Linda and I would correspond. On occasion, I would call from the pay phone just down the hall from my room. It's seems as the weeks rolled by our hearts grew fonder. I told her I planned on getting a Christmas leave because I still had about thirty days on the books and maybe more.

Just after my return from McCoy, I had a roommate assigned to me. A tall skinny Texan just out of tech school. Like most Texans I had ever met you never had any problem knowing what's on his mind. We got along pretty good and we had some things in common, he liked girls and poker. I know, I know, I got this thing going on through the mail in Florida, but I didn't think it would hurt me to just look around. Stockton, the Texas roomy really did love poker, you might say he was obsessed with it. Any kind of poker. Our room became the poker room once a week though it was restricted in the squadron to gamble.

Stockton and I hung out together a lot. One weekend we were hanging out down by the American River, at a place called Paradise Beach. Many young people came there to swim and party. On this day the party broke up early. Why, I decided to try to swim across the river, I'll never know! I challenged Stockton to swim it with me, but he declined. Into the water I went and soon I would be in the middle of the river and that is when it got scary.

The rivers current was flowing fast and strong. I knew instantly I could be in trouble. Then suddenly, this calm came over me. I knew that all I had to do was go with the current and try to ease my way over to the bank.

However, though I was safely to the other side, trouble was still ahead. When I looked back there was Stockton in the middle of the river and in panic mode. I screamed to him to relax and let the current take him to the bank. It was getting worse. I knew I had to go after him. When I got to him he was thrashing in such desperation, I could hardly hold on to him. Then to add to my problem, I was having trouble keeping my head above the water. I yell at him to stop fighting and let me get us to the other side. That is when I saw the fallen tree laying out in the river. As we neared the branches I could grab hold. Finally, we could pull ourselves up on the tree and then follow the trunk to the river's bank. I told Stockton, "what happens on Paradise Beach stays on the beach". We never discussed that day again.

I had two other friends in the building. Doug Thorne from Findlay, Ohio, whom I met in the day room just about every night to watch the Tonight Show with Johnny Carson. Later, Doug and I became roommates and he would become my first best man. Then there was Leon Stokes, who I met incidentally when the pay phone down the hall, kept ringing. After about the third time it started ringing, I went to answer it. It was some woman bawling her eyes out over the phone telling me to tell Leon, she was going to kill herself. "Who in the world, is Leon"? She told me his room number, I knocked on his door and when it opens there was Leon in his boxers, half asleep. "The phones for you", you got a suicidal maniac on your hands out there".

"Oh man, she's always pulling stuff like this, I can't seem to get rid of her", as he left the room to answer the phone.

Even though I lost contact with Leon shortly after I left the Air Force, I did happen to run into him at the Maverick Club one night about six months later.

In December of 1964, I took a two week leave to see Linda. I planned to ask her to go with me to visit my parents. To get to Florida I found out I could fly free on military aircraft. At our HQ, the admin officer arranged for me to hop a flight to San Antonio; from there I would take a C130 to Patrick Air Force Base in Florida. From Patrick, I would take the Greyhound to Orlando where Linda and her Dad would meet me. My travel plans worked out beautifully coming off without a hitch.

On the following night Linda and I took a stroll down to the park. We sat on the bench talking and cuddling and that's when I decided to propose. When I slipped the engagement ring out of my coat pocket, it was a Hollywood moment. With a cool December breeze in the air and a moonlit night causing little sparkles of light to dance all over the park lake, and the park lamp light located just above our heads making my beautiful girl's dark eyes shine, the feeling of young love was in the air. Her response caught me by surprise...she started laughing, "does this mean what I think it means? "Why sure it does", I assured her. "I've been thinking about this ever since we met, that's why I'm here and that's why I want you to go meet my family". Now she's crying, and I am thinking, "What's wrong with this girl".

Just then she takes my right hand, while I wipe her tears from her eyes with the back of my left hand. "Hey what's the matter kid? "John, I can't accept this, not until you talk to my Dad". Lifting her up from the bench I exclaimed, "Well let's go ask him".

Linda's father was a soft spoken and gentle soul, I really liked him. Her mother was a quiet woman, who was always wanting to get me a cup of coffee. When we sat down with them and I ask for their daughter's hand in marriage, his first response was, "she has to finish nursing school first". "No problem" I insisted, looking for some affirmation from Linda, which came as a short hug. Looking back to her father, I stammered, "so can I take that as a... yes"? They both nodded, and Linda shrieked "YES!" Meanwhile her mother poured us all coffee... and served us pie a la mode.

The next evening Linda's parents took us to the Greyhound, and we waved goodbye. From the bus window, I could see Linda's mother with her face in her gloved hands, crying. Her father pressed himself against the bus window following it as the bus began to slowly back from its parking space, "take care of my girl John and be safe". As he spoke, his breath caused the bus window to fog.

We talked for several miles about everything; mostly of how all this was going to work out. I had about fourteen months to go in the Air Force and she had almost the same amount of time before graduating, so it looked like maybe in June of 1966 we could have our wedding.

In Birmingham though things got weird, as the tone began to change, one could feel this wasn't going to be fun. I could see in Linda's face that she was thinking my folks were not liking this idea one bit. To describe the atmosphere of the next few days as tense would be kind. Oh, I think my parents liked Linda alright, but they just weren't happy with all this talk of marriage.

It saddened me the way everything turned out and it saddened Linda too, "I want to go back to Florida John". I bought two tickets one to Florida and another to California. We both wept as we said goodbye and for the second time in my life a girl named Linda got away.

Back on Old Route 66, like one of Yogi Berra's most memorable 'Yogi-isms', "It's déjà vu all over again".

After getting back to McClellan, Linda and I corresponded by mail for three months, then her letters stopped. Well... I guess there won't be a wedding in June of 1966 after all...so I thought, but I would be wrong about that too.

It was late March of 1965 and I had gone up to the day room early around 9pm to watch TV. "Mays", turning to see the CQ, he said, "it's the Colonel, he's on the phone", "who"? "It's the Commander, he's waiting for you, better get your tail down there". "What is going on" I thought? "Hello"? I hear a voice on the other end say, "Mays, let me get right to the point, I need a volunteer". I've a man on another crew who's going to have to go on this new TDY coming up. The problem is his wife is about to deliver his baby and I need a replacement for him." "Where you going Sir"? "I really can't say its top-secret Mays". "I have a top clearance Sir", "Alright its South-East Asia". Those words immediately transported me back to Okinawa. I was thinking "I love those Asian women". "Alright I'm in Sir". "Then be at HQ first thing tomorrow, and John thanks for helping me out on this and thanks for your service". Wow, he's never called me John!

Now, I should have known what was going on in the world, but frankly I was totally out of the loop on current events and didn't know that the situation in Vietnam had escalated into war. Maybe that's why I didn't take all the rigorous training to serious for the next week. Nerve gas training, parachute training on how to pack the chute and then repeated practice of jumping from a shoulder height platform onto the ground and into a sawdust pit, learning to make smooth falls. When the time finally came for us to leave, I had a disappointing discovery. My Commander was not going to be my Aircraft Commander. The man who asked me to volunteer and to go on this mission. The man I flew with off the island of Cuba. This same man who was now my Squadron Commander was not going with us, not on this trip. Instead we will be led by this gung-ho Major, who thinks the Air Force can only fly by the book.

After we loaded our gear, which included not only our duffle bag, but now our own personal issued Air Force parachute, which we were told by the Major, "unless you want to spend the rest of your duty in the stockade, we better not let that chute or the M14 rifle out of our sight". With only a few minutes left before roll call, I noticed a phone booth just off the ramp, so I quickly ran over and made a collect call home to say goodbye to Mother. As we lifted off and made our assent over Sacramento I began to feel a bit melancholy, a guess from hearing Mother's voice.

Our flight will take three days, with four stops, Hawaii, Wake Island, Guam and Taiwan. It will be an extra two weeks in Taiwan before we finally arrive at Vietnam.

All anyone must do is mention Hawaii and you have visions of beautiful black haired, sun bronzed women in grass skirts dancing the hula, accompanied by ukulele music while dining on poi, Kalua pig, lomi salmon, the sweetest pineapple you've tasted, cold beer, or choice of colorful cocktails with tiny umbrellas.

124

Walking on the beaches of Waikiki Honolulu is a mixture of luxury and breathtaking scenery...bikinis!

On our arrival Major Gung-ho gave us orders that we were to be on base restriction and would have guard duty at the plane. Major Gung-ho also threatened that anybody late for roll call at 0600 hours the next day would spend the remainder of our military careers in a Marine stockade.

We all complained to each other "It's Hawaii, and if he thinks we're going to just sit here all night, he's nuts, we will take our chances". That same morning, we were at the base-exchange as soon as it opened, cashed our travel paychecks issued to us before we left California, we each then bought one of those colorful traditional Hawaiian shirts. Then the three of us "violators" of a military command, made our escapade plans. Right after the last man stands his two hours of guard duty; we rent a car and do some bikini watching on the beach. Now it's late afternoon we soon found ourselves in Honolulu, in the middle of swaying palm trees and white sandy beaches. By the way the city isn't lacking in Tiki bars and dance clubs. On recommendation from a couple of sailors led us to this hot spot with a Hawaiian rock n roll band and lots of girls, we were in paradise.

As the night ended a couple of the girls wanted to go for a ride in our rented convertible. Good idea, so we left the bar about midnight, thinking we would soak up some ocean views for a couple of hours and who knows we might get lucky, if you know what I mean, then drop the girls off at their homes, turn the car in, hit the hay, and be at roll call at 0600 no problem, no harm done.

125

With the top down and their hair blowing in the breeze these two aloha beauties directed us to a picturesque remote beach. As we pulled off the road I could feel the wheels sinking into the sand. Except for the moonlight and the stars, it was pitch black dark. In the distance, we watched the moonlit white foamed waves crashing onto the rocks and beach. I wasn't worried for I figured we had time to test the "waters so to speak" and then get the car unstuck. As it turns out, "if it hadn't been for bad luck we wouldn't have had any luck at all". This car was buried and looked like it was going nowhere. All our efforts to push it, rock it, spin the tires, completely failed. We even thought about leaving it and hitchhiking back to base, except the guy who rented it had to give them a copy of his military ID. Finally, we had exhausted all our ideas and began to yell for help. Then from out of the dark, the Marines showed up. "We could hear you all the way to where we were, looks like you need some help".

There were four of them, superhero size men, who put their backs to the rear of the convertible, they lifted on the bumper and the convertible rose out of the rut. They quickly pushed us back on the highway. Hastily we all piled into our seats shouting, "Ooh-rah", a battle cries common in the United States Marine Corps, as we sped away.

We raced down the two-lane coastal highway like we were going to a fire back to Hickam Field. We took precious minutes to drop off the girls whose names I never knew. The clock is ticking, and I've been having horrible visions of that Marine stockade, it's now coming up on 0500 hours, I thought however, "we might just make it".

The guy who rented the car dropped us at the transient barracks, we grabbed our gear and the driver's gear, pulled our flight suits over our civilian clothes and ran to the tarmac. As we walked up to where the crew was assembling, they all gave us a curious look as if to say, "Where have Y'all been". As we tried to compose ourselves our driver would soon walk up and join us, he quickly donned his flight suit just as "Major Gung-ho" was arriving in a chauffeured jeep.

Soon our wheels were up, we are flying, we are airborne. Next stop Wake Island and there we would continue the party. The next morning, we were on our way to Guam where we would finally get some sleep, but only because the island was having a tropical rainstorm.

Leaving Guam rested, we were grateful to know that we would be in Tainan, Taiwan, for two weeks before going on to Vietnam. Tainan was historically the oldest city on the island and commonly known as the "Capital City" because for 200 years before Taipei became the capital it was the capital of Taiwan. The city faced the Formosan Strait in the west and to the southwest of the island about a thousand miles is our destination, Tan Son Nhut Air Base located near the city of Saigon in South Vietnam. The United States has made this their major base during the Vietnam War.

The only duty we had here in Taiwan was a shift of two hour a day guard duty and only every two days, leaving the rest of our time to do what we wanted. Of course, we knew what we wanted...booze and girls. Someone told us about a place on the beach where you could swim and go body-surfing. The place also had a Tiki bar with cold drinks and eats.

There were girls there too, both local Chinese and American. The Americans were either military like ourselves or military dependents from families stationed there.

All day we partied and surfed and then one of the guys brought a guitar, which I laid claim to and became the group entertainment. The guitar was nothing like the guitar I had bought just before we shipped out. I had made a deal with the Sherman Clay music shop where I had purchased the acoustic Gibson. I traded it in on a Gibson ES 335T. This ax stands as one of Gibson's all-time most iconic models. I loved mine, it was the sunburst F-holes, hollow Maple body, double cutaway with Rosewood fingerboard. It came with two hum-bucker pickups. I also bought an amp and reverb unit. I was ready to start making music as soon as I said good bye to "Uncle Sam".

But for now, I was enjoying playing again right here on the beach. At night, we spent most our evening at the "NCO" Club. (non-commissioned officers) This club was awesome, with several bars and a cafe. It also had a large dance floor with music played by an amazing orchestra led by a Japanese conductor who doubled as master of ceremonies. The band featured this gorgeous Chinese singer who sang the Classic American Songbook.

On this night, the orchestra was having an amateur talent contest and the first prize was a 40oz bottle of Seagram's VO. This was enough incentive for all my guys, to start coercing me to sign up, "you could win it Mays". I argued, "no way", but to no avail, the guys signed me up. When the conductor asks what I wanted to sing, I told him how about, "I Left My Heart in San Francisco".

I remembered they had played a chart on this Tony Bennet number a few nights before. My performance came of pretty good. I got a standing ovation from my guys, but when I won the contest they were ready to celebrate. Later in the evening the conductor asks me to do an encore.

Of course, the guys insisted, so I did Elvis's song, "Wooden Heart", a song best known from his 1960 film G.I. Blues.[lii]

"Can't you see I love you

Please don't break my heart in two

That's not hard to do cause

I don't have a wooden heart

And if you say goodbye

Then I know that I would cry

Maybe I would die

Cause I don't have a wooden heart"

"While I sung, both Sweet Linda, and Orlando Linda, came to my mind". However, my singing for the night wasn't over.

After the talent show victory we all decided to go to the city. Outside of the club stood a row of three-wheel cycles. There was a double wide seat for two passengers between the rear wheels just behind the driver's seat. Feeling the effect of the VO whiskey, we hired about four of them trikes and had a race. By paying the drivers extra and telling them there was a big tip for the winner who was first to the hotel downtown, was all the motivation they needed. The hotel was really a casino, with an excellent dining/showroom, complete with a Vegas style variety show. There were acrobats, magicians, jugglers, and singers all accompanied by a big band. When we arrived, we ordered steaks and wine and as we dined the hotel manager spoke to me in his broken English;

"Ah so, you buddy say your big winner GI...you sing at base tonight win first prize. Ah so, base conductor my friend. How about you sing with my orchestra GI. Please you sing I introduce you".

Of course, when the guys heard this, there was no way out. So here I am performing on this magnificent stage with these amazing players, in the main show room of the Chinese Casino in Taiwan. I repeated my winning song I sang just hours ago at the NCO Club; the entire audience began to yell an applaud. It was an experience I will never forget; all my guys were proud and jazzed.

Days later we were touching down on the runway at Tan Son Nhut Air Base! Slowly we taxied, rolling down the tarmac toward the ramp. The Crew Sergeant barked, "Mays open the aft door, let some air in here". You must in Vietnam there are only three temperatures hot, hotter and hottest, and today was one of the hottest. Inside the aircraft it felt like a sauna. As I opened the door, the humid hot air hit me in the face, but it wasn't unwelcome. As I stood in the door I saw bunkers made of sandbags and behind them were armed soldiers, some with machine guns. In fact, about every three hundred feet there would be another, then another, "hey guys you got to see this, what the heck". A couple of the guys came to the door to look, "what did you expect Mays, a red carpet and a brass band, there's a stinking war going on here".

Soon we would be parked and escorted to our quarters, you might have guessed, that's right, another Quonset hut. Inside there were several steel framed bunk beds, with mosquito netting; every bunk had a mattress, sheet and a pillow. Just as we are getting into the building and claiming our space, a sound of a loud siren blasts through the heavy humid air. Our escort shouts, "drop everything and follow me." Out the door we ran like a stampede of elephants, across the yard and hunkered down in a large sandbag bunker with a steel roof. We were in the war.

I've been asked was it stressful over there. Listen to me, there is no safe place in a war zone. You don't have to be at the front, in the jungle, in the air or on the sea, to feel the stress of war. Just trying to walk about and not show the anxiety you've got pressed down inside your gut, you bet it's stressful. Seeing every imaginable kind of soldier from several countries, most of them not much more than kids all armed to the teeth. You bet it's stressful. It's stressful watching the helicopters bringing in the wounded and those killed in action, trust me all this works on your mind and you don't even know it. The Veterans Administration website explains PTSD. "Post-traumatic stress disorder is defined as having flashbacks, upsetting memories, and anxiety following a traumatic event. Believe me war is a traumatic event. For hundreds of years, these symptoms have been with soldiers from many wars and described under different names, punchy, raddled, shell-shocked and so on. However, the Vietnam Veterans with these symptoms were the first to have the term 'PTSD' applied to them. Despite the passing of more than fifty years since the war, for some Vietnam Veterans, PTSD remains a chronic reality of everyday life".[liii]

"Code Name Big Eye"

Our mission in Vietnam is clear for our crew, our forces in the north had an advantage in that their radar coverage could detect most U.S. strike aircraft flying at 5000 feet or above virtually anywhere in the country, using a system that was difficult to jam. U.S. forces did their best using radar ships in the Gulf of Tonkin and ground sites in Thailand, but both had serious gaps in their coverage because their radar systems were line of sight. This glitch resulted in the Air Defense Command to set up from the 552nd AEW&C at McClellan Air Force Base, California, to fix the problem. That's why we are here, to fill the gaps.

Operating in pairs, our Big Eye crew would fly a 50-mile race track pattern approximately 30 miles offshore known as the Alpha orbit. The second flew the Bravo orbit track at 10,000 ft. farther from the coast, acting as backup for Alpha EC-121. This provided a practical detection range of 100 miles, just enough to cover the Hanoi urban area and the main MiG base at Phúc Yên.[liv]

Our missions from Tan Son Nhut began 21 April 1965, using the call signs Ethan Alpha and Ethan Bravo, which became standard. After refueling at Da Nang Air Base, Ethan Alpha made a wave-top approach to its orbit station, where it remained five hours. Because of the threat of interception by Russian fighter aircraft, MiGs, my EC-121 was protected by a Lockheed F-104 Starfighters, and if for any reason the Mig Combat Air Patrol, could not rendezvous, we would cancel the mission. One of our big challenges was the air conditioning system aboard the EC-121, it was virtually useless in this profile and the heat produced by the electronics, combined with the threat of being shot down, made Alpha orbit missions highly stressful. On 10 July 1965, had its first airborne-controlled interception, an EC-121 provided warning to a pair of U.S. F-4C fighters, resulting in the shooting down of two MiG-17s.

The Big Eye Task Force remained at Tan Son Nhut until February 1967, when the threat of Viet Cong ground attacks prompted a move to Thailand.

Because I was due to be discharged in March of 1966, I too was moved back to the states before Thanksgiving Day. I would have a lot to be thankful for and glad to be back in California.

Chapter 9

Now that I'm back in the States I wanted to get busy preparing for my life after the Air Force. The Air Force had offered me a hefty incentive to make it a career, but I had other plans. After winning the talent contest in Tainan my confidence in my talent as a singer had been revived. But, I needed to broaden my music knowledge and improve my guitar playing. I started studying music theory, composition and practicing my guitar every day. I knew I needed to build my repertoire and I did. I added to my set lists, everything from the standards, the fifties, country-western, rhythm and blues and even blue grass.

Around the same time my roommate Doug mentioned that a theatrical group was auditioning for the musical play "Bye, Bye Birdie", a musical satire telling the story of a rock and roll singer who is about to go into the army. When I inquired I found the director was still looking for a singer for the role of the rock star Conrad Birdie. I got up enough moxie to do the audition and luckily, I won the part. To say I was jazzed when I walked out with a copy of the script under my arm, wouldn't tell you what I really felt.

Her name is Marion Lee Camp, I called her Bunny. Our romance was a whirlwind affair. I was intoxicated by her charm, her cute mannerisms and her lovely features. Bunny had this wonderful family, great parents, Charlie and Alice and sisters Charlene, Janice and Pamela. They lived in the real "leave it to beaver" California neighborhood, where every home sat behind manicured green lawns with rose gardens while nestled under the shade of big leaf fruitless mulberry trees.

They accepted me from our first meeting. When they found out about my winning the role of "Conrad Birdie" they were equally enthusiastic. However, the curtain would quickly fall on our elation when after just two weeks of rehearsals I would be victim of a very unfortunate car accident.

The night of the accident I had been out drinking with a buddy at the Maverick Club. As it turned out just before the time for the bar to close, my buddy had scored with some chick and had arranged for her girl friend to give me a lift back to base. I was pretty much wasted from too many shots of "Wild Turkey", so I wouldn't realize that my driver was in no condition to drive. At the intersection of Watt Avenue and "A" street, she makes the turn to wide and crashes into this large concrete traffic controls box. Her car hit the object with such force that my face smashed the windshield. Though I was awake through the entire ordeal, I couldn't remember the ambulance ride to the base hospital. e I do recall hearing someone say how bad I looked, "when this guy wakes up its going to be ugly". She was charged with drunk driving, but the bad news for me, she was the wife of an Airman serving in Vietnam. I was totally unaware of any of this the night I got into the car. After the medics finally sewed me up they let me make a call. I called Bunny and ask her to call Doug, he would escort her to the hospital. Bunny told her parents and they insisted that she bring me to their home. I was thankful for their kind offer. I told them how the accident happened as best I could. Before this case was closed, I had to tell the story several more times. I answered questions to the Air Police, the First Sergeant, and the squadron Commander. They were particularly unhappy that I was out with another GI's wife. I told them I honestly didn't go out with her, I didn't know her, that I was introduced to her by my friend at the club and she just offered me a ride. Thankfully, my friend and the woman substantiated my statement.

The wounds I received were deep gashes on my head, forehead, over my right eye and cheekbone. The windshield glass had made dozens of small lacerations over my entire face. Fortunately for me, in time most of the smaller scars would disappear and the larger one over my eye would become hardly noticeable. The play's director and cast were grieved over my injuries and of course saddened that I would not be able to perform. I hated that fate had stolen my opportunity. I never went to watch the play performed, I just couldn't. It was more than I could bear.

On March 22nd, I left the Air Force, four years to the day. They gave me mustering out money which included almost two months of unused leave and a promotion to Airman 1st Class. But, more important to me, than the promotion or money was the Honorable Discharge. I had also received a few medals over the years; the Good Conduct medal, which made me smile when I thought, "if they only knew". The Outstanding Unit Award, the Vietnam Medal, and the USAF Air Medal, which is a military decoration medal awarded for meritorious achievement while participating in aerial flight. I also earned my permanent wings for flying in a combat zone and don't forget I had my G.E.D., and topping it all off I would be leaving the Air Force with a real since of pride and accomplishment. I had kept my oath and completed my duty to my Country. Because of my service I would receive many benefits from the Veterans Administration in the years to come. The GI Bill would help me finance my first house. The GI Bill supported me financially when I went off to Bible College.

Today the VA takes care of my medical needs and sends me a pension each month for my diagnosis of PTDS, which they proved had injured my life for many years.

Some months after my discharge my wounds are healed, and all my bandages are off. I was reading the employment want ads in the Sacramento Bee when I happened to notice an ad looking for entertainment at the 007 Club, "to inquire call". Now, if you are from that period, you know how popular the James Bond, Mr. 007 movies were. I thought, "why not, let's give it a shot, you know, get back in the saddle so to speak, after all what did I have to lose". I called the number, told the owner about my act as a solo singer and guitar player and then I simply showed up. Like most drinking establishments when you enter them they are usually dark, so it took a few moments for my eyes to adjust to the dimly lit room. The first thing I noticed were a few people standing or sitting at the bar. Looking around the room I saw others lounging on large colorful cushions next to short legged tables. They were listening to a long haired hippy fellow playing an autoharp and singing Dylan songs. I watched and listened and thought to myself, "he's pretty good".

After the folksinger's set, the owner of the bar gave me time to set up my gear. When he asks how I should be introduced, I answered, "I go by Johnny, you can call me Johnny Mays". That was the name I had worked out with the play director a few months back and that name is what I am generally known by to this very day.

"Here's Johnny", the audition went off great and the owner offered me eight weekends for ten bucks a night and all the beer I could drink.

Listen… you must start somewhere… right? Believe me, up till now I played for free or tips only, so this was a good start.

After the run at the 007, there would be several solo gigs which followed, none of them paid much more. I knew if I was going to continue my musical pursuits I was going to need a day job. At one of my gigs, a group of guys walked in. They were salesman from an auto dealership. One of the guys came up to me at my break and said, "my name is Bob, I have to tell you, you're pretty good, have you ever thought about selling cars"? "What do you mean" I asked. "Well I thought if you would like to make a little extra money you could come and work for me, work the days you want, it won't interfere with your music and we both could make a little more money".

That next week I went to work for Bob Irons and sold British cars. I remember one midweek night just about closing time when two college age girls came in looking at the prominently displayed canary yellow, 1966 Jaguar E-Type. Those girls must have spent a half hour past my closing time, bouncing on the seats, blowing the horn and pretending they were driving around London. I told the girls that I had to close the store, but please come back tomorrow. "You don't think we're going to buy this car, do you"? I had enough of these two, in fact I was growing weary of the car business in general. I answered, "Frankly Scarlett, my dear, I really don't give a damn"! With that snarky remark, they stormed out. The next day I had an early morning shift at the showroom.

While I sat in my sales cubicle having my morning coffee, I noticed the Jaguar being pushed off the display floor.

"Hey where are you going with my car." "Johnny did you have a couple young ladies in here about closing time last night"? "I did, they were pretty annoying". "We know, their father came into our El Camino store, and bought this beauty for his daughter, she had told him about the mean salesman at the downtown store".

As they left with the Jag I could see my commission going out the door with them. Lesson learned, "never judge a book by its cover". That was my last day for me as a car salesman.

When June of 1966 came it turns out I would be getting married after all. No, not as I had first planned with "Orlando Linda", a date we had set for our wedding almost two years ago. Today I would be getting married to Marion Lee Camp. I remembered as Bunny and I were standing at the altar, I kept thinking, "this is the wrong girl", as I reminded myself, her name is not "Judy". If you can remember the childhood prophecy given to me by "The Voice", when I was still a kid, "your wife will be Judy from Sacramento".

Someone once said to me, maybe your first marriage failed because you only had a platonic relationship. I had to look that up. "Platonic describes a relationship that is purely spiritual and not physical. This word platonic refers to the writings of Plato, an ancient Greek philosopher who wrote on the interesting subject of love. Platonic love and platonic friendships are marked by the absence of physical or sexual desire."[lv]

Well, that wasn't our situation. I couldn't have described our marriage platonic because, she was already pregnant and nine months later we would have a baby.

No buddy, there was plenty of physical and sexual desire, we had those bases covered. No, the problem we had…was me, something was very wrong in my head.

I tried to keep our marriage together and thought maybe a move would help. So not long after the wedding I talked her into moving back to Alabama with me. I found a job at the Alabama Music Center in Birmingham. The job was an apprentice position as a musical instrument repairman. The store paid me fifty dollars a week with a promise of a raise if I would agree to let them send me to the Conn band instrument repair school. Though I agreed, I knew that would never happened because I had a pregnant wife who would hardly let me out of her sight even to go to work. Then to add to my woes, I was paying rent on a two-bedroom apartment which we were sharing with my brother Gary who just graduated and moved to Birmingham with us. Out of the fifty bucks a week I was trying to save half for the baby coming, so I knew I needed to find a better paying job.

My brother Gary was working at a department store as a clerk. I was sure happy to have him with us, he was my best friend and a real source of strength to me. I guess because of all his health challenges with two bouts of rheumatic fever and open-heart surgery to remove scar tissue around the heart valves. Oh, by the way he would have to endure a second heart surgery in a couple years to replace those valves. The new plastic valves would make his heart sound like a ticking clock with every heartbeat. I saw him as one of the most courageous individuals I had ever known. Gary encouraged me to try to find something else, even though being around music was where my heart was. I followed my brother's advice and I found a job at the milk dairy, training to be a milkman.

To get to the dairy every morning for training I had purchased a cheap bicycle. Darn the luck, on the very first day, I parked my bike and chained it to a street sign, only to find it after with both tires flat. Some malicious person had sliced them open. So that put me afoot again. I've often wondered what kind of person finds humor or gets a thrill out of destroying someone else's property. I remember my first thought, "if I could get my hands on that son of a gun I'd strangle him". Anyway, it wasn't that far to walk, only ten blocks or more, but I made it every morning without missing a classroom session. Now it was time for my ride along, to get hands on experience as a milkman.

One early morning just as the sun was beginning to dawn. My trainer and I were coming up a hill, when I heard a thunderous bark. Reaching over to grab a metal milk bottle carrying crate, which milkmen use to protect themselves from mean dogs or in some cases irate husbands of forlorn housewives. "You won't need that here with this big guy, he's got no teeth"! Apparently, my trainer was familiar with this big fellow, he told me the dog had a history of chewing on milkmen, postmen, or anyone else he took a disliking too. So, to curtail his aggressiveness the dog's owner had his teeth pulled. Sure enough, as we approached the top of the hill, standing there in the shadows of the dawn, a huge, dark English Mastiff, bellowing like an ox. With every bellow, the drooping hides around his mouth, exaggerated by the lack of teeth in his jaws, made his jowls flap in the wind.

With every bark, as he tried his best to ward off these unwelcome intruders to his turf, these large flaps would make a flapping fluttering sound around his face. I felt sorry for the old boy that day, but I have used his story often in my sermons to describe the devil. I would tell my congregation the devil goes about like a roaring lion, but his roar is worse than his bite, because our overcoming Savior has defeated him by pulling his teeth. I preached the Devil can threaten you with fear, but he can't harm you if you believe.

Meanwhile, Bunny had returned to my parents' house for a doctor's visit just before the time of my graduation from the dairy. When graduation came I was assigned to a dairy outside of the city to the north of Birmingham. My route would be a rural route. I knew I could neither walk to work or ride my bike way out there, not at two o'clock in the morning. I shopped around for a car, but with no luck. I only had a little savings and absolutely no credit. One salesman suggested a motor scooter. Well I found a very old Cushman motor scooter and bought it for fifty bucks with the agreement that the purchase was, "as is". I had to drive it several miles back to my apartment and as I drove I felt there was something wrong, the motor sounded good, but the transmission was having problems. I was sure it was the centrifugal clutch. This type of clutch is a drive engagement mechanism which automatically engages a drive transmission at a certain RPM level. This allows the engine to idle without spinning the wheels. I thought maybe if I could tighten it up or somehow get the slipping to stop it would be alright. As I rode into the driveway it would be the last time I would ever ride the scooter. For hours in the cold, while the night fell about me, I tinkered with no success. I became angry and frustrated. I began cursing and screaming, kicking and beating it with my hands till finally I could do no more, it had beaten me.

Exhausted, I fell across my bed and the next thing I really remember was waking up in my Aunt Ruth's house with Dad sitting at my side. Apparently when my brother Gary came home from work, he found me sprawled across my bed, but he couldn't communicate with me. "He just stared into the air and said not a word", he explained, "it was like he was in a trance". My brother was scared about my condition and called Aunt Ruth and my Uncle Curtis. My Uncle Curtis was a WWII veteran and he recognized my symptoms right away. He told my brother he had seen this before with soldiers who had become overwhelmed with stress. They took me right away to their home and called my Dad. By the time I finally came out of it, the night had passed, and the morning had come. Dad told me we're going to Hamilton as soon as I felt better. I might have forgotten to mention that my parents had left Birmingham about the time I had gone to Vietnam and they had moved back to "Woods Creek" and back to Pa's old house. My Dad's cousin Bryce had purchased the old house after Pa died, and basically gave it to my family rent free just to have someone on the property.

Being back at the old house, brought home to me so many fond memories, still… I knew it would never work for us living with my parents. I wouldn't be able to deal with all their expectations they would have of me, but not only me, but Bunny too. Bunny told me she didn't want to have our baby in Alabama, and that she wanted to go back to California. I put her on a bus and told her I would come-back as soon as I could.

So here I go "Leaving Woods Creek" again, and now for the second of what will be four times in a span of a decade I would be riding the Greyhound west on Route 66.

143

As I've said before going back is never the same. Even though we would have a beautiful baby boy, things between Bunny, her family and me would never be the same. I named our baby after my Dad, I called him John Oliver Mays II. Please understand something, I have never hated my Dad, I loved my father. You may remember that it was his courage that saved my life before I was born. My Dad was there at one of the lowest points of my life at the bedside in Aunt Ruth's house. My Dad was no psychologist, he didn't know what was wrong with me, nobody understood why I thought the way I thought and would do the things I would do.

My brothers would tell me years later that the only time they ever saw their daddy cry was when he would stand up in the Pleasant Grove Baptist Church and ask the congregation to pray for me. As life would have it, I would preach my Dad's funeral in that same church. In fact, we laid him to rest in the cemetery on the hill just outside that church. I was proud to give my first born my Dad's name. I knew it may never mean to either of them what it would mean to me.

Returning to California would be my second chance to try my hand at being a professional musician. Had I known what it was going to cost me I probably would never have pursued it. Yet on the other hand music has opened so many more opportunities for my life and would be the impetus by which I would discover my salvation. Trust me, everything you have heard about a musician, are in most cases true.

Long before the sixties, way back in the forties and fifties the term "Beat Generation" characterized many of the youth of America as anti-conformists.

144

These youths were congregating in jazz clubs like the Birdland, the Open Door and the Royal Roost. The performers who played these clubs, Charlie Parker, Dizzy Gillespie, and Miles Davis and their band members, not only shared in the growth of the music, but they also shared their own language. Terms like; square, cats, cool and do you dig. This was the seed bed of the fifties and Rock N Roll. Music has always set the sounds of youth, the fashions of youth, the language of youth and the thinking of youth. In the forties we were, "beat", thus, "beatniks", the fifties we were "cool", thus the term, "cool cats" and now in the sixties we were hip, popularizing the term "hippies".

It was the dawning of the Age of Aquarius and the dark side of the sixties, which was a decade of historical tragedy. With the Vietnam war, assassinations of Martin Luther King, John and Bobby Kennedy, along with national civil unrest which was the news of the day. The 1960s brought us tie-dyes, sit-ins and large-scale drug use with the Hippies smoking marijuana, kids in ghettos pushing heroin, and Timothy Leary, a Harvard professor, urging the world to take a trip with "Lucy in the Sky with Diamonds... LSD. These were dark and tumultuous times.[lvi]

The music of the decade however was awesome, played by some of the most iconic musicians from the British invaders, the California Surfers, the Motown Funk Brothers and Bakersfield Country music. In the sixties California had a honky tonk bar in every town and neighborhood. Plenty of places to perform and I would play in many of them anywhere and everywhere.

The music wasn't the problem in my marriage. It was what the music attracted, women, drugs and booze. Too many nights away from home caused the divorce papers to finally

145

arrive into my hand. Bunny was done with me, done with my life and done with my music and honestly, I didn't blame her. She deserved a better man than what I had become.

As much as her leaving and taking my son away from me hurt my selfish ego, I found it to be, in a heartless way, a liberating relief. I hope that doesn't sound too crass, but my intention is to show you just how far from my upbringing I had fallen.

I was always sorry for the way I hurt Bunny, she loved me. It's tough for a person when you give someone all your love and hope with all your heart, hoping that it's going to lead somewhere great, and then you find out this person is not who you thought he or she was. I was not the person she thought I was. Even I couldn't tell you who I was, or what I believed.

The truth, at the time I couldn't really tell you if I was a believer in anything, in particularly the God of my childhood, for all of that seemed so distant, so far away from me right now.

The person I thought I was...was gone... somewhere along the way I had lost me. The man I had become was never me but someone else impersonating me. My mind was swirling about, there was "a bad moon on the rise".

"I see a bad moon a-rising
I see trouble on the way
I see earthquakes and lightnin'
I see bad times today

Don't go 'round tonight
It's bound to take your life
There's a bad moon on the rise

I hear hurricanes a-blowing
I know the end is coming soon
I fear rivers over flowing
I hear the voice of rage and ruin

Don't go 'round tonight
It's bound to take your life
There's a bad moon on the rise

I hope you got your things together
I hope you are quite prepared to die
Looks like we're in for nasty weather
One eye is taken for an eye

Oh, don't go 'round tonight
It's bound to take your life
There's a bad moon on the rise
a bad moon on the rise[lvii]

My first time to play the Howdy Club, was a solo gig on a Sunday afternoon, but now I am introducing them to a full four-piece country band. The McClendon brothers, Jerry on lead guitar and Oscar on the drums, with Roger "Ramjet" Quick playing the bass and me on rhythm guitar and vocals. We were pretty good, and had good crowds especially on the weekends.

One weekend a large group came in taking up many tables. Roger had told us before our first set that he had some family and friends coming in. They all appeared to be having a good time, laughing and dancing, they were loud but fun. Their applause after every number we played made performing that night more enjoyable. Usually honky tonk audiences don't normally applaud. The litmus test for a good night and to know that your music is being received is known by how many dancers are on the dance floor and how many drinks they are sending up to the stage. If you have more than three drinks sitting on your amp at any one time, you're having a good night. But as far as the bar owners are concerned, the only music that counts are the sound of the cash register ringing and when that stops the gigs up.

When our break time came the group began to holler, "introduce us to the band Roger"! Roger had us shaking hands with everyone there. "This is my sister Judy, Jude meet Johnny Mays", we both smiled, as I quickly turned toward the bar. This would be my first encounter with my Judy.

Two or three months passed before I would have the chance of meeting her again. By then I was already performing with a new band in a different club. These guys were awesome players, on lead guitar, Lee Pate, whom I called" Chief" and was considered by everyone as one of the greatest guitarist in Northern California. On the drums, James "Jimbo" Schlarp, agreed by many as not only one of the top drummers in Northern California, but an awesome singer. I was playing bass now and singing. Our front man was, Lee Roy Toten, who I called the, "Don Rickles" of country music.

I never understood how Lee Roy could get away with the things he both said and did to an audience. I told him once as seriously as I could, "Lee Roy if you are going to talk like that to our audience, please don't stand in front of me". I said, "one of these nights someone's going to take a shot at you, they're going to miss you and hit me." I was as serious as a heart attack, but Lee Roy would just laugh and say, "that's a good one Pard". Lee Roy called everyone Pard.

My next encounter with Judy came as I was visiting a friend of mine whom I called "Momma Bear". She was a cocktail waitress in a cowboy bar called the Outpost. As I was walking up to her apartment door, above my head I heard someone yell; "hey you"! As I stopped, turning my head and looking up to the apartment balcony, there stood Judy Quick, Roger Ramjet's sister.

Judy: "Aren't you the guy that plays music with Roger"?

"Not anymore, I mean…yes, I use too, but I'm with another group now. Your name is...Judy, right"?

Judy: "That's right, nice seeing you again, I'll see you later". She then turns and walks back into the apartment before I could say another word.

Inside, Momma Bear and I are having coffee. I had paid her for the diet pills, for that's why I had come. Suddenly there's a knock on the door. "It's a pretty young woman for you Johnny". When I get to the door, it was Judy again. "My mom wanted me to ask where you are playing and maybe we could come see you sometime before she moves to Tahoe with me".

"You live in Tahoe"?

Judy: "My home is there, and I work in the casino there".

"That's cool, I'm playing at the Roadhouse in West Sacramento.

Judy: "I always heard that's "a strip club". I was feeling the chagrin in her voice.

"Oh…Ohno…I mean you're right, it has been…. but it's a country music club now. Would you like to go with me tonight, I can pick you up"?

Judy: "Sure, I'll go with you. What time?

"How about eight o'clock tonight. I'll pick you up!

I hesitated to tell her we would be going on my 1965 Suzuki S32 motorcycle. Luckily for me she was dressed in jeans and a nice jacket when I arrived. When she saw the motorcycle, she looked a bit reluctant, but ran back up the stairs and came down with her short dark black hair wrapped in a scarf, framing her beautiful ivory face with her piercing blue eyes. When she straddles the bike, she leaned forward wrapping her arms about my waist, and all I could think about was, "don't mess this up".

The night went off without a hitch, the guys were impressed that she was Roger's sister and with that knowledge and the fact that she was with me there was an air of respect being shown to her. She wasn't a barroom girl. Later back at her mother's apartment we simply said goodbye. We never exchanged as much as a hug. She promised me she had a good time and she hoped we would meet again. I felt the same way. Unfortunately, she would nearly get away from me. It would be months later before I would see her again.

This time the marquee outside the Metropolitan Club, would read "The Johnny Mays Trio".

Finally, I had my own band again and we would work together for more than five years in different venues. It was the same players less one Lee Roy, his uncouth shenanigans finally separated us from him and we thought we would tried to do it on our own. With Jimbo and I on vocals and Chief on his awesome guitar we had a big sound for just a trio.

The Metropolitan was packing out and who would show up one night, about half of the group who visited the Howdy Club more than a year earlier.

There she was, my Judy, and as excited as I was to see her, my heart literally broke when she told me she was engaged to be married in two months. I couldn't believe my ears. Almost shouting I could hear myself saying, "what do you mean, I mean what about us".

Judy: "What do you mean...us"?

"I mean, I was thinking about something...I had something on my mind."

She just shook her head and told the girls she came with she had to go. I watched her walking away I thought this "can't be happening". For the next two weeks, I couldn't keep my eyes off the front door of the club. Every break I would walk out to check the parking lot to see if she might drive up.

Then one night...there she was, with a girlfriend, in fact it was her brother's wife. When I came to her table I tried to control my enthusiasm, yet when she told me she had

cancelled her wedding plans, I simply grabbed her and
declared.

"Listen you, and don't you forget it, you're my girl from
now on", don't even think about being anyone else's
girl, you're my girl".

From that point on we saw each other every week. I would
never lose her again, though I almost did, except by the
grace of God. I've often wonder if that story about her
getting married was true, or if she was just fishing. I never
asked, because it didn't matter.

The Metropolitan gig played out soon after that. For the
next several months, "The Johnny Mays Trio" moved
around a bit. Somehow, we found out about a rich Oregon
farmer, from Milton-Freewater, a small town near
Pendleton, Oregon, who had opened a large club
and needed a band right away. We accepted the
invitation and the rich guy flew us up. The owner had
someone meet us at the airport, we grabbed our gear and
got to the club just in time for the first set. Also on the
show was a female impersonators group who looked more
like a bunch of ugly face dudes in miniskirts, it was
hilarious. After the first set I told my band, "these guys
won't last past their opening set". When the fellows ask me
how I knew. I told them, "man didn't you see that audience,
it's all cowboys and lumberjacks". Sure enough, when
those sissies came off stage, they came off running,
grabbing their dresses and jumping into their van. "Where
are you going ladies", "were getting the heck outta here,
did you see that audience". The guys in the band started
laughing until we cried. To be honest we didn't stay much
longer either, after our second payday, we rented a car and
got out of that one-horse town.

One of the most interesting gigs we landed was with a couple of old road dogs, Larry Ford and Venus. A club owner by the name of Lloyd Hickey, hired Larry Ford and Venus to play at his Forty Grand Club, and suggested to Larry that he hire "The Johnny Mays Trio" to back them up.

Larry called their act "Venus and the Baja Country Jesters". Larry was a standup comedian who also played guitar and alto trumpet. He also prided himself at being a singer.

Venus was a four-foot dwarf from Mexico City, who played the straight role in Larry's comedy portion of the show. She also did a Mexican hat dance around a sombrero which was as tall as her. She grew up in the Mexican Circus and it was a real side show, but our audiences loved it. We played a couple months at the Forty Grand Club. After that Larry took us on the road and we played some military bases, and then wouldn't you know it, Larry booked us over the Christmas/New Year's holiday at Harvey's Wagon Wheel Hotel and Casino in Lake Tahoe. It was perfect, when I told Judy, she offered to let me stay with her at her mother's apartment. During those days Judy had a 1965 white Mustang which I drove to the casino on our opening night. Opening night was a blast, we played on a stage right behind the bar facing the casino floor. From the stage, I could see Harrah's Club across highway fifty, but in the middle of opening night I could see nothing. Tahoe was having a blizzard and there was zero visibility outside the hotel. After the last set, I went to get the mustang and I almost never found it, for it was buried under a snow drift. From that night on I took the taxi.

153

At Harvey's we rotated with two other groups. One was a four piece all black musicians from Philadelphia. They were a real family, two brothers and two cousins.

The other group rotating with us was a trio of a male piano player, with a good looking female singer, and a drummer.

On this night, my guitar player and I were standing outside of our dressing room which by the way all the dressing rooms were in the basement under the stage. As we stood near the spiral stairs that led up to the backstage door, we watch the brothers as they came down. When the last brother passed by us, my guitar player said, "Johnny did you see that dude, he doesn't have long to live". "What are you talking about Chief"? "You can tell by his belly, he's got cirrhosis of the liver". My hand to God this dude was dead in two days. The brothers ask Jimbo our drummer to finish out their run, so they could get enough money to take him back to Philly to be buried.

After Tahoe, we all left Larry and Venus and "The Johnny Mays Trio" landed a gig in Reno, Nevada at the Nashville West night club. So, I decided then to make Tahoe my home and commute. Judy and I got a little apartment and things were going great, except my conscience started bothering me about our living arrangements and I decided I was going to pop the question. Well it just so happened that Leon came to hang out with me on the weekend. I had introduced Leon to Judy a couple of months prior. The three of us were good friends.

I was off on Monday and Tuesday so we all hung out together, grabbing some lunch and enjoying the snow-capped Sierra Nevada mountains and beautiful Lake Tahoe. That night Judy had to work so Leon and I were hanging out in the casino where Judy was dealing blackjack. I had told Leon privately of my plans and he said go for it

After a few drinks at the bar, I walked up to her table and I whispered, "when you get off work we're going to get married". She just looked at me and laughed like I was nuts.

By the time her shift was over I had gambled what money I had on the roulette tables. I ask her to loan me a hundred bucks. With borrowed money from my future bride, the three of us went across the street to Harrah's Casino, I got a little lucky, ran up what I had borrowed, to about three hundred dollars, and hurriedly we ran out of there.

"Let's go". She hesitated, as I pleaded, "please let's go now". Even though she was reluctant and not really knowing what to do with me, she went. We were all quiet as we drove the twenty miles to Carson City, where we got our marriage license. Still Judy was not saying much even as I woke up the preacher at the wedding chapel, by now it's a Tuesday morning, August 18, 1970. What we have here is a half sober groom, a reluctant bride, a tired best man, a preacher's wife who is a total stranger and a preacher who is half asleep in a wedding chapel at about four in the morning.

I was one very lucky guy that night. This woman that" The Voice", had promised me when I was just a kid, was now my wife, my Judy. I will love her all my life. I had dreamed of her all my life even though she had just been a promise made to me by an unknown… "The Voice", many years before. Even more than I knew I could, I would love her, over the past soon to be a half century. I could not have lived without her. If she were to be taken from me, it would be like taking breath from my lungs. I would suffocate without knowing she was near and within my reach. She became my home, no matter where I would travel or how far the music or ministry would take me from her over the many years. Whether in some obscure Russian village preaching the gospel, or as I stood on the equator in Africa, or walking the Great Wall of China or visiting the Forbidden City in Beijing or the Temple of the Emerald Buddha in Thailand, or at the Wailing Wall in Jerusalem, she was always in my heart. Even my travels to the green fields of Ireland, the quaint country side of the British Isles, a lonesome hotel room on The Isle of Man, or on a Russian train going to the shores of the Black Sea. Traveling the breadth of Europe my mind was always on her. Mile after mile as I drove the length of America, the two things which kept me anchored and gave me strength, was the grace of God and knowing that somehow my getting home to my Judy was still in my future.

"The man who finds a wife finds a treasure, and he receives favor from the LORD".

Proverbs 18:22

Chapter 10

Danny Hart a rock n roll bass player who thought of himself as a song writer, talked me into driving him back to Nashville. I suppose every country player would like to give the "Music City a shot, so I borrowed Judy's Mustang and we left. We were nearly broke by the time we got to Hawthorne, Nevada. Luckily while we are having our breakfast in the casino, Danny hits a keno ticket. So, with a few more bucks in our pockets we continue. Somewhere in Texas we pulled off the highway Route 66 at a roadside bar/café, Danny wanted a beer. I should have taken a hint when all I saw were pickup trucks in the parking lot! Once inside, all I saw were cowboys sitting at the tables and leaning on the bar. Around the pool table stood three pretty good sized old boys shooting pool. When they saw these two long haired dudes standing at the door, all I could here was, "whistles and "hey Mable….is that your girlfriends coming in here" …as the waitress turned to see who the cowboys were whistling at! Immediately as if by telepathy, not saying a word to each other or the cowboys, Danny and I started backing out the door, climbing into the Mustang, looking over our shoulder only to see if any of those pickups were behind us. As we sped away all I could imagine is me hanging by a short rope from one of those tall Saguaro cacti we had been seeing across the desert. I didn't slow down until we were crossing the Alabama Stateline.

I had plan to go by Pa's old house to see my folks. But when we drove to it they were no longer living there. Some folks who looked like the cast from the movie Deliverance, told us that they believed the Mays family lived in the city.

It was dark around nine o'clock when I found them living in some newly constructed projects in Hamilton. When I knocked on the door, my Mother came to the door. She just stood in the opening and stared at me, then took notice of Danny who was standing just behind me, she never said a word. After a few moments, I realized she doesn't know who we are. She doesn't recognize her own son. I mean how bad off have you become, to be unrecognizable to your own Mother. Of course, it'd been a few years since Bunny and I were with them at the old house. "Mother, it's me"! She steps back from the door. "Mother, it's your son…it's Bill". That's when I saw my Dad coming to the door fasting the belt on his trousers, he had already gone to bed. Dad recognized me right away and then Mother reached out to me, it finally dawned on her who I was.

It was great to see everybody, and we got caught up on the news. Somehow, they had learned that I had been divorced and remarried. They didn't say much about it. They didn't know what to think about Danny, so in two or three days we continued to Nashville.

It was cold when we arrived. We drove around the city and found The Ryman Auditorium the original home of the Grand Ole Opry, referred to reverently as "The Mother Church of Country Music."

Truth is… the building originally was a church. The Union Gospel Tabernacle opened 1892. It seems that back in 1885 there was a riverboat Captain by the name of Thomas Ryman who owned several saloons and a fleet of river-boats. In that same year there was also a revivalist in town by the name of Samuel Porter Jones. Preacher Jones was conducting tent revivals which were interfering with the Captain's business, seeing how drinking and gambling were considered a sure-fire way of going to hell. The Captain and a few of his hooligans decided they would put a stop to all these hallelujah folks. They went to the tent with the idea of heckling the preacher out of town, but The Lord turned the tables on them. When the gospel was preached, they fell under conviction and the old Captain was converted into a devout Christian, and soon after the Captain pledged to build the tabernacle, so the people of Nashville could attend a large-scale revival indoors. When Ryman died in 1904, his memorial service was held at the tabernacle. During the service, Reverend Jones proposed the building be renamed The Ryman Auditorium, which was met with the overwhelming approval of the attendees. Preacher Jones died less than two years later, in 1906. Quite a story.[lviii]

The first thing we did after sightseeing was locate an old friend of Danny's who had some success in Nashville. Danny told me he owed him fifty dollars. We found him, Franklin Delano Reeves, better known as Del Reeves. Del was known for his hits "Girl on the Billboard" and "The Belles of Southern Bell". Del invited us to come to his office to get the money which was in the same building as the country division of United Artists. We got the fifty dollars.[lix]

Later that day in a café on Broadway we met a group of musicians who all lived in a large Victorian house owned by one Nashville songwriter Don Chapel.

Among his best-known compositions is the George Jones hit "When the Grass Grows Over Me." which was nominated as the CMA Song of the Year in 1969. That was the same year that George married Tammy Wynette. She

159

had been previously married to guess who, that's right Don Chapel, just two years before.[lx]

Well Danny and I hung out at the Chapel house for about a week. But when I realized that this dozen or so great musicians and singers that lived in the house were all unemployed, I figured it was time for me to move on and get back to California. I told Danny goodbye then and decided to go south back through Alabama one more time before going on west. In Alabama is where the Mustang broke down. I only had a little money left, so I decided to leave the car with my folks and take another Greyhound on Route 66 west. How many time do I have to repeat this insane circle. Thankfully I was home to my Judy but unknown to me then in just a matter of a couple of months I would be back, it's totally crazy.

Right away I landed a gig at the Maverick Club in North Sacramento with a new band, regrettably my life was out of control. I was spiraling deeper into the horrible pit of drug abuse and sin. It came to a climax at a jam session at the Outpost one Sunday afternoon.

Someone or, some "Thing" ...hissed. "Try this Johnny", so I opened my mouth and popped it in. Looking back, I honestly think it was the Serpent himself, the Devil. Within a matter of minutes, I would find myself in the most horrifying state of mind that anyone could ever imagine. It was as if hell had opened its gates and every demon horde that had ever seduced me over the course of my lifetime showed up.

Darkness was all around me, I could sense nothing good, nothing pure, and nothing holy. I felt God had left me and I was terrified. Unable to perform, I drop my instrument on

160

the stage, left the club running, fighting back the vicious images that were flooding my mind. Speeding back to my apartment, I quickly demanded that Judy who was pregnant pack quickly, so we could leave California. She tried to console me, but I strongly insisted. She packed a few things then taking her four-year old son Robert Paul by the hand and led him down the stairs as I brought the luggage. I had adopted Robert who was the youngest of Judy's three sons. Her two older sons from her previous marriage, were now living with their father.

I fled with my little family in terror wanting to distance myself from the damnation I was experiencing. My only thought as insane as it may sound was, I had to get back to Alabama, I knew there is a God at "Woods Creek". I had convinced myself that this was the only way I could protect my family from Satan's grip. After the many years of the sins of substance abuse, alcohol and a history of mental stress combined with a dose of lysergic acid diethyl-amide, also known as LSD, purple haze or orange sunshine, all of this was stealing my sanity, and now all my madness was coming to a head. This wasn't my first experience at acid, but it would be the last, because hell had come, and death was at the door.

We rode for hours on Route 66, Judy hardly speaking to me directly, she didn't know what to say. Seventeen hours after we left, Santa Rosa, New Mexico was now coming into our view. It was here she insisted we stop and sleep. Until then I had only stopped for fuel, food and toilet breaks.

My 1962 Volkswagen bug which I had purchase about a week before we left, was getting nearly thirty miles per gallon.

After arriving in Alabama, we found my parents at the projects. My Dad was now working for the State of Alabama Highway Department. My mother was a seamstress at a company making women's night clothing. My brother Kenny was now an Alabama State Trooper stationed in Birmingham. My brother Gary was living in the same government projects with his new wife. My brother Joe was now about seventeen and my sister Peggy was about thirteen and of course they both still lived at home.

Being in Alabama gave me a little quiet time to get my emotions under control. I could finally sleep. Both Judy and I soon found jobs and my Dad pulled some strings with the housing authority and we moved next door to my parents. Dad signed a banknote and we bought a house full of furniture. On May 21, 1971 at the hospital in Guin, Alabama our son Christopher Cody was born which was the best thing that had happened to us for a long time. But, the "bad moon was still rising".

Devastating News

I was awakened by Judy, "John your dad is at the door". I jumped up ran to the door, "Son somebody is on the phone from California, something urgent concerning Marion". I ran next door, I grabbed the phone, "hello", my gut was wrenching, I knew something bad had happened.

"Johnny this is Timothy; Marion's parents wanted me to call you and tell you that she and little John Oliver have been in a terrible accident. Your son John Oliver is fine, but his darling mother is dead. She was killed by third degree burns. However, by the grace of God just before the car burst into flames a bystander saved John Oliver out of the wreckage. The man had tried desperately to free

162

Marion, but the car exploded into flames before he could rescue her. John, I'm sorry to have to be the one to tell you this, but as far as your son is concerned don't worry about him, in fact Charlie and Alice don't want you coming around for a while, they feel it would be too difficult for Little Johnny."

Tim was Marion's sister Charlene's husband. While he talked I could feel my life energy draining from my body and my mind, just as it had in 1966 when in Birmingham I struggled with the scooter and collapsed under all the stress which I had been under during those days. When I hung up the phone I turned to my family, I said, "Bunny is dead.... she's dead, killed in a fiery crash"! I broke, as a tsunami of guilt flooded my brain, as my heart began bursting with grief, in my mind all I could think, "it's all my fault, if I had been a better husband this would have never happened"!

These thoughts were all that made sense to me. "I've been the bad guy, not her. I'm the one who should be punished not her". This girl had finally got over me, she was starting a new life, a new husband, with our beautiful son and even the car that killed her was a new car. I was devastated by the shame of how I had treated her, our son and her family. My hope was gone, my soul was sick with despair, for there was absolutely nothing I could do to change things. In this mental and spiritual condition, I was sinking deeper into the mire, feeling lost and helpless. No one could comfort me, I deserved this pain.

Before the summer's end I was even more determined to get my family back to California. I had finally and completely realized since the day we were all "Leaving Woods Creek" that this place would never ever be home to me again. California is my home, not here in Alabama. I had tried to fit into this place, time and time again, but it seemed that no matter how hard I tried to make it, it just never worked. I knew I had to get away from this place and get away fast. As soon as we could we left Hamilton without saying goodbye. We waited until after my parents had gone to work then Judy and I drove to St. Louis on our way to Judy's brother Lanny who lived in Waterloo, Iowa. I hated to leave that way like we were escaping convicts on the run. In St. Louis, we waited for a money gram from Judy's mother to come, because of a flat tire we had on our way here, we were a little short of money. While waiting in the city park we ate sandwiches which Judy had packed. Judy watched Robert play, while she tended to our new baby. I found a Bible and literally with nothing else to do, I randomly opened to the book of Job. Here I discovered in the Bible that as soon as Job received the terrible news about losing his children and his wealth. He immediately responded by seeking God in worship saying;

"The Lord gave, and the Lord has taken away; blessed be the Name of the Lord". Job 1:21

I mused on this passage quietly all the way to Waterloo, I found some solace in the scripture. When we got to Iowa we discovered her brother was out of town, and his house was locked. I found a window left opened and could squeeze in. Once inside Judy called her mother in California and somehow, she found Lanny. Lanny would call us to tell us to make ourselves at home.

He finally arrived to find his house burglars sitting at his table eating his food. His kindness soon made us forget our embarrassment of showing up the way we did. In Iowa we found jobs, I as a bartender and she as a cocktail waitress.

In a month or so we had enough money to continue our final exodus back to Tahoe.

You would think by now that I would have had enough heartache for a lifetime, and that I would have learned my lessons...no...no... not this fool! At least for now I was sober, though I was still smoking a little weed, I had to, it was the only thing that relaxed me. Judy and I were getting along pretty good, she was very happy and comfortable to be back with her mother. She even suggested I should go back to Sacramento and see if I could find a gig. I hoped she wasn't just trying to get rid of me. We didn't talk anymore about Alabama or Bunny, so off I went while she and the kids stayed with Bernice her mother.

You hear comedians make jokes of their mother in laws. Not me. I was blessed to have not one but two wonderful mothers-in-law. Bunny's mother Alice Camp a wonderful woman. Alice was strong, honest and smart. Even though she was displeased with the way things worked out between her daughter and I, I knew she loved me. After Bunny died Alice raised my son like her own. When Johnny was sixteen, she called me and said, he needs his father now John, she was not a selfish woman. After she passed, I spoke at her memorial service and wept bitter tears because I owed her so much.

Then there was Bernice Rowe, Judy's mother. Bernice was a widow of an Army sergeant. Bernice was a strong and independent woman who never showed any sign of feeling sorry for herself. She was not a meddlesome person either. Her philosophy was "live and let live". Her door was always open to her family. She loved sports and was quite clever at handicapping the football games. Her grandsons were always calling her to get her picks. She loved to play

165

card games and the nickel slots. Her best friend was a lady we all called affectionately Aunt Van, though she was no blood kin at all, they had been friends all their lives. When Aunt Van passed I was out of the country, so Judy handled the services for her. However, I was standing at the bedside when Bernice passed. I remember just before she took her last breath I felt the presence of Angels, they had come to escort her to her new home. I wept for this woman, because I loved her.

But for now, knowing Judy was safe with her mother Bernice, I left Tahoe heading down the mountain. On the way down the hill I met a California Highway Patrolman coming up the hill. As soon as I saw him I knew I was in trouble. You see in all this time I had let my California driver's license and license plate tags expire. I knew I had traffic warrants out on me for different infractions and to top it off I had an ounce of weed in my pocket. If he found that grass on me I would be in trouble for sure. Back in the seventies the law frowned on people in possession of marijuana. So immediately I pulled over, so I could hide the dope. On the floorboard of my car was a pile of trash, all kinds of empty fast food bags, cups and newspapers, so I tossed the weed into a brown McDonald's bag and buried it at the bottom of the pile. Just about then I looked in the rearview mirror in time to see the CHP pulling up behind me with his red-light flashing. I watched him as he walked up to the car with this sardonic grin on his face. Smiling he takes out his ticket book. "You know your tags are expired"?

"Yes Sir, and my driver's license is expired too", as I handed him my registration and driver's license. He closed his ticket book, had me step out of the car. He then ordered

166

me to place my hands on the roof of my car, he searched me, handcuffed me and then took me to his car and strap-ped me in the back seat. I watched through the security screen as he thoroughly searched the vehicle, groping about in the front seat and then the back of my car. I could only watch and pray, "please don't let him find my grass". Soon the officer was back to his vehicle still smiling when he spoke, "I'm guessing you know you're going to jail...and the car is going to be impounded." "Yes Sir" I said.

Soon I was back at Tahoe in the hoosegow, that is jail. After they booked me they gave me a phone call. Over the phone I told Judy the story, so she came in a taxi, paid the fifty bucks bail and they released me. We rode from the jail over to see about the car. They wouldn't let me take the car, but allowed me to get some personal things out of it, of course the only thing I was looking for was my weed.... but it was gone.... disappeared. "You got to be kidding me, the CHP got my grass, no wonder that guy was always smiling". Now, it was me who was smiling as I returned to the taxi. "What's so funny", Judy asked, as our taxi left the impound yard, "oh nothing really". That day would be the last time I would see my 1962 Beetle and the thought of the sneaky CHP officer, now had me laughing.

It didn't take me long to land a gig. Old Lee Roy employed "The Johnny Mays Trio" to back him up at the "Forty Grand Club" on Del Paso Boulevard in Del Paso Heights a suburb just North of Sacramento. The proprietor was a man named Lloyd Hickey, I've mentioned him before. The Forty Grand was opened twenty-four hours a day, seven days a week, with cafe, card room, pool room, barroom with a dance floor and stage. There was also Lloyd's office which his musical guests and the house bands used as a dressing room. There was a back door to the office which we used to step out for a smoke.

The house band played Tuesday thru Saturday. The second band played on weekends during the house bands fifteen-minute breaks and they also played the afterhours which was just a big jam session that went until six in the morning.

Our group was the house band and now "The Johnny Mays Trio" was doing business as" Lee Roy and The Rhythm Kings" again. The second band was "The Blasingame Brothers. We all took pride in knowing we were one of the highest paid bands in town. Our long weekends started every Friday afternoon, that's when we taped The Forty Grand Show on Channel 40 for a Saturday broadcast to the Sacramento Valley.

Lloyd Hickey also booked touring artists for the weekends. "The Johnny Mays Trio" (now known as the Rhythm Kings) backed them all. Stars like, Rose Maddox, David Frizzell, Molly Bee, Jerry Wallace, Freddie Hart, Buddy Allen and the list went on. Other stars who traveled with their own bands perform with us. Bands like Ernest Tubb and the Texas Troubadours, Willie Nelson and Little Jimmy Dickens. Sometimes traveling bands would just show up to party and jam, like the Buckaroos and some cast members of the Hee Haw television show. We were the best country show in town and the Forty Grand was the place to be.

After seven years of pursuing this business, I was finally making some decent money and was now getting myself sorted out. I rented an apartment, so Judy and the children could come home. Lloyd gave her a part time job dealing

Hi-Lo poker in the card room on the weekends, so she had extra money. Things were looking up for us. I got all my traffic tickets paid off, got my driver's license back, and eventually I would purchase a car, our own furniture and a colored TV. I really believed the worst was finally behind us…. but not so fast old pal, "I can still see a bad moon rising".

Time was flying by and it's now 1973, but sad to say I was still playing the part of bad boy. One-day Lee Roy said, Lloyd is bringing in another band for a few weeks just to change things around a bit, keeping it fresh, but don't worry I've got us a road-tour. The problem was my guys, the trio didn't want to go on the road. We would for the time being having to go our separate ways. I was looking forward to the trip, just to get out of town. Truth was things were getting a little strained around the apartment. I thought that maybe a little time apart would be good for us at home. I could sense we needed some space, at least that's what I wanted to believe. When it came to the new band, I had recruited some excellent musicians, these guys were pros, all business. Just before we were to leave, Lee Roy stopped by the house. "Hey Pard, you wanna get your fortune told"? What did he say? I didn't really believe in all that hocus-pocus stuff, but I thought "it couldn't hurt", so I went along.

When we pull up to the house we could hardly find a place to park. When we got into the house the living room was full of women. They looked to me like the real desperate housewives...then maybe not, though I was sure they were of the sort that believed in Ouija boards, horoscopes, magic and such, lots of people do. Me, I was a skeptic. One by one the women were called out and finally they called us.

169

As we walked into the dining area I saw this short, stocky, Gypsy woman, sitting behind a Formica topped kitchen table with chromed legs. She had two matching chromed leg dining chairs with shiny yellow backs and seats sitting across the table from her just waiting for the next chumps to sit down. Beneath her head scarf was long black stringy hair encasing a ghostly face with an ash colored complexion which supported thick heavy framed glasses with lenses that looked like the bottoms of coke bottles. The extreme magnification of those lenses made her eyes look too large for her head. When she spoke, she sounded like a Kentucky coal miner with black lung disease. As we sat, she paused and said to Lee Roy, "I can't tell your future with him in here", as she looked over at me. I look at her, then Lee Roy, and said, "I'll wait for you in the other room". r "Alright Pard", I'll come and get you when she's through with me". In a few minutes Lee Roy hollered and I went back to the kitchen. There was Lee Roy leaning on the kitchen counter, "have a seat Pard". As I sat down I pushed my five dollars across the table to the fortune teller. While she shuffled her deck of cards, I was staring at the huge cross hanging around her neck. Suddenly she lays down the deck, then pushes my five dollars back to me and says, "I can't tell you anything about your future, I've nothing to tell". I stood up to leave, but just before we stepped out the door she said, "hey you", both Lee Roy and I turned, "that's right you, pretty boy...don't stand in one place too long or you'll get hurt", then she looked back down at her cards as we left the house.

"Holy cow! .... Pard...., what did you do to her, you really ticked her off". I just shrugged my shoulders and was glad to have my five bucks back in my pocket.

170

When we got to Pueblo, Colorado we were to perform for two weeks there, then two weeks in Phoenix, then another two weeks in Albuquerque, then back to California. The first week was great, but we were all looking forward to Monday our day off, which was also payday. Early Monday afternoon there was a knock on my hotel door by two of the band members. "Johnny, we think Lee Roy is cheating us, he's not paying us what he said he would". "I don't have a problem with mine, just go talk to him, he'll sort it out with you". "No, Johnny, you talk to him"!

When I go next door to talk to Lee Roy and tell him about the bands grievances, explaining to him that they felt like they weren't getting what had been promised them, "they believe you've shorted their pay". When I said that he took offense thinking I was personally accusing him of being a thief and a liar. I tell you, I should have listen to that Gypsy woman because I made the mistake of standing too long in one place.

As I was hitting the floor it was only Lee Roy's roommate the drummer who was there to help me. Immediately he jumped between me and Lee Roy stopping him from hurting me any further. As I picked myself up from the floor bleeding and angry, I called Lee Roy a few uncomplimentary names. Then I threaten him, by telling him, you better not be here when I get back because I will put a bullet in your eye. As I left the room with my mouth swelling, my nose bleeding, and my right eye turning black and blue, I was madder than a hornet.

However, once I was in my room, and after cleaning up my face, I had cooled down and decided it wasn't worth it. I spent the rest of the night with cold packs on my face.

It was already nine o'clock when we walked on the stage the next night. After the first set the owner asked to the whereabouts of his star performer. We said we hadn't seen him today, but we expected him to be here, "he must be under the weather", the drummer said. "What happened to you Johnny", the owner now noticing my swollen lip and black eye. "I had a little accident". "Alright you guys, all I can say, is Lee Roy better be here tomorrow night or you guys are fired"; As he walked off cursing. We couldn't find Lee Roy anywhere, though his car was still there, and his car keys had been left in the hotel room, we all got a little worried.

That next night at the club he didn't show. The owner was going to fire us on the spot, but relented when we begged him to let us finish out the week, so we could afford to get back home. After closing night, we loaded Lee Roy's car and headed back to Sacramento. The booking agent canceled the rest of the tour, though we tried to get him to let us finish the road tour, no deal he said, "not without Lee Roy, it's over".

Chapter 11

After returning from Pueblo, the atmosphere in my home had changed. It seems that Judy and the children were now attending church at the Landmark Missionary Baptist Church. Judy told me the story of how it happened. "It was Saturday before when two young elementary age girls came to our door. They wanted me to come down stairs and talk to their Sunday School Bus Captain. I ask the girls why didn't she come up herself. They told me if I went with them I would understand why. So out of curiosity I went to meet this mysterious bus captain. What I found was this amazingly beautiful twenty something woman in a wheel-chair. She had this irresistible smile which just melted my heart... she looked so sweet I just wanted to hug her

She introduces herself as Marna and the girls as "Rosie and Beth...she called them her little helpers and that every Saturday they would go about the neighborhoods inviting children to come to Sunday School on the bus. I ask her the schedule, she told me the bus comes at nine o'clock because it takes about an hour to collect everybody and get to the church by ten o'clock. Marna ask me if I thought I could come and I told her why not. For the last two weeks the kids and I've been going, and it's been great".

As Judy spoke I could see a glow on my wife's face like I have never seen. She went on, "guess who was there last Sunday singing and playing his guitar"? I said, "I can't imagine". "Joe Blasingame, can you believe it John, Joe Blasingame in church. He told everyone how he had given his heart to the Lord. As soon as church was over, I ran over to him and ask him if he remembered me? He said, "sure.... your Johnny Mays' wife". Joe ask me how you were doing, and I told him you were on the road, and that I was no longer dealing cards, just staying home and being a mom. He told me I should bring you to church".

I had never heard Judy go on like this, it just wasn't her style. "Yeah, I might go with you sometime". I should have never said that, because every time she and the kids would leave for church she would ask if I was coming. Though I didn't go, deep down I wanted to. A couple of weeks passed by, and she approached me again. "Johnny, I thought you would be interested, there's going to be this gospel band at church tonight and I thought "maybe we could go"? I told her "sure.... okay". I mean after all I really had to, because I'd been promising her for some time.

I will never forget that night. I was really surprised as to how many people were in the church and how many of them came up to me to say hello. Many of them recognized me from the old Forty Grand television program and they all mention what a beautiful wife I had.

When the band started playing I must admit I had heard better, but still... there was something powerful in their songs. I recognized that power from the old days when I went with my friend Royce to his mother's Pentecostal church. It was the same feeling as I had back then. While I reminisced, I tried to hide the tears that wanted to leak from my eyes. I touched Judy's arm, leaned over and whispered, "I'll be right back". Out the door I went, grabbing a smoke, I waited for Judy to come out, so we could go home. Driving back, she didn't say much, so I volunteered by saying "thanks for inviting me, I really enjoyed it". I didn't tell her why I had left, she didn't ask me, but somehow, I felt she knew.

A few days later I get a call from an old friend, Danny Hart. You remember Danny, we had gone to Nashville together, well, he had not been long back from there. "Hey bro, I got a gig for us if you want it"? I said yes, without asking, where, for who, for how long or for how much. "Alright I'll pick you up tomorrow, I need you to play rhythm guitar, and do some background vocals, we already have a lead singer. Bring some black trousers, black shoes, a white belt, any style of long sleeve shirt".

I didn't care what I had to bring, I just needed to go. When Danny arrived at the house he asks me to drive. We were about fifty miles down the road before my curiosity got the best of me. "Hey bro, where are we going". Danny said, "get ready dude, this will blow your mind. We are going to meet the rest of the band in Redding. There, we will join... hang onto your hat, the Merle Haggard Show, can you believe it"?

"How the heck did you land a gig like this".

Danny: "It was all Lloyd Hickey's doing, some agent from Hollywood called and ask him if he could put a band together for the Haggard Show. Apparently, there was a car accident and the cats who were playing the front show are in the hospital".

"Do you know who they were"?

Danny: "Lloyd told me, but I was so freaked after he offered me the job I can't remember who he said it was".

I never learned who it was, it was bad luck for them, but good luck for me.

Getting to Redding, California we joined the rest of the musicians and the country artist who had been brought in as the opening act, Johnny Carver. Johnny had recorded a cover of the Tony Orlando and Dawn monster hit, "Tie a Yellow Ribbon Round The "Old Oak Tree". His version of the song enjoyed duplicate success on country radio, simply titled "Yellow Ribbon" and was a top 10 hits on the Billboard Hot Country Singles chart in June 1973. Carver's version also reached Number One on the RPM Country Tracks chart in Canada. We had us a legitimate country star. We rehearsed "Yellow, and two or three other tunes for a couple of hours. Carver seemed impressed with the band and the vocal harmonies I offered.[lxi]

Later that night we got to meet the boss. No, I'm not talking about Merle, but the television celebrity "Bob Ubanks", the star of the very popular show "The Newlywed Game". In fact, his show had been one of mine and Bunny's favorites when we were newlyweds, "God rest her Soul". Bob was the tour director and the Master of Ceremonies of the Merle Haggard Show and tour promoter.

Bob asks. "Johnny, "I like the tone of your voice, did you ever do any announcing"? "Sure" I said, joking "when I was a kid I use to pretend I was a disc jockey. "Well that's good enough for me, I got a little job for you", and he handed me a paper. "Look this over and read it to me". I paused to look it over, as he asks me to do, then in my best announcer's voice I said enthusiastically;

"LADIES AND GENTLEMEN, THE STAR OF ABC'S NEWLYWED GAME, BOB UBANKS"

"That will do great Johnny. I want the band to vamp a little something, you read the script, then I will come out and start the show...I appreciate it"!

Danny and the guys gave me high fives as we broke for the day to find something to eat, drink and smoke. Our opening night was a huge success. I introduced Bob as we rehearsed, he welcomed the audience, made a few announcements, then introduced Johnny Carver. When Carver closed our set, Bob was back out to bring on Merle Haggard and his band "The Strangers", the crowd was on their feet.

A little side story...while Merle was performing, I found the tours audio mixer. The sound man gave me a headset and punched everything out but Hag's voice. I knew as I sat there listening to his voice, I was hearing a lyrical genius and a legendary performer, it was a once in a lifetime up close and personal moment with pure artistry.

Leaving Redding I drove all night arriving in Salem, Oregon about 6am. Aware that we have two shows today, a matinee around 2pm and the evening show about 8pm which would be the tour's final performance of the season. The concert would take place on a stage erected on the racetrack in front of the grandstand at the Oregon State Fairgrounds.

Danny and I found a motel room, I jumped into the shower, I finished only to find Danny already crashed across one of the beds sleeping like a baby. After getting dressed I sat down on the edge of the bed, lit a joint, hoping the weed would help me unwind. That's when I noticed the Bible on the night stand.

At that very moment, I had a sudden flashback of the city park in St. Louis and the Book of Job. Funny though, this Bible was already opened to the first chapter of the book of "Ecclesiastes" chapter one, as if someone wanted

177

me to find it. I thought to myself, "how strange is that",
as I picked it up and began to read, the first eleven verses.

*"The words of the Preacher, the son of David, king in
Jerusalem. Vanity of vanities, saith the Preacher, vanity
of vanities; all is vanity. What profit hath a man of all his
labor which he taketh under the sun? One generation
passes away, and another generation cometh: but the
earth abides forever. The sun also arises, and the sun
goes down, and hastens to his place where he arose. The
wind goeth toward the south, and turns about unto the
north; it whirls about continually, and the wind
returns according to his circuits. All the rivers run into
the sea; yet the sea is not full; unto the place from whence
the rivers come, thither they return. All things are full
of labor; man cannot utter it: the eye is not satisfied with
seeing, nor the ear filled with hearing. The thing that
hath been, it is that which shall be; and that which is
done is that which shall be done: and there is no new
thing under the sun. Is there anything whereof it may be
said, See, this is new? it hath been already of old time,
which was before us. There is no remembrance of former
things; neither shall there be any remembrance of things
that are to come with those that shall come after".*

"That's heavy", I heard me saying out loud, as I looked up
to see if Danny heard me.

Then taking another toke off the joint, I read it aloud again,
*"All the rivers run into the sea; yet the sea is not
full"*; then I noticed this portion of verse eight, *"the eye is
not satisfied with seeing, nor the ear filled with hearing".*

Now listen to me carefully…at that time in my life I
wouldn't have described myself as a spiritual man, but

178

I had no trouble understanding these words, and had I thought about it I would have said, "Amen". The truth was that ever since my "Leaving Woods Creek", in my quest for adventure, my search for happiness, and my craving for acceptance, I now found myself sitting on this bed in the hotel with the Bible in one hand and a joint of marijuana in the other hand, and all that was left in me was a sickening emptiness. I had come to a place in my life where there was nothing left in me.

After the matinee, everyone on the show had found the momentum. We all knew we would be on our "A" game for the evening performance and it was great. Everything about it was great, the sound was great, the music was great, all the performers were having a great night. Carver and Haggard both killed it. I noticed the audience when we were on stage that they too had bought into the show with an electrifying enthusiasm. As we took our bows and exited stage right, standing in the shadows off stage was Haggard, as I walked by him, he looked at me and said, "good show, you did good". That was music to my ears!

As I watched, "The Working Man's Poet" do his magic, I was saddened as I watched his last encore and knew that it's all over. Soon the roadies would swoop in and start packing. The instruments and lights were put carefully into their cases, mike cables were being gathered and put away.

I watched security people herding the few lingering folks from the grandstand. I stood alone pining, that my one and only shot with the greatest show I had ever performed in was over, the curtain had fallen, the spotlights were turned off. I stood alone a solitary figure. I noticed Danny huddled with Ubanks and Merle. Danny looked my way, then motioned me over, then Bob said, "good show", as Merle smiled. Danny had arranged for us to get a picture with them and called a nearby roadie over to snap it with one of those Kodak disposable cameras Danny had made sure to bring. One lone picture, that's all that will remain of that evening as I stood on a racetrack in Salem, the City of Peace. Like the scripture I read earlier at the motel.

"All things are full of labor; man cannot utter it: the eye is not satisfied with seeing, nor the ear filled with hearing. The thing that hath been, it is that which shall be; and that which is done is that which shall be done: and there is no new thing under the sun". Ecclesiastes 1:8-9

Getting back to Sacramento I felt I just couldn't go back to Judy's apartment right away. I wasn't ready to deal with everything, besides Danny had already booked us into another honky tonk gig promoting Johnny Mays as one of the stars of the Merle Haggard Show, which I told him it wasn't true. He told me it helped to close the deal with the club owner and it would be a good promotion. I didn't say any more about it.

I decided to rent a little house, more like a shanty, out in the country, which was a pickup truck bed camper that the owner had built some rooms around. The camper portion had the kitchen, tiny toilet and shower. Its location was the best part about it, it was inobtrusive and peaceful, surrounded by California Live Oak trees and the smells of fresh cut hay from fields across the road. No... the shanty wasn't pretty... though it was cheap, the quiet is really what I needed. It was October and the weather were cooling and welcomed after the long hot summer.

180

One morning I came into the camper and sat at the table. Sipping on my coffee, I opened my stash box to roll a joint so to get my morning started. I wasn't alone. Laying on the floor under an old blanket out in the room was a friend. As I sat drinking my coffee and inhaling the smoke off the marijuana joint, I heard "The Voice" whisper in my ear, "so this is what you want"?

I knew where I had heard this voice before, it was the same voice which spoke to me as a child. Instantly my entire life like a movie reel, began to play in pictures on the screen of my mind. As the pictures flashed by year after year, I interrupted, "no"! Answering "The Voice's question, "this is not what I wanted, this is not what I had in mind when I was Leaving Woods Creek. "The Voice" … "so why do you keep doing it then, why don't you stop"?

I sprung from my chair, woke my sleeping friend, "get up you got to get me home". Within the hour I was standing at the front door of Judy's apartment.

Knocking on the door, Judy was soon opening the door. "Can I come home"? I asked hopefully. Judy just shook her head as she stepped aside to let me in. "What are you talking about John, this is your home". At the same time, she is pointing to the children, "and this is your family".

We talked a lot that night, I told her about the Haggard Tour and the Bible in the hotel room.

When I left the shanty that morning I had grabbed what things I had there, because I knew I wasn't ever going back, though I didn't mention that to the driver who brought me home. I pulled the Bible out of my bag and showed it to Judy. I told her it was like the one in the hotel which I had read. It was what they called a Gideon Bible which meant absolutely nothing to me at the time.

I would learn later more about the Gideon's and their mission to place Bibles just like the one I had in hotels and motels. In fact, as I thought about it I remembered the Gideon's giving me a small Bible at Fort Wayne right after I took my military oath. We were getting on the bus to go to the airport and there was a guy standing at the bus door giving Bibles to us as we stepped into the bus.

Well, Judy started telling me how things were going at her church and about her pastor James Wilkens. She wanted me to meet him sometime. I can tell you, right about then, the thought of talking to a preacher didn't excite me too much. Then Judy said, "Johnny you should pray". I said, "yeah...you're probably right". The truth was I didn't have a clue how to pray. I remember as a little boy my grandmother Phoebe would pray a prayer with me at bedtime.

"Now I lay me down to sleep.

I pray the Lord my soul to keep.

If I should die before I wake,

I pray to the Lord my soul to take".

There was also a prayer I would pray in my times of desperation over the years, "Lord get me out of this and I will never do it again".

Now that I think about it, He often answered that prayer, but I would inevitably do it again. I didn't pray that prayer much because I knew I would be lying to God.

I thanked Judy for the evening we had spent together, and we went to bed. Soon we were asleep. I often over the years would awake in the night, then I would scoot over close to her. Her back would be toward me and I would place my ear up against her back and just listen to her breathing. I could feel her heart beating. I could hear her life. I would think about how much I loved her, though she would never believe it anymore and couldn't trust me when I would tell her I loved her, because truthfully, I didn't know how to show her love, in fact I didn't know how to show love at all.

I slept well that night and rose to realize it was in late morning, almost noon. She would make me coffee. I told her, "I've been thinking Jude about some of the things you said about church. I thought I might take a ride on my bicycle, get a little fresh air and go visit a person whom I met in the Forty Grand that was always talking about the Bible. Maybe I'll take my Bible and go talk to her." "You are going to talk to a… her…", Judy asks suspiciously. "John, listen to yourself, you met a girl in the Forty Grand. John, think about what you are saying, you want to talk to a girl, you met in a bar, about the Bible".

"No, no it's all cool Jude", I insisted…I guess her father is a preacher or something, and she use to come around the Forty Grand, talking about Jesus, the Bible and stuff, she lives right over by the Forty, I know her husband". I didn't tell Judy it wasn't until this chick was drunk, that she would start crying and talking about Jesus.

Honestly it happens in bars more than one might think, drunks talking about religion as if they know what they are talking about. In fact, many of the musicians I knew told me they use to play in church or sing in the choir.

As I left the apartment it was a beautiful autumn day, the temperature was moderate, a gentle breeze caused my long hair to lift off my shoulders as I rode my bike. At the woman's house, no one responded when I knocked. I hoped they still lived here, I was seriously wanting to talk to her about the Bible. I had been sure to bring along my "stolen Gideon Bible" as I jokingly referred to it.

After several minutes of waiting for someone to come to the door, I sat down on an old sofa they had on the front porch. I figured I would wait a while longer in case some-one just might show up. Sitting there I leaned with my head back against the window just above the sofa. I closed my eyes and reflected on Judy's recent remark, "you should pray John". I thought what would I pray if I did. The only thing I could think of in that moment, the only thing that crossed my mind, was the name of Jesus. So, I began to pray Jesus. Over and over, I chanted the name Jesus. That's all, nothing else, only Jesus, Jesus, Jesus, Jesus, Jesus. For several minutes with my eyes closed tightly I would reiterate the Name of The Son of God.

That's when the vision came, followed by "The Voice". The vision which appeared on the screen of my mind came in vivid colors was a, "Tree". It was very large, very tall and compelling. As I looked at it, I had the sensation "The Tree" was pulling me into its branches and foliage. After the vision was "The Voice" with its gentle whisper, "do what I tell you to do", then again, "do what I tell you to do". Unnerved by the vision of "The Tree" and "The Voice" I open my eyes and I jumped off the porch, grabbed my bike and thought to myself, "I got to get out of here, I've got to get back to Judy, she is the one real thing in my life and the only person I could trust". Speeding away from the house "The Voice" spoke again, "do what I tell you to do, do what I tell you to do"! I finally capitulated, "okay, okay, I will, tell me what you want". What followed my inquiry was a long period of silence? For several blocks I rode with nothing but silence to accompany me, then abruptly, the silence was broken by the lyrics and music of a song I had heard while on my visit to Nashville years ago. It was an old southern gospel tune. Under my breath I began to sing it as I continued my ride toward my Judy.

"Troublesome times are here

Filling men's hearts with fear

Freedom we all hold dear now is at stake

Humbling your hearts to God,

saves from the chastening rod

Seek the way pilgrims trod, Christians awake

Jesus is coming soon, morning or night or noon

Many will meet their doom, trumpets will sound

All the dead shall rise, righteous meet in the skies

Going where no one dies, heavenward bound"

While I sung a powerful feeling of euphoria swept over my body and mind. The more I repeated the chorus, the stronger the feelings came. I was now singing boldly as if I were being intoxicated by its message;

"Jesus is coming soon, morning or night or noon

Many will meet their doom, trumpets will sound

All the dead shall rise, righteous meet in the skies

Going where no one dies, heavenward bound"[lxii]

Again, and again, I repeated that chorus welcoming the joy and peace that came with it, until "The Voice", spoke yet again, "stop here". As I pulled to the sidewalk to stop, there in the yard I saw this grandmotherly aged woman, her silver hair in a bun, donning an apron over her blue dress. She was busy pruning her rose bushes and as she paused her work, she looked over to me. I saw in her face that she was annoyed at my uninvited presence. There I sat on my bicycle looking like a prisoner of war caused by a lifestyle of alcohol, drugs and country music, so there was no doubt my being there bothered her. When I spoke to her, the first words that came from my mouth were the words I had been singing," Jesus is Coming Soon". It was obvious she wanted to ignore me. "Did you hear what I said"? I spoke with insistence so that she should pay attention to me, "Jesus is Coming Soon". With that she turned with pruning shears pointing straight at me as she responded, "everyone knows that", and with that she waddled off toward her house.

As I watched her leave I was certain she had to be wrong, "not everybody knows that"! I for one sure didn't know. I continued both my riding and my singing with even more determination than ever to do what "The Voice ask me to do, "do what I tell you to do". As I rode and sang I hadn't realized I had lost my direction to my home.

"Stop here"! Now, for the second time "The Voice "spoke. When I came to a stop, I noticed a young boy probably the age of ten or so, walking along the sidewalk. As he approached me he had a warm broad smile upon his angelic face, his deep blue eyes seemed to consider my soul. "I like your bike", his voice was softened with kindness. I said, "Jesus is Coming Soon". He said nothing immediately, just continued to admire my bike, then he looked up at me, "I know", I go to Sunday School". Then he walked away. As I watched him disappear around the corner at the end of the block, "I thought... who was that".

In the next moments, I became overwhelmed with anxiety, "Oh my God" I thought, "Jesus is Coming Soon"! In my panic I felt the urgent need to warn everybody, "Jesus is Coming". I would herald my new revelation, "Jesus is Coming", down the street, block after block. Can you imagine the scene? Picture this long-haired hippy, racing down your street, screaming at the top of his lungs "Jesus is Coming"? I was sure many of the people who saw me thought I was a mad man, who thought he was Paul Revere. Yet there were plenty of others who waved back to me with smiles, even laughter, seeming to affirm my news. I don't know how long this went on, but by now I had ridden to the outskirts of the neighborhood and found myself on a lone one lane levy road traveling in the exact opposite direction of Judy.

A new sense of calm had come over me followed too by embarrassment. I didn't want to go back the way I had come. What I noticed next was a trail leading down and away from the levy. Could it be a short cut home? Let me try!

As I rode down the trail I soon found it necessary to dismount from my bike, for the trails surface was rutted by erosion. Walking and leaning on my bike I came upon a Mexican couple with a small child. The man was fishing in the stream that flowed alongside the levy. I could sense his alarm by the sudden appearance of this gringo at his fishing hole. Without stopping I pushed my bike on down the trail. As I passed them I spoke, "Jesus will make us fishers of men". "Where in the world did that come from", surprising myself by my remark.

Soon I was completely out of sight of the fisherman, when suddenly it was as if some very strong hands gripped me by the shoulders. I felt as though I was being forced to the ground. Though I could see no one, I knew something powerful had come upon me. When my body hit the ground, my inward being exploded forth in extremely painful emotions. My eyes turned into opened faucets pouring streams of agonizing tears. My guts wrenched with heartache. Obviously deep-seated sorrows that had been locked within me for years, were now manifesting uncontrollably. I began to beg, "stop, stop, please stop, you're killing me." I grab-bed my head and squeezed both sides trying not to lose my mind, I repeated "stop, please, stop.

Then as quickly as it came, everything went quiet. The tears ceased leaving my face wet from weeping. I picked myself up while slowly pushing my bike, I had to get out of there. As I continued, the trail disappeared into a field of tall grass, which made it impossible to push the bike. I carried it until my way was blocked by a wall of cockleburs. With my right hand holding my bicycle, I began wielding my left arm like a machete.

188

I made a path through the wall of brush and cockleburs. There, finally, I had broken through. Stepping past the wall, I found myself standing in a small green meadow hedged by a forest and caressed by the dark murky stream. Then to my astonishment, there in the middle of the field about twenty yards from the water's edge, was "The Tree" from the vision. As hard as I found it to believe, there it stood, like a giant lone sentry, guarding over the field and the stream. It was just exactly as I envisioned back on the porch. While I stared stupefied by what was before me, "The Voice" spoke, "build an altar". "What's an altar"?

Then from my mind came the instructions. I knew exactly what to do. I turned back through the wall, as my eyes fell on the levy. The levy was constructed of granite rocks both large and small, reinforcing the mounds of earth that composed it. I knew in my heart that "The Altar" had to be one of those rocks and the rock altar had to be placed exactly at the foot of "The Tree".

Quickly I tried to lift several rocks, but they were too heavy. I finally found one that I had strength enough to flop over. By flopping it from side to side I moved my rock along the path, through the hole in the cocklebur wall, making progress along the edge of the stream toward its place at the foot of "The Tree". Suddenly "The Rock "seemingly leaped from my hands as it rolled into the dark murky water. "Oh no, not after all this work". I turned to go find another rock, when "THE VOICE" spoke again…

"I HAVE GIVEN YOU YOUR ROCK"!

"OH MY GOD"!

Right at that very moment and for the very first time in my life I had the courage to believe and confess the identity of "The Voice" that had been with me since I was a boy.

"MY LORD" I cried, "it's in the water and I don't know how deep it is". I looked down at the water about two feet lower than its muddy banks, I notice laying in the brush a long-broken branch. I picked it up and used it to measure the water's depth. It looked to be about four feet deep. So off came my shoes, my socks, my shirt, as I rolled up my trouser legs and slipped off the bank of the murky stream into the water. I groped around unable to see the bottom. When I found THE ROCK, it was light as a feather as I lifted it from the muddy bottom. However, as soon as it broke the water's surface it's buoyancy would leave, and it became too heavy to lift. I decided to move THE ROCK next to the bank. I employed every strategy of leverage I could think of, but with no success. As I stood in the waist deep water, both physically and mentally bankrupt, exhausted beyond description! I cried out, "MY LORD", I can't do this by myself". This would be my first spiritual lesson. "That only with God are all things, including miracles possible". In that same moment the story of Samson came to me. It was probably one of the stories I heard from the Salvation Army ladies on Beecher Street back in the projects in Adrian when I was about five years old. It came to my mind. I prayed, "MY LORD", give me the strength of Samson." The last thing I remember while standing in the stream was my hands touching the stone beneath the dark murky water. The next thing I realized "THE ROCK" was at its perfect place at the foot of "THE TREE", and I was kneeling beside it. With my Gideon Bible in my hand, my clothes soaked, I was physically, mentally and emotionally…completely diminished in every

190

way. I was at the end of me. I took a deep breath, wiped my hands on my wet trousers, took a long look at what God had done. Opened the Gideon Bible. It opened randomly to the pages of the ninth chapter of Mark and I read;

"One of the men in the crowd spoke up and said, "Teacher, I brought my son, so you could heal him. He is possessed by an evil spirit that won't let him talk. And whenever this spirit seizes him, it throws him violently to the ground. Then he foams at the mouth and grinds his teeth and becomes rigid. I asked your disciples to cast out the evil spirit, but they couldn't do it." Jesus said to them, "You, faithless people! How long must I be with you? How long must I put up with you? Bring the boy to me." So, they brought the boy. But when the evil spirit saw Jesus, it threw the child into a violent convulsion, and he fell to the ground, writhing and foaming at the mouth. "How long has this been happening?" Jesus asked the boy's father. He replied, "Since he was a little boy. The spirit often throws him into the fire or into water, trying to kill him. Have mercy on us and help us, if you can." What do you mean, 'If I can'?" Jesus asked. "Anything is possible if a person believes." The father instantly cried out, "I do believe, but help me overcome my unbelief!" When Jesus saw that the crowd of onlookers was growing, he rebuked the evil spirit. "Listen, you spirit that makes this boy unable to hear and speak," he said. "I command you to come out of this child and never enter him again!" Then the spirit screamed and threw the boy into another violent convulsion and left him. The boy appeared to be dead. A murmur ran through the crowd as people said, "He's dead." But Jesus took him by the hand and helped him to his feet, and he stood up. (verses 17-27)

When I finished reading I cried out to The Lord, I said, "MY LORD", that's me"! Immediately, as in the story, I fell across "THE ROCK". The power of God unleashed itself on the demonic spirits that imprisoned me. The Mighty God was delivering me out of a horrible pit of sin and shame. The Blood of Jesus was washing me, cleansing me, as He was saving me. I raised myself up from the "Rock Altar", as God breathed into me a new life, the old life was gone, my sins were forgiven, the weight of guilt and remorse left me. I was being translated out of darkness into "THE LIGHT". The Holy Spirit filled me with His Presence, I was born again.

Then the Power of God stood me to my feet, and directed my eyes to the granite rocks holding the levy. "My son, each of those rocks are a person like yourself for which MY SON JESUS died. As I separated you and your rock, so shall we bring others out of their sins for their salvation". As I stood there listening to God speak I knew He had anointed me and called me to my mission. Jesus had reclaimed my life on a fall day in October of 1973. There was no turning back.

I lingered there for some time and I knew it would be dark soon. As I was leaving this Holy Place, I knew I had been with God Almighty. I started back the way I had come, this time I was the only fisherman there, "the fisher of men". When I reached the lanc at the top of the levy I noticed a tow truck coming towards me, it stopped, and the driver spoke to me through the window, "what are you doing way out here Johnny"? I recognized him from the clubs, "I am headed home" I told him. "Toss your bike on the back, jump in and I'll take you home", within minutes I was standing knocking on my door.

Judy came to the door, seeing me standing there. She told me later, "In that moment, when I saw you, I knew our lives would never be the same."

I tried sometime later to go back to the levy to find "that tree and that rock, I never found it! Remember, it's like "Leaving Woods Creek", there's no going back, because it's never the same."

Chapter 12

Four the next month I could not put the Bible down. I consumed, breathed and rested with God's Word. Not since I was a child back at Pa's old house on "Woods Creek", have I had such a peace of mind and a renewed sense of wellness. It seemed to me that Judy and I were enjoying each other more and the fellowship we found among the church folks filled our hearts with joy. My life was quieted by the love of God. From the first day, I encountered the living God beneath "The Tree" at the "Rock Altar", I couldn't stop weeping or praising the Name of Jesus. My tears of joy came with every thought, every passage of scripture, in every church service, or each time I would look at my children, I would weep with thanksgiving. I was a broken man and of contrite spirit, filled with gratitude because of God's goodness. I had an overwhelming sense of indebtedness. I wanted to do something for Jesus.

One morning while shaving, The Lord spoke to me, "Son, you have some unfinished business". "What do you mean Lord". "I want you to come clean with your wife. I want you to tell her of your betrayal and how you have broken your marriage vows". I couldn't believe what The Lord was asking of me. Surely, He wouldn't do this. I tested the Spirit, for I knew if I told Judy of all the ways I had cheated on her, she wouldn't be able to forgive me. "Lord, can this really be You"? Knowing my heart, God answered, "She deserves to know the truth, and deserves the right to make her own decision of staying on with you or leaving".

For many days after that I dreaded the thought of doing this, but the time came. I began my confessions but before I could finish and without saying a word, she left the room. The next morning, I awoke on the couch and from the kitchen I could hear the fan above the stove humming, the smells of bacon frying in the pan and coffee brewing. Judy called me to breakfast, then sat down at the table with me. I waited nervously. "John, I prayed for us last night. I prayed for our family. I ask God to help me. The Lord has told me He forgave you and He ask me to forgive you and I do. I knew it was her faith and her obedience to the Heavenly Father that was working here. Judy has always been the best of us. Though we tried to never discuss that day, it would on occasion find its way to the surface. Finding trust in me would never be easy for her and being suspicious of my motives still haunts our relation-ship to this very day and who could blame her.

Less than a week later, I would face the next challenge to my commitment. When the phone rang Judy answered, "John, it's Jimmy Snyder, he wants to talk to you". "Jimmy Snyder calling me"?

I first met Jimmy Snyder while I was still in the Air Force. Jimmy and his band were performing at the Maverick Club the night I had the car accident with the drunken Airman's wife. Over the years Jimmy and I had become well acquainted. I couldn't say we were like the best of friends, but I did have a strong professional admiration for his talent, he was the real deal. I would say he was one of the best singers I had ever heard and a fantastic musician. In 1970 Snyder had his biggest hit, "The Chicago Story", a song about a soldier's wife seeing him off to war, with a twist ending that was controversial at the time of the single's release. In February of that same year Snyder was nominated the "Most Promising Artist of the Year" by

Record News, Cashbox, and Billboard Magazine. In 1980, just seven years after he called me that morning, Jimmy and his band the Palomino Riders won their first Academy of Country Music award for "Best Non-Touring Country Band in the nation. Any musician working for Jimmy would have a secure gig. As I took the phone, I thought I saw concern in Judy's eyes. [lxiii]

"Hello"?

Snyder: "This you Johnny Mays"?

"It's me Jimmy, how are you",

Snyder: "It's been a long-time, what are you doing, are you playing anywhere right now"?

"No, I'm not playing right now, I'm just hanging out at home.

Snyder: "Hey man listen, I got a job or you. I need a bass player like yesterday, and Johnny you'll make more money than you have ever made playing music. You know I've always liked you're playing and I've watched you grow up in this business. Johnny, we've known each other a long time, since your Air Force days isn't that right".

"That's right, it's been a long time and a lot of water under the bridge. But to answer your question Jimmy...well it all sounds great.... and on any other day, I would have jumped at the opportunity to work with you. But my whole life has changed, I'm a Christian now and I'm going to church with my wife".

Snyder: "So, what do you mean, you got religion or something, that's no big deal, it won't be a problem with me...so what do you say, come on, let's do this"?

"I'm sorry...but I'll have to say no to you. I hope you can understand…listen, three or four months ago I would have gone wherever you wanted me to go. But I just can't do it right now my friend".

Snyder: "You sure I can't talk you into it.

"It's like I said Jimmy, right now I just can't, I hope you find the player you need, and I wish you all the best, but I'm sorry my answer is still no".

Snyder: "Alright then, well thanks anyway, it's nice talking to you Johnny Mays, maybe will see each other down the road, good bye".

(I would see Jimmy again years later, at a benefit for Lloyd Hickey after Lloyd's death.)

As I hung up the phone, I just stood there, staring at it on the wall, "can you believe this" ….as I turned I see Judy smiling at me and pouring me a fresh coffee. "He offered me a job, after all these years, he wanted me in his band."

"I heard what you told him, but listen, God has something better for you and for all of us, The Lord has a plan for our lives." I nodded in agreement and remembered the calling The Lord gave me while I stood at "The Tree". Judy would tell me many years later that when she heard me turning down the opportunity to play music with Jimmy Snyder that morning, she knew for sure that I had truly changed, and that God was doing a great work in my life.

I would continue with my studies in the Bible especially in the Gospel of John and the Book of Acts. I was particularly absorbed in the passages where Jesus is telling his disciples that after He was gone away He would be sending the Holy

Spirit to be a friend, teacher and guide to them and that they would receive a GIFT from the Father. After Christ died and rose from the dead He instructed his disciples to remain in Jerusalem for the promise He had given them.

"Once when he was eating with them, he commanded them, "Do not leave Jerusalem until the Father sends you the gift he promised, as I told you before. John baptized with water, but in just a few days you will be baptized with the Holy Spirit." So, when the apostles were with Jesus, they kept asking him, "Lord, has the time come for you to free Israel and restore our kingdom?" He replied, "The Father alone has the authority to set those dates and times, and they are not for you to know. But you will receive power when the Holy Spirit comes upon you. And you will be my witnesses, telling people about me everywhere-in Jerusalem, throughout Judea, in Samaria, and to the ends of the earth." After saying this, he was taken up into a cloud while they were watching, and they could no longer see him. As they strained to see him rising into heaven, two white-robed men suddenly stood among them. "Men of Galilee," they said, "why are you standing here staring into heaven? Jesus has been taken from you into heaven, but someday he will return from heaven in the same way you saw him go!" Acts 1:4-11

In the following verses, I read also of the experiences the disciples had regarding this promise.

"On the day of Pentecost all the believers were meeting together in one place. Suddenly, there was a sound from heaven like the roaring of a mighty windstorm, and it filled the house where they were sitting. Then, what looked like flames or tongues of fire appeared and settled on each of them. And everyone present was filled with the Holy Spirit and began speaking in other languages, as the Holy Spirit gave them this ability. At that time there were devout Jews from every nation living in Jerusalem. When they heard the loud noise, everyone came running, and they were bewildered to hear their own languages being spoken by the believers". Acts 2:1-6 NLT

This Word of God excited me so much that I began to pray asking God if I could receive such a gift as the disciples had received. I told The Lord if there was something more that He had for me to please help me to have it. I wanted all that He had for my life more than anything in the world. I knew that if I was ever going to be able to do what God had called me to do back at "The Tree", I was going to need His help and His power.

After that prayer, within days Joe Blasingame drop by our apartment. "Johnny, I'm headed to a prayer meeting at a friend's house and I thought about you and Judy and thought maybe you would want to go". I looked at Judy, and she excused herself. Joe and I left without her. When we got to the house, the people were already praying quietly all over the house, the entire place was filled with the Presence of God.

I found a spot in one corner of the house and knelt on a shag carpet woven with about one-inch long strands. While kneeling I heard God say, "get lower", I thought to myself, "get lower, what does God mean".

Trying to comply I got onto my hands and knees, when God said, "get lower", and again I thought, "what is He talking about"! So, this time, I sprawled myself flat on the floor face down.

I began to pray, when again God said, "Get Lower"! "What do you want Lord, I don't see how I can get any lower". That's when I decide to part the shag carpet fibers the way a man parts his hair and then I stuck my face into the part and I said, "Lord, I don't know how to get lower"! Then the voice of God spoke, "Good! "Now praise Me"!

With that I began to quietly praise and worship The Almighty God, and just like on the day of Pentecost, God manifested The Power of The Holy Spirit and from out of my belly came worship like an artesian fountain erupting within me. Suddenly I was on my feet shouting and worshipping God in an unknown language. The folks in the house soon joined me in this surge of worship, and for hours we praised the Lord. When Joe and I got back to Judy, she asks "have you been drinking"? "Oh Lord no", and tried to explain to her but I was too excited and finally Joe had to intervene and explain what had just happened. I told her, "Judy, I feel the way I felt the night when Sister Blasingame was standing over me and said, "son your life will never be the same", do you remember that Jude? You remember that night a few weeks ago, we were with Joe and his mother. God delivered me from smoking that night".

Judy and I decided to move to south Sacramento to be closer to the new Pentecostal church we had started attending. The pastors Cub and Marva Stone, were two very beautiful people, they literally took us under their wing, these two baby Christians and began to disciple us. They made room for us to grow.

We learned so much during the times that we were with them. I helped Marva with the music and worship. Judy taught a group of children in the Sunday school. Pastor Cub even encouraged me to share my testimony about "The Tree" and "The Rock". He would also introduce me to a group of believers from a ministry called "Prison Ministries".

The leaders of this ministry were both ex-cons, whom had found Christ while serving time in prison. God had led them to return to those same prisons and preach the gospel. When I met them, they were just beginning a new phase of their ministry as a home missions work of the Assembly of God organization. Their vision was to open a halfway house for Christian ex-cons coming out of the joint. They saw it as a buffer between their former prison life and their new life outside of prison. The half-way house would be a home for them, in a safe and spiritual environment, helping them return to society and avoiding the pitfalls of the mean streets. The leaders had purchased a building which was conveniently located near downtown Sacramento. It was built originally as a funeral home, filling up nearly a half of a city street block, very spacious with many rooms and offices, with a nice chapel auditorium, along with kitchen facilities and toilets with showers. There was also a private two-bedroom apartment upstairs. I began attending all their midweek services and going to the prisons with them on most weekends to sing and play my guitar and share my testimony.

Meanwhile I had been thinking about and talking with Judy about Bible college. I learned that Judy's first church the Landmark Missionary Baptist Church had started a Bible College and were accepting enrollment.

The Bible school had also been accredited by the Veterans Administration as a qualified school for veterans who wanted an education there. I jumped at the opportunity. I of course knew Pastor Wilkins and so there was no problem for me getting in.

I will never forget my first day at the school, in the admin office, while getting all the paperwork for the GI Bill funding sorted out so I could pay my tuition, I could have never imagined who I would meet there. Bob Irons, the sales manager that had employed me as a salesman many years before. He was a Christian now and a member of the church. After enrolling in school, I thought it was wise for Judy and me to attend the Baptist Church too, so we did.

To help with the finances I decided to take a job driving for the Yellow Cab company at night. Which brings me to this story and my experience with, The Blanket Man.

My shift was over, so I returned to the yard at the taxi company to leave my taxi and go home. After getting to my car I had to first scrape a hole in the frost on the windshield of my old Chevy Impala, and then hurried behind the wheel. The engine churned slowly in the frigid night air; then finally, ignition. Man, I couldn't wait to get home as I wiped the fog from my breath off the inside of the windshield. Slowly I drove down the street, straining to see out of the scrape hole in the frosted pane. It was like navigating through a knothole. I crept toward the motorway. Out of the corner of my eye, I noticed a silhouetted figure. "What was that"? "Where did that come from"? Then the voice of God spoke to my heart, "Go back." I asked, "What did you say"? "Go back and get him". "Come on, Lord, I don't want to go back". Then silence from God.

"Oh man, I pouted, why does He do this to me"? I came to a stop and put the Chevy in reverse. "Whoa...it is easier to drive in reverse because there was no frost on the mirrors. "Careful now, as I looked for the shadow on the roadside," I was talking to myself. Slowing to a stop, I rolled the window down about three inches on the passenger's side. In the cold dark, I could see frosted vapors of a person's breath coming from under the blanket that shrouded the blackened eyes peering through my window. Shivering from the cold, I stammered, "Where are you going"? "The Aquarian Effort," came the response from out of the shadow. I remembered, the Aquarian Effort is a drug rehabilitation home, or something like that. "Okay, get in"! The door opened, and as I pulled away, his door closed. I asked, "Where is this place?" "I don't know," the shrouded shadow responded. "Oh man," I thought, "what am I going to do with this person"? From His silence, God spoke again, "Take him home with you." "Home"! …. I exclaimed silently, not wanting to believe what I heard. "Judy will kill me"! …. Of course, my wife would never react like that, but after all, I was looking for any excuse to justify myself for not doing what God had told me to do.

As we drove up to our condominium, I turned to the Blanket Man and said, "You're going to stay at my house tonight. Tomorrow we'll find the place you're looking for." As I walked into the apartment, it was filled with the warm smells of home. Behind me was the Blanket Man standing silently, looking about. My eyes look up the stairs; upstairs is everything I cared the most about in the whole world. Up those stairs are the treasures of my life tucked away in their beds, sound asleep. The hood light from the stove was shining out from the kitchen. Judy always left a light burning. In the light, I could see the man, as the blanket that had him shrouded came down from around his face. He was a young man, in his early twenties, obviously tired, with a bewildered look, and his clothes and blanket are caked with mud. "Hey man, whatever you do, don't sit on the furniture. Put your blanket on the floor. I will get you a pillow." After I got him bedded down, I went upstairs. Looking at me through sleepy eyes, Judy murmured, "Who is with you". I whispered, "We will talk in the morning, go back to sleep". Laying down and feeling the warmth of the bed wrap around me, I began thanking God that I was home. I was painfully sleepy, but I kept imagining the Blanket Man standing over me with a knife.

I tried to sleep with one eye open, just in case. When I awoke, I flew out of my bed and landed at the bottom of the stairs, "You got to be kidding me". Blanket Man was sitting on the couch, staring into space. "Hey, I told you, don't sit on the furniture". I sighed, "Oh well, what is done is done".

I made some coffee for the two of us, and soon Judy was down with the children, getting them ready for school. My family watched the young man with curious faces as he ate the cereal and toast we made for him. I guess they didn't ask any questions since this was just one more, like the many times before, that their Dad would have somebody sitting at their breakfast table, another lost soul he had found along the way. After the children left for school, I took the man upstairs to the shower.

While he showered, I called Pastor Cub. I told him the whole story, and in about an hour, he was at our place with clean clothes in hand. The pastor had boys about the same size as my Blanket Man. He looked good all cleaned up.

We tried to carry on a conversation with him and we even tried to pray for him, but the man could not communicate or even remember his own name. Suspicious as we were about him, we concluded he was harmless, but it was obvious that he suffered from amnesia, without a doubt from the use of drugs. He had no attention span at all but would simply drift off and be lost in a cloud.

Some days after, I called the leaders of Prison Ministries and told them my story of the man in the blanket and asked if they could help with a place for him to live. The ministry agreed to put him in the program, and I agreed to come and get him for church and prayer meetings. His condition did not change, and after several weeks, I was wondering what to do with him. Then it happened. On this day as I closed the prayer meeting in my home, we all stood in a circle, our hands joined, and our heads bowed to pray.

Without warning all hell broke loose! Our prayers were interrupted with a blood-curdling scream! Everyone in the circle opened their eyes in horror to see the Blanket Man falling to the floor. His countenance took on a monstrous appearance of the deepest shade of purple I had ever seen, as his swollen tongue began protruding from his face. He continued to scream as if he were choking. "Oh God," I shouted, as I flew out of the prayer circle right on top of the man like jumping on the back of a horse. I grabbed his chest with my hands and I shouted at the top of my lungs, "SATAN, LET HIM GO, IN JESUS NAME!" Just as quickly as this episode began, the power of God overcame the man and the demon loosened him. Softly and beautifully, a veil of golden light fell over his face; then God's peace that passes all understanding filled the young man's mind.

Paul (that is his name) awoke and walked out of his spiritual bondage into the kingdom of God. The Name of Jesus and the power of God had set Paul free from the death grip of satanic bondage. From that moment on, we were introduced to a marvelous individual filled with the love of God, intelligent and sure of himself. After several weeks of fellowship, church services, and Bible studies, I came as usual to bring Paul to the church. As we left the halfway house to get into the car, Paul broke the news. "Johnny, I am going back home tomorrow". I argued, "Oh...you don't want to do that Paul, you are doing so well here"? Paul assured me, "No, please don't worry Johnny, I am okay, it's time for me to go back home. I know now I am going to be fine".

A month or so after Paul left, I got a very nice thank-you card from him. He gave the glory to God for everything that was going on in his life now that he was back at home. Then he added a PS:

"Johnny, I want to thank you for all you did for me. When you found me that night on the roadside, my life was like a piece of meat hanging on a barbwire fence".

I do not think I have ever heard a wasted life described so correctly. Without Jesus, life has no meaning, no purpose. Only when we are free by God's grace does life began to take on true purpose and have a real meaning. My Blanket Man was free. Paul was walking with Christ, clothed now in the righteousness of Jesus Christ his Savior.

Meanwhile back at Prison Ministries, I had been asked to join the team for a weekend of preaching and singing in the prisons. On our way back, the ministry leaders Joe and Charles talked to me about joining their team with the idea that Judy and I would move into the upstairs apartment and act as overseers of the house and be friends to the men. I could have an office and see to it that the house chores which are assigned to each man were done. I could go to Bible school in the morning because all my classes were over by 1pm, and they didn't mind that we continued at the Baptist church. So that's what we did, both Judy and I felt it was God's plan. One other nice blessing, I didn't have to drive the taxi anymore.

Pastor Cub and Sister Marva were sad to see us go but gave us their blessing and now in the fall of 1974, almost a year to the day since God had first entered our lives the blessings of God were happening at a swift pace.

The fundamentals of the faith being taught at the college were Biblically sound, so I was getting a firm foundation in the truth. I did soon find out however that Baptist doctrine didn't accept the Biblical teaching of talking in unknown tongues which was common among Pentecostals. They reasoned that those manifestations had stopped with the passing of the Apostles. I certainly didn't hold to that idea for two very good reasons.

First, I felt their exegesis of scripture was bias because of their Baptist traditions and secondly, I knew from personal experienced what happened in the prayer meeting, with my face stuck in the carpet, and I was certainly convinced it wasn't the devil, for I had a lifetime of the devil in my life and he was never that loving or kind to me.

Nevertheless, the school had a strong opinion on the subject and the church had a strong zealous advocate who was anti Pentecostals in every way…period.

In fact, he was so adamant about it that he went so far as to preach from the pulpit that speaking in unknown tongues was from the devil. I felt like I was under suspicion by many at the Bible College and our church of being a tongues talker, only because of my association with Prison Ministries, even though no one had ever heard me speaking in my Heavenly language. When I heard about this pastor's message I felt very sad for the Holy Spirit. Then I learned that this same pastor's wife was very ill.

One evening after a midweek service while getting into my car to leave, I looked down the parking lot to where the church parsonage was and where this pastor lived. The thought of his sick wife crossed my mind, when God spoke calling out the pastor's name to me, "I want you to go to Pastor Tom's house". "Lord, I can't do that, the man hates me". But with no response to my rebuttal, I started to the house. I stood on the steps knocking on the door. The thought within me was I really wanted to run back to my car, was interrupted when I heard from behind the door, "Come on in, the doors open". It was the pastor's voice. Slowly I pushed the door open and stepped into the room. Immediately I noticed the surprised look on the pastor's face when he saw me. I then noticed his wife laying stretched out on a couch, looking deathly ill. I was feeling awkward at my being there and I apologized for my uninvited visit. "Sit down Johnny". I took a seat on the love seat by the door. For the next few moments we just sat, neither of us spoke. Then I said, "maybe it would be better if I came back at another time Pastor Tom". "No, Johnny, I want you to pray for my wife"! With that word and without hesitation I moved toward his wife, I could feel the power of the Holy Ghost coming upon me. I placed my left hand on her forehead and lifted my right hand to the heavens.

I prayed as God's anointing was filling the place. I opened my eyes to find the pastor kneeling in prayer behind me. It was a powerful prayer. I was sure when I left, that a healing miracle had just happened. I wish I could tell you his position on Pentecostals changed that night, but they didn't. Nonetheless, from the pulpit, that very next Sunday, he gave testimony of his wife's healing, and there she was on the front pew, a picture of health and a testimonial to God's goodness and mercy.

At Prison Ministries God was doing great things and many miracles were happening. We had ministered in The Grey Stone Chapel behind the walls of Folsom Prison. While I sang and gave testimony, my eyes caught sight of one of the men in the audience. He stood out in a very special way. Though everyone in the crowd were all dressed in prison denim, this man had a noticeable aura about him. I would never forget that man.

A few weeks later, an elderly woman came into my office at Prison Ministries. She told me she had been to Folsom Prison to visit her grandson. Her grandson told her that Johnny Mays had been singing at the prison, so she learned where I was, and had drop by specifically to meet me and to say thank you. Then she began to tell me her grandson's story of how he'd left Alabama to go to Hollywood, he wanted to be an actor, but he fell in with a group of hippies. Almost in tears now, she sighed, "the leader of the group was this self-proclaimed guru by the name of Charles Manson". She continued, "my grandson Bruce, came to the cult by way of Scientology". She said he was eventually kicked out of Scientology because of his drug use. She mentioned too, that even though he wasn't there at the Tate or La Bianca murders; he was however convicted in 1972,

and was sentenced to life in prison for the murders of Gary Hinman and Shorty Shea. Now with tears in her eyes, her lips quivering, shaking with emotion…" he's
found Jesus Brother Johnny…. he gave his life to The Lord".

The team would return to Folsom Prison by request of the warden. To my astonishment the man with the aura I had seen on my last visit, came up to me and thanked me for talking to his grandmother. You can't imagine how shocked I was to find out who he was. It's been more than forty years now since we first met. Bruce is still in prison.

In March of 1975 Judy and I learned we were going to have a baby. She was born on November 6th and we were astounded that we had a daughter. She was the most beautiful thing my eyes had ever seen. What little hair she had was a beautiful copper color, she had gorgeous green eyes, she was our treasure, she was a wee Irish lass. She filled our hearts with so much joy, and our boys were so happy they had a sister. Judy named her Libby and I named her Star. Libby Star Mays your family was in love with you, our sweet baby girl.

Just before Christmas I moved my family from the apartment at Prison Ministries to a home near Roseville. In Roseville, I had taken the position as youth pastor at the First Baptist Church. Since I was still in Bible College, my time spent there was more part time.

Upon the completion of my studies in Bible College I took a teaching position at Sacramento Christian School. My class was a combo of seventh and eighth graders. This was as much an educational experience for me as it was my students. Though I enjoyed teaching, I had one student who gave me nothing but trouble. His mother was a young widow, her husband had been killed in a motorcycle accident. She had two children, my student Billy and a younger sister. She had enrolled Billy in my school thinking the discipline there would help him get better grades. I was always having to discipline this boy. I commuted every morning with one of the other teachers, her children and my son Christopher. One morning on our way to school, God spoke to me concerning Billy with a passage of scripture;

"A soft answer turns away wrath: but grievous words stir up anger". Proverbs 15:1

I thought, "okay, I'll do it your way Lord". So, from that day forward I never raised my voice or threatened Billy anymore. I did have him sitting right beside my desk and he stayed after school every day to finish his school work, by request of his mother. She begged me to help, because he would never do it at home. One day as we were both working, God spoke; "tell Billy you know what his problem is". I looked over at him… "Billy", he looked up at me from his work, I know what your problem is". Billy waited to hear, for he couldn't have known that I was waiting to hear myself. Then God spoke, "tell him his problem is he hates ME, and he blames ME, for his daddy's death". I repeated the context to what God had told me…" Billy your problem is you hate God, you blame God for your daddy's death". When I said that, this young boy and by the way a very handsome, athletic young boy, broke. His hard-shell countenance begins cracking like a shattered hard-boiled egg. He began to weep. I prayed with him and told him that God loved him and God had wept too when his daddy died.

211

I told Billy before you were your Daddy's son, your Daddy had become a child of God. From that day on Billy changed, he surrendered his life to the Lord.

After two years of teaching school, I desired to learn more about a pastor's role in ministry, so I took the position of music director or music pastor as it's sometimes called, with Dr. John Wilkins at his church the Amazing Grace Baptist Church. Dr. John had been one of my teachers at the college, he was also the Dean of Students and the brother of Dr. James Wilkins the President of the College. The Wilkins brothers came from a family of five brothers, all of them preachers. Dr. John had taken a real liking to me as the results of a college chapel service.

The first thing every Wednesday morning our college would have a typical Chapel Service, with singing, announcements and of course preaching. Every student and staff member were required to attend. Very often there were visitors who would come as well. Usually one of the teachers or church pastors did the preaching. This time though things would be different. For some reason Dr. John had ask me to preach. I could hardly believe it, but was honored by the invitation. The chapel messages were usually no more than twenty minutes long and Dr. John took exception to anyone who would go past the allotted time. That thought made me nervous and then to think about preaching in front of all those students, staff, preachers, and perhaps others as well added to my concerns. I knew if I was going to do this I would have to put all that fear and trepidation under the control of the Holy Spirit. I prayed much about the service and I believed that God had given me just the right text out of the Epistle to the Colossians chapter one. The title of my message was;

"CHRIST IN YOU THE HOPE OF GLORY"

"Whereof I am made a minister, according to the dispensation of God which is given to me for you, to fulfill the word of God; Even the mystery which hath been hid from ages and from generations, but now is made manifest to his saints: To whom God would make known what is the riches of the glory of this mystery among the Gentiles; which is Christ in you, the hope of glory: Whom we preach, warning every man, and teaching every man in all wisdom; that we may present every man perfect in Christ Jesus: Whereunto I also labor, striving according to his working, which works in me mightily". Verses 25-29

I wish I could tell you what I preached that day, after all I had prepared notes, but I never used them. From the time Dr. John introduced me and I had greeted everyone, the only thing I remembered was reading my text. From that point on I don't remember a thing. As soon as I began to preach God's Word, the Chapel was filled with God's Presence and power as the Holy Ghost took over. The next thing I knew I was yielding the pulpit back to Dr. John. I was paralyzed by my lack of recall as to what just happened. When the students left to return to class, there was a deafening silence. Seriously, you could hear a pin drop. Nothing was said by anyone. My next class was Elemental Theology, my teacher was Dr. John. In the class-room, it was as quiet as a funeral parlor. Usually these young preachers were a boisterous lot, joking around and carrying on, but not today. I sat waiting and praying that someone would say something. The silence was finally broken when one of the brothers said, "Brother Johnny Mays, I never heard anything like that before".

"What did he mean by that, did he mean it was the worst thing he had ever heard, or maybe something else, I didn't know how to take his remark". Then when the other students started chiming in with compliments and giving me thumbs up for a great message, I became inwardly pleased. Yet I wasn't a hundred percent convinced until Dr. John came into the classroom and as the guys got quiet again, he said, "Brother Mays, that was a good word, thank you for the message". Finally, I could breathe again.

Working at the church with Dr. John was a real blessing. Once he called asking me to meet him for coffee. He told me there was something important he wanted to talk to me about. I told him I would be there and as I drove to the café, I was thinking of how mysterious he had been.

As I neared the meeting place, The Lord spoke to me with "a word of knowledge". In the Bible, the "word of knowledge" is a spiritual gift listed in 1 Corinthians 12:8;

"For to one is given by the Spirit the word of wisdom; to another the word of knowledge by the same Spirit";

It has been associated with the ability to teach the faith, but also with forms of revelation like prophecy. It is closely related to another spiritual gift, "the word of wisdom". Among Pentecostals the "word of knowledge" is often defined as the ability of one person to know what God is currently doing or intends to do in the life of another person. It can also be defined as knowing the secrets of another person's heart.

The "word of knowledge" I received that day was, "the pastor wants to ordain you, but he has a problem with the rumors that you speak in unknown tongues". I was pleased to know Dr. John's intentions. Up till then all I had was a license to preach from his brother Dr. James Wilkins and the Landmark Missionary Baptist Church.

As we sat drinking coffee for several minutes I was beginning to think nothing was going to happen, when finally.

"Brother Johnny the reason I wanted to talk to you is to tell you that you've been doing a great job at our church and (he pauses) well you see I feel like the Lord told me I was to ordain you, and I really want to do) that but, (he pauses again but I have to ask you a question, (stuttering) he says, "do you speak in unknown tongues"?

Without hesitation, I said, "yes I do".

Almost flustered now he says, "I just knew you were going to say that". "I'm sorry Pastor, I know that's a problem for you".

"Brother Johnny, "it's a big problem for me, because some of the other pastors in our fellowship weren't too happy when I told them my plans to ordain you".

"Pastor John, it seems to me you've got a bigger problem than the brethren". For a moment he looks at me with a puzzled frown.

"What do you mean Brother Johnny".

"Well, what I mean is, didn't you tell me The Lord told you to ordain me"?

That's right, The Lord told me to ordain you."

"So as far as I can see it's not the brethren that's your problem, your problem is are you going to obey the instructions of The Lord."

On the night of the ordination there are two candidates. Myself and a man from our congregation.

We sat on the pulpit platform facing the congregation while behind us were the pastors representing the area fellowship of churches. There were a few absentees. You see the way it works among independent Baptists. All the preachers from our fellowships submit questions to be asked of the candidates by the moderator, in this case Dr. John.

The questions asked typically were about your conversion and what you think it means to be saved. There are questions about the history of your family. They want to know what makes you think you have a calling, and then they would get into doctrine and theology. It was all-encompassing. Everything was going great, then came the one question that was making Dr. John and the other pastors nervous.

"Brother Mays could you tell us, what is your position on speaking in unknown tongues"?

My answer went something like this, "Speaking in tongues means speaking in a way or in a language that is not normally understood by the speaker or the listeners, unless there is an interpretation".

Before I could continue, Dr. John moved on to ask the other candidate an altogether different question. At the end of the questioning the brethren laid their hands on us and prayed, the church gave us beautiful ordination certificates, and we were done. I was now an officially ordained Baptist preacher.

Chapter 13

Over the years I have had to support my ministry and provide for my family by working at various kinds of jobs. I drove taxi, worked in construction, sold life insurance, sold ice cream from one of those ding dong trucks. I umpired city league softball and occasionally a high school baseball game. I drove big rigs, buses, installed aluminum siding, worked in lawn care and landscaping. I would do anything to make a buck, so I could preach the Word and at the same time keep a roof over my family's head, food in their bellies, clothes on their backs and shoes on their feet. In every endeavor, The Lord was with me. When I couldn't find work, then I had to live by faith and trust in The Lord and the kindness of God's people.

For example, one Sunday on our way home from The First Baptist Church, both Judy and I were concerned with what we were to do for lunch, our pantry was bare. When we arrived home, our hungry kids began to complain, "when are we going to eat Dad"? I told them, "we're going to eat soon boys, but first we're going to thank The Lord." I had them join hands and we prayed. While I was praying, the doorbell rang, one of the boys broke from the circle opening the door. There, standing at our door was one of the ladies from the church. "Pastor Johnny, I was just headed to get some lunch and thought I would come and take the Mays family with me". "How about it kids, where would you all like to eat." God had answered our prayers, "we all like "Okie Frijoles". It was an American/Mexican buffet.

At the restaurant I told the boys, "fill up boys this is it for the day". Later that evening that same Christian lady brought several bags of groceries to our house.

Then after few weeks that same lady and her husband found out that my Dad had ask me to come to Alabama and preach a revival at his Church. This couple blessed us by insisting that we take their Volkswagen Camper bus for the trip. They convinced us it was spacious, it was equipped with bunks, a cooler for food, and gets great gas mileage. We would leave about a week before Christmas. As we drove the old Route 66, which is now US Highway 40, I told the story the of first time I rode the Greyhound to California. After refueling about one o'clock in the morning, I pulled out of Amarillo, with a tank full of gas and a hot cup of coffee. Just about forty minutes out without warning the engine shuts down. I coasted to the side of the highway, "what's wrong John"? "I don't know let me check". Grabbing my lantern, I walked to the rear, opened the bonnet and tried to hand turn the motor at the belt pulleys but nothing moved. Hurriedly I returned to the cab, it was cold outside. "I think we've got a big problem, the motor is frozen, so we better pray". For an hour, I waved my lantern to every passing vehicle on both the westbound and eastbound sides of the highway. No one would stop. I looked across the flat fields on both sides of the highway, if a light was shining in the Texas night I would see it.

I must admit I was worrying more about the cold. I watched Judy as she snuggled the boy's closer to each other under their blankets, and added more cover on her and Libby. In the distance, I saw headlights coming toward me, there was a wide median between us, I frantically waved my lantern

219

in a triangular pattern signaling distress. As the vehicle passed, I watch in my side mirror as it goes away, then I see him crossing the median and turning in my direction. I didn't take my eyes off him until the vehicle stopped just at the rear of the van. As I exited the van I noticed a young man in a cowboy hat stepping out of his pickup. "I saw your light, looks like you got a problem", he said in his Texas drawl. "Thanks for stopping, yeah, I think my motor is gone, I have little children and my wife and it's getting cold out here". I am sure he could sense the anxiety in my voice. "Well it's winter time in the Texas panhandle, but don't worry I'll be right back, I got a chain at the ranch and I'll get you towed to town. Groom, Texas is about five miles up the road. They got a garage there and a motel and a café".

True to his word he came right back, hooked us up and towed us to the garage. He then dropped us off at the motel. Thank the Lord there was a vacancy. I offered the cowboy money for his help, though I was glad when he wouldn't take it, because after I paid for the room, I knew my travel budget couldn't handle many more unexpected expenses and the truth was this ordeal had just begun.

The next morning, I bought coffee, milk and cinnamon rolls from the café. I said hello to the same fellow who checked me into the room, he was now the cook at the grill behind the counter. He told me the man's name at the garage... "tell Fred I sent you". As I walked into the garage, the smell of gas, oil and grime, reminded me of Daddy's old Lion Service station. The only things in the large garage bay was farm equipment and tractors. My van was right where I left it earlier that morning. Seeing no one around I yelled, "anybody here"?

220

From beneath an international harvester tractor came a man, dressed in grease covered overalls, in a tattered red Pendleton shirt with a quilted vest over it. On his head, a halfcocked John Deere baseball cap with matching grease and grime. "That your rig out there"? "At the café, this morning, Sam told me you would be coming". "Yes, it's mine". Removing his cap, he began scratching his dark wavy hair with a tint of silver in his sideburns, he says, "well Sir you see the problem is I don't know anything about those foreign jobs. Farm equipment and trucks are more to my liking, but I can give you a tow back to Amarillo, they got a Volkswagen garage there. We can go about three this afternoon. I have to finish a few things here first, if that's okay with you". "Sure, that's fine, I'll meet you back here at three".

In Amarillo, the news was not good. The engine had to be replaced. I called the owners back in California and told them I was very sorry but there was a breakdown with the van. They apologized to me, of all things, and ask me if Judy and the children were okay. Then they ask me to put the manager on the phone, after which the manager gave the phone back to me. "Johnny, I am sending a bank draft to the dealer's bank for the cost of the repairs, I am also sending you and Judy a thousand dollars to help you all out, so I don't want you to worry. And by the way the van will be ready in two days and when you pick it up he will have your cash for you too". I thanked my friends and apologized once again for the trouble I had caused. Kindly, they assured me it was not my fault and were glad to help. When I returned to the motel and told Judy, she was happy that things were working out.

When evening came, we all decided to go for a walk, just a few blocks from the motel there was a gathering at the church. As we entered the church we were greeted by an usher who welcomed us, gave us a program and directed us to a pew. The sanctuary was decorated with green, a nativity scene dressed the table in front of the pulpit, the choir wore maroon robes with white collars. It was a wonderful evening of singing the Christmas carols and it was a blessing to hear the reading of Christ's birth.

"And there were in the same country shepherds abiding in the field, keeping watch over their flock by night. And, lo, the angel of the Lord came upon them, and the glory of the Lord shone round about them: and they were sore afraid. And the angel said unto them, fear not: for, behold, I bring you good tidings of great joy, which shall be to all people. For unto you is born this day in the city of David a Savior, which is Christ the Lord. And this shall be a sign unto you; Ye shall find the babe wrapped in swaddling clothes, lying in a manger. And suddenly there was with the angel a multitude of the heavenly host praising God, and saying "Glory to God in highest heaven, and peace on earth to those with whom God is pleased." Luke chapter 2:8-14.

Afterward we were given an invitation to join the congregation for Christmas cookies, coffee and hot chocolate. Then we met the pastor. "I was talking to Sam, he told me you were at the motel, he tells me you're a Baptist preacher on your way to Alabama to hold a revival and your vehicle was in Amarillo being repaired". He says smiling, "you have a beautiful family", to which Judy and I both thanked him. I thought to myself, "man news travels fast in Groom".

222

Then as if he is reading my thoughts, he says while looking past me, "Sam at the motel and Fred the mechanic over there go to our church".

I followed his gaze and sure enough standing across the room stood Sam and Fred. When they noticed Judy and me they walked over, "Nice to see you all here tonight" said Sam. "Listen, don't you worry about anymore motel renting. I've taken care of that; you and your family are welcome to stay ever how long you need. Fred here told us your van we be ready in a couple of days". Fred nods while munching his cookie. "Oh… and by the way, I opened a tab for you at the café, so you don't have to eat bologna sandwiches for two days. We can't let you do that". How in the world did he know Judy had gone shopping at the little grocery store with the children while I was in Amarillo…? Of course, the young fellow at the grocery store went to their church too. Judy had mentioned seeing him when she was helping our kids with their hot chocolate. "Pastor we are overwhelmed by your congregation's generous care and kindness." "Don't worry about it Brother Mays, when I learned that one of God's servants had a need, I made some calls". For the rest of the evening the conversation moved to questions about how long I had been in the ministry, which church we attended, where I went to Bible College, the questions kept coming from everyone.

Getting back to the motel we were all soon to bed. While I lay on the pillow I thanked The Lord for the family of God. The next two days we ate at the café and put it on the tab. Many of the church folks came around to the room to welcome us to Texas, and their town. One afternoon some ladies stopped by with an assortment of baked goods. The

223

pastor stopped by to tell me that when it was time for us to go to Amarillo, he had cleared his scheduled to take us. I thanked him again and told him I had never seen such Christian love, he smiled and said; "you're in Texas now preacher".

When we got to Amarillo the car was good to go, there too was the thousand dollars from the owners of the car just as they promised. Judy and I said goodbye to the pastor and thanked him profusely. Before we left Amarillo, Judy wanted to buy the children winter coats and we did. As we were coming closer to Groom, I mentioned to Judy I needed to stop by the garage and settle with Fred. In the garage I found him buried under the hood of an old farm truck. When he saw me he said, "I see you all got your wheels under you again". "Thanks to you Fred, say I need to settle up with you on the tow to Amarillo, what do I owe you".

Fred leaned back on the old truck wiping his hands on a grease rag, scratching his head, he smiled, "I think twenty dollars will cover my fuel, yep that'll do it I figure". As I gave him the money, I repeated myself, "Fred you all here in Groom are amazing, your kindness, and hospitality, was truly Christ like.

I will never forget you and I will tell people wherever I go about the family of God in Groom, Texas". As I pulled onto the eastbound lane the road sign read Oklahoma City 215 miles. While I drove Judy and I began singing the Bill Gaither song, The Family of God.

"You will notice we say

"brother" and "sister" 'round here;

It's because we're a family

and these folks are so near.

When one has a heartache we all share the tears,

And rejoice in each vict'ry in this fam'ly so dear.

I'm so glad I'm a part of the fam'ly of God!

I've been washed in the fountain,

Cleansed by His blood.

Joint heirs with Jesus as we travel this sod,

For I'm part of the fam'ly, The fam'ly of God."[lxiv]

It was a happy reunion with my Alabama family, they were excited to see the kids and having us there at Christmas time made it even more special. The revival began the day before New Year's Eve it was a Sunday morning and lasted until Friday night. I like to tell preachers that my first revival started in 1978 and didn't end until the next year. One of my greatest joys happened in that first service. When I gave my first invitation, a big fellow jumps up off the back pew, runs down the aisle to where I was standing, picks me up off my feet in this huge bear hug. I look in his face and tears of joy were running down his cheeks.

That big guy was a man I had loved since we were boys, my brother Gary. We both stood there weeping as the church gathered around us and prayed. My Brother Gary would go home to be with The Lord in 1980. I wept!

The following Sunday my family and I were invited to preach in a church in Decatur, Alabama. Some men of the church had invited me to join them at the County Jail for a service which started about two hours before their church service. I left Judy and the children at the church for Sunday school.

At the jail, the men began showing their identifications to a female officer standing behind a heavy plexiglass window. She had them sign in on a clipboard. When it was my turn, she took a long look at the California driver's license, and frowned, "we got us a problem this morning gentlemen. I can't let your guitar playing friend into my jail". The brothers, asked "why"? "The sheriff's orders, no one from out of state is allowed, besides he couldn't take that guitar in there no how". The brothers pleaded but to no avail.

I was left standing there as they departed through the big steel door with two deputies leading them out of the waiting room. One of the men volunteered to stay with me. "You ready to go back to the church Brother Johnny? There's no sense us waiting here, it'll be an hour before they come back". Just as I was ready to consent, I heard the voice of God speak, "DON'T MOVE, STAND STILL". The word was so strong, I told the brother, "not just yet God is doing something". When he asks what did I mean God is doing something, I told him what God had spoken, "don't move, stand still".

When the Lord gave me that word, I was still standing in front of the plexiglass window, just far enough away so the people who were coming in for visits could squeeze in front of me. Every moment I stood there, seemed like forever. Soon the officer came back to the plexiglass window, "is there something else I can do for you Sir"?

"Yes...you could let me into this jail.... can't you call the Sheriff"? "The sheriff is out of town, she snapped, besides it would do no good".

With my feet frozen in place, and my accomplice sitting in the corner chewing his nails, wondering if I had lost my mind. I noticed activity behind the plexiglass window. A couple of deputies had gathered with the lady officer.

Then making his entrance the "Jailer" himself joined them. This man was big and carried on his hip, a giant ring of keys. As I watched them leave the office area, the next thing I know, the big steel door next to me opens, and there is the jailer and two deputies. "Alright, come on in, bring your buddy, and go ahead bring your guitar." He then instructs his deputies, "take him where he wants to go, just don't let him out of your sight".

With my guitar in hand, I'm inside the jail. Stopping at the first cell block I see a dozen men, some on their bunks, other sitting at a table playing dominoes. They were all smoking cigarettes, so a haze of smoke filled the cell block.

Without a word spoken to them I began with the song, The Lighthouse. When I started singing, God, joins us in this jail service that morning.

"There's a lighthouse on the hillside.

That overlooks life's sea.

When I'm tossed, it sends out a light,

that I might see.

And the light that shines in darkness,

now will safely lead me home,

227

If it wasn't for the lighthouse, my ship would be no more".

It seems that everybody about us says:

Tear that old lighthouse down.

The big ships don't sail this way anymore.

So, there's no use in it standing around.

But then my mind goes back,

to that dark stormy night, when just in time I saw the light.

Yes, it was the light from that old lighthouse,

that stands there up on the hill.

"And I thank God for the lighthouse. I owe my life to Him.

Jesus is the lighthouse, and from the rocks of sin.

He has shown the light around me, that I might clearly see.

If it wasn't for the lighthouse,

tell me, where would this ship be"?

This great song was written in the downstairs bathroom of a church then called "The Pentecostal Tabernacle" in Salinas, California. The Hinson Family singers had been rehearsing songs that Saturday evening and when Ronny Hinson disappeared for several minutes, only to return to the church sanctuary brandishing a long fluttering piece of toilet paper, with the words to The Lighthouse which would become Gospel Music Association's song of the Year for 1972". Years later, my Judy would become the director of the school in that same church which is now called The First Assembly of God. [lxv]

As I sang this song, the power of The Holy Spirit filled the cell block. Every man in there was moved by God's Presence! The men left their bunks and dominoes, snuffed out their smokes and were now standing at the bars as if they were being drawn to God. Down the corridors I could hear other inmates yelling, "bring him down here, bring him down here"! Before we left the jail, we visited every cell block on the floor. When we returned to the church, the men who had taken me to the jail that morning learned the story from my accomplice, they were astonished to say the least. "You'll never believe this he told them, but God broke us into jail this morning". All the brethren rejoiced at the mighty power of God.

We had a great weekend at the church, but now we are on our way home to California. Driving back to the west coast would have been uneventful, except for the leg from Little Rock to Oklahoma City, which took several hours because we got caught in a blizzard. It was long and arduous and there were moments when I thought we weren't going to make it. Yet we learned that by prayers and the grace of God we would survive. So, we continued west on old Route 66.

Back in our home, Judy and I were determined to begin our own church. I received a call from Joe and Charles at Prison Ministries. They ask if we might consider being the pastors of the church they had started in the chapel, they were calling it "Freedom Church". We agreed we would take it. The congregation was largely ex-cons and people from the streets. I organized a worship team, and started a gospel band which we named, The East Gate Gospel Band. Judy started a Sunday school and the people began coming.

For months the church grew, then just before Thanksgiving, Joe and Charles told me they were closing the church. I ask them what was their reasons. They told me they felt it was wrong for them to have begun it in the first place. They apologized and said in two weeks they were pulling the plug and that should give the people time to find somewhere else to go. I argued with them. "The people who come here come because they don't fit in anywhere else". My plea falls on deaf ears. My heart was broken, what am I going to do. I announced the bad news to the congregation and told them they were welcomed to come to my home for church and Bible study. Sadly, they didn't come, because for most of them my home was too far away, and they had no transportation. We would not forget them. For several years after that on Thanksgiving Day, Judy and I would go to the streets of Sacramento and feed and minister to the folks who lived there.

Meanwhile, we were holding meetings in our home and a few people attended. On the other hand, The East Gate Gospel Band was busy doing a lot of performing. With Raymond on the piano, Bob on bass, Steve playing drums, Lola and Rita were singing the harmony vocals. I played guitar and sang. We were doing concerts in parks, auditoriums and occasionally a local country western television show on KCRA Channel 3 in Sacramento.

One weekend I was invited to Stockton to preach for Pastor Ardley Reynolds at the Windsor Pentecostal Church. After the service, the pastor asks if I knew anyone interested in buying some church pews. He was replacing his old pine wood pews with new cushioned pews. He said he'd sell them to me for ten dollars each. Driving back to Sacramento I kept asking myself why I had bought those pews, I had no building to put them in. I rented a Uhaul and brought those pews to our house and stacked them in the garage. Judy just laughed, "I guess you know what you're doing." I laughed with her... "I haven't a clue". A few days later while sitting at home thinking about the pews, The Voice of God spoke, "Go look at the church building you've been driving by in Rio Linda". I remembered the building, it was out in the countryside. I had driven by it on an occasion and had seen the for-sale sign in the yard. I didn't think any more about it after that, because I've hardly been able to pay my house rent, much less buy a church building.

Nonetheless, at The Lord's prompting I did what The Lord ask me to do. As I turned into the driveway of the church, I noticed an old man standing on the front steps, fiddling with the door knob. "Is he trying to break in?

"Hello...excuse me...hello".

When he hears me, he then turns...then guessing he asks, "you here to buy the church"?

"If you are come on in and look around".

"Thank you, maybe I will".

In my mind I'm thinking, "why are you wasting this old man's time". Then the old man asks: "Are you a preacher? Are you needing a church? How many people you got? How large is your congregation? I'm asking eighty thousand for it, is that too much for you? I just had a man here looking he didn't have no money I told him to hit the road". Like machine gun fire his questions came, before I could answer the first one he would ask the next.

Honestly, it was as if he didn't care what my answers would have been.

While he talked, my eyes were not believing what I was seeing. It was a large sanctuary but in terrible disrepair. The plaster from the ceiling had fallen in several places, every wall needed paint, there was a mixture of seating; folding chairs, military office chairs, a couple of very old pews and the carpet was a patchwork quilt of remnants.

"I've got about twenty or so people mostly women, children and one old man. I really can't buy anything. I just felt The Lord led me to come and look".

Old man: "I tell you what you do, you bring your people here and have church and I'll take half your weekly tithes and offering for rent, how's that suit you."

"That suits me just fine… by the way do you mind if I bring in my own pews"?

As we shook hands, I could sense relief in the old man's eyes. I drove away with the keys of the building in my hand as I watched him take down the for-sale sign. No lease papers, no application, no credit check, no references required, for we both knew The Lord had done this thing.

My group was excited when we moved our pews into our new church. They first began to remove the old tattered carpet then swept and mopped the concrete floor.
The old building had been built as a turkey hatchery originally. It was made entirely of concrete, it was strong as a bomb shelter. "What are we going to name our church Brother Johnny"? "I'm going to call it "Harvest Chapel", because the Bible says;

"You, wake up and look around. The fields are already ripe for harvest"! John 4:35

Everybody with me that day said, "Amen"! In the first two months the church doubled in size and by the time the new year rolled around we were pushing a hundred. They were coming from everywhere because God was anointing our worship and preaching. Everyone who came felt like this was their home.

We finally decided to carpet the place. My friend Charles from "Prison Ministries" owned a carpet business. He made a deal with me to sell and install an industrial carpet for a thousand dollars.

I was excited, but I knew God was going to have to provide the money. Our church was growing fast, but the offerings were not. Our folks were mostly on welfare or unemployed. Many of them were old hippies, street people with a history of substance abuse. Thank God there were some with businesses, good educations and jobs. The day before the carpet was to arrive one of those hippies came into my makeshift office and said, "Pastor Johnny I got a tithe for you", and he gave me a thousand dollars in cash. He had received a disabled check that payed him retroactively ten thousand dollars and he was here to honor God with his tithe.

The next day we had everything out of the building sitting in the parking lot waiting for the carpet to arrive. In the back of our building but attached to the church were extra-large rooms which were being used by a drywall company which I found out was owned by the old man's son. While we were all sitting outside on the pews, the drywall company owner stopped and ask me what was going on.

He asked if he could look around inside. I walked with him into the church...he grunted, "this church needs more than carpet...listen don't put any carpet in here till my crew does a little work. I'm going to sort this place out for you at no charge. All I want from you, preacher, is to get ceiling lights." Then he left as abruptly as he came. When the church doors opened that Sunday, the congregation walked in on new carpet from the front door to the stage. Above their heads was a new ceiling with brand new lights. In the air was the smell of fresh paint. All this compliment, of a faithful hippie, a practically total stranger and his crew of drywall installers. The church continued to grow. Near the end of our second year one of our men who was highly educated decided to start a Christian School. The drywall company donated the use of one of their large rooms. The drywall owner also owned a house next to the church and since Judy had earned enough college credits, she open a preschool in that house. Things were really moving and we all gave God the glory.

Chapter 14

The worship band was largely The East Gate Gospel Band and they were awesome. Sadly, our piano player Raymond whom I had known from our old honky tonk days, became very ill with cancer and would in just six months from his diagnosis pass away. The funeral was large because of Ray's very large family and everybody from our former musical world attended. We were all saddened. I remember visiting Ray just before he passed. He was in recovery from just having exploratory surgery. When he saw me he said, "Pastor Johnny", "God told me to tell you, "keep your eye on the sparrow". I loved Raymond.

Soon Jimmy Callahan an awesome piano player and singer came to us and joined our team. Oh, and by the way Callahan was blind. He told me he always wanted to be a school teacher, he had graduated from Boston College with a degree in history, but in the end, he became a piano player and he was gifted. We were glad he was with us.

A couple of years before all this began at Harvest Chapel, one morning as I awoke, I had a vision, of an old bar, you know a saloon? With the vision came the name "Jacob's Well." For two years I kept my eyes open thinking there had to be a place. Well just down the road from Harvest Chapel on a side street I stumbled upon it. There it stood, the old bar, all boarded up. God spoke, "here's your "Jacob's Well".

Every week I drove by that bar, but no one was ever around and there was no contact number posted anywhere.
In fact, there was no kind of signage.

Then it happened. I noticed a car parked to the rear of the building. I found a man working there and he informed me that the owner would be there on Saturday. I was there on Saturday. Driving up to the bar I saw parked at the front a sleek automobile. The front door was propped open, so I went in. Inside it was just as I envisioned, a beautiful old fashion bar, with a mirrored back bar. It had bathrooms, kitchen, with two rooms in the rear. As I stood looking around a handsomely dressed Mexican man came from the rear of the building. I introduced myself and told him my vision and plans. He liked my ideas but said I was too late. The reason he was there, he was waiting for the realtors and the new perspective owners from the Veterans of Foreign Wars organization. They planned to purchase it for a new VFW Club. He hoped to close the deal today. Saddened by the news, I gave him my card and ask him to call me if anything should change. He discouraged my hopes by unwaveringly repeating that the deal was done all but signing the papers.

As I drove away, I knew in my heart that something was wrong. God had told me this was "Jacob's Well". Two weeks passed when the call came, "Pastor Johnny, this is Alphonso, you spoke to me a couple of weeks ago about my bar. If you're still interested it's yours, I'm here right now". Without hesitation, I told him I was on my way. We talked about the price of the rent and I told him it was a fair price. However, I also told him, that because the place was in such shambles and that I was going to have to spend a lot of money getting it fit enough to open, that I thought it was also fair if I didn't pay any rent for six months. He finally agreed to my terms, I signed an agreement and he gave me the keys.

By God's grace I had several skilled people in my church and they had Jacob's Well looking just as I had first seen it in my vision and more. They built a stage, where every Friday and Saturday night we had live music. Everyone who worked there was a volunteer. Every morning except on Sunday, we opened our grill with a breakfast, lunch and dinner menu. We had customers at 6am every morning for "all you could eat biscuits and gravy with a ten-cent cup of coffee". We had people in there all day. I recall one day a biker dropped in and asked for a beer. Our waitress Lola told him we didn't serve alcohol, but we had great coffee, soft drinks and milkshakes. He asked her, "what kind of bar is this". So, Lola gave him our church's testimony. He became a regular.

One morning at breakfast one of our customers who owned a bait shop and small engine repair service just down the street, spoke to me while eating his breakfast. "Say, Brother Johnny, about your church Harvest Chapel? Brother Johnny do you think if I came to your church sometime, the roof would fall in"? I laughed, and told him I thought he'd be safe enough for it had already been tested by some notorious characters.

The next Sunday both he and his wife were there. He wore a new pair of denim bib overalls and a crisp starched white shirt. When I gave the invitation, he sprung out of his seat and gave his heart to the Lord.

There were stories after stories like this from "Jacobs Well", people getting saved while playing a game of pool or during one of our concerts. It was awesome. Talk about notorious characters.

I was about half asleep and my mind in a fog from a long afternoon of deskwork when I heard a phone ringing. The phone rang, maybe two or three times, before I realized it was my phone. I answered. "Hello". "Pastor Johnny?" the voice asked. "Yes." "Pastor Johnny, I need your help. The doctors have told us Clarence has about an hour to live." The name Clarence gave me a clue to who was calling. "Can you come Pastor Johnny?" she asked desperately. "Of course, I am on my way!" "Wait, Brother Johnny, there is one problem." "What's the problem Sister M"? Sister M had been attending my church for about one year. She is a native American Indian, married to a white man from Oklahoma. She is a wonderful woman, truly devout to the church. Her husband was known to be one tough "Oki". Their boys had reputations of being a rowdy bunch. The good news, they were all attending church. Sister M replied apologetically, "Many of the family don't want you to come." "You know, Brother Johnny, they believe differently than you do. You Hallelujahs, as they put it, are not their kind." Hallelujahs is a term used irreverently, like Holy Roller. Which was used by those who scoff at the practices of the Pentecostal Church. "Okay, Sister, but how does his wife feel about it,". "Oh, she wants you to come." "Then I am on my way."

I had met Clarence, her brother, a few times before at Jacob's Well. Remember that the ministry importance of Jacob's Well, was the fact that it was a free zone for people who were not your typical churchgoers. All of Sister M' folks would come on occasion to the Saturday night concerts at the Well. In fact, all of Sister M' clan really found their way to my church through the outreach at Jacob's Well. As I walked down the hall to Clarence's hospital room, the hall was lined on both sides with family.

I remember that day vividly. It was like running the gauntlet. Like fiery arrows the stares and glares flew my way.

Halfway to the room, I passed the priest who had just performed the last rites for Clarence. Neither the priest nor I spoke as we passed. In the doorway stood Sister M with Clarence's wife, her eyes filled with tears, and hopelessness. I shook their hands and said. "Give me a few minutes with Clarence, and then we will talk." As I approached his bedside, the site was dreadful. His stomach had swollen, creating a large mound beneath his blanket. His jaundiced face gave the appearance that death had shrouded over him like a heavy yellow blanket. Kneeling beside his bed, I drew close, my face near his, and spoke, "Clarence, Pastor Johnny here." His eyes opened. "Clarence, I am going to be straightforward with you man. The doctors have given you an hour. I'm talking an hour Clarence, and then you are going to meet God. Are you ready to meet God?" He strained to look, his glazed eyes meeting mine, and then in a whisper hardly audible, he said, "Brother Johnny, I can't meet God like this." His answer brought me some relief. "Clarence," I said, "God has given us a promise from His Word, *"that whosoever calls on the Name of the Lord shall be saved"*. Don't you want to be saved Clarence?" He whispered, "Yes." "Let's pray, just call on the Lord with all your heart." I bowed my head and began to pray. I could not hear Clarence praying, but I could see the tears streaming down his yellow skin, leaving a trail of repentance. My heart went out to this broken man. Oh, I know people who are very skeptical about deathbed confessions. My answer to them is, just wait until it is your deathbed, and then see how you feel about it.

After a few moments encouraging Clarence, I stood to leave his bedside when the Lord spoke to me in that still small voice, "Are you not going to pray for his body?" "Lord," I said, "I don't have that kind of faith." "Ask Clarence if he wants you to pray for him." "Clarence, do you want me to pray for your body?" Clarence nodded. "Yes." At that moment, I knew Clarence had more faith than I did, so I prayed two prayers. One prayer I prayed for Clarence and one prayer for me. I prayed that God would raise him up, and I prayed he would help my unbelief. By the time I left the two women and said goodbye, the hall was almost vacant. I walked out of the hospital, and no one spoke or looked my way. Clarence lived through the night, then twenty-four hours, then forty-eight hours; and after seventy-two hours, Clarence was out of the hospital and attending the funeral of two of the people who were standing in the hall the day I came to pray for Clarence. The irony was sobering. I have often referred to Clarence as God's ninety-day wonder. For ninety days, Clarence never let an opportunity pass him by to give God the glory for saving him. He witnessed to his entire family of the redeeming quality of God. Only then, God took Clarence home to heaven. He met God boldly and with gladness of heart. He never returned to the hospital; he just quietly departed to his heavenly home completely healed.

The East Gate Gospel Band was invited to perform, can you believe it, behind the old Maverick Club. Some rich guys were putting on a BBQ free to the public. They had the club house band performing and because my band, "The East Gate Gospel Band was well known, he invited us to perform the closing set. Well, by the time we got to the stage, the audience was shall we say, feeling pretty good with all that free beer and BBQ.

After we finished our set a fellow walked up to me feeling the booze he says, "Johnny when you and the singers were singing Amazing Grace I could see my deceased mother standing on stage with you singing that song, it was her favorite". He was hard to understand because he kept slurring his words because of the booze. "Where's your church he asks". I told him, but I thought, he will never remember!

The following day was Sunday. I arrived early to Harvest Chapel, there in the parking lot was an old beater of a truck. I notice three heads as I looked through the rear window. When I got to the truck they all stepped out. "Pastor Johnny I told you I'd be here". "This is my wife Laura and our daughter Becky, oh...my name is Jessie". I welcome them to our church. While we talked, others would soon come. They stayed for Sunday school and church. However right in the middle of my sermon, Jessie stood up and left the building. I thought to myself, "that didn't take long", but soon and to my surprise he returned.

After church was dismissed I would greet people at the door, Jessie stopped and said, "Pastor I apologize for getting up in the middle of your service, but I forgot that I still had my pistol in my pocket, and just didn't feel right about it so I took it to the truck". "Not a problem Jessie", thank you.

One Saturday night at the "Well" as Callahan and I were on stage doing a duo set, through the front door walks Ola Louise. Ola and her husband Paul "Okie Paul" Westmoreland owned a huge honky tonk right around the corner from Jacobs Well, called The Detour Inn.

Okie Paul was a songwriter and was best known for his song "Detour (There's A Muddy Road Ahead)", written in 1945, which became a big hit for Spade Cooley and was afterwards covered by Patti Page and many others. [lxvi]

Well, Ola walked to the end of the bar and took a seat on the last bar stool. She was dressed to the nines. Ola had her own country band and performed in her club, she was the personification of a "barroom Queen". But tonight, she was in our place. I whispered to Callahan, "do Amazing Grace". When he sang, the anointing of God came. When Ola turned on her barstool her mascara was running. I spoke to her and invited her to the Chapel. The next day at church, during the invitation she gave her heart to the Lord. Thank you, Jesus.

One story that touched my heart came from my video game vendor, whom I had been bugging about getting me a juke box. He came one afternoon, and I just happened to be there. "Pastor I need a favor". "What can I do for you"? He told me that he wanted me to do a funeral for his father. His father had been terminally ill and had committed suicide. He told me because his father was Catholic, he couldn't let the priest do his funeral because he would preach my father into hell. I learned Catholics believed suicide was a sin that couldn't be forgiven. I promised him I would. After the funeral he tried to pay me. I insisted there was no way he could pay me. A few weeks later he showed up at "The Well, and what did he have on the back of his truck a magnificent Seeburg Jukebox. "My Dad would want you to have this. Can you give me a donation receipt, it's yours Pastor Johnny for helping me out"? I reminded him there was no charge, but he argued it wasn't for me, but it was for "Jacob's Well".

I accepted the blessing and loaded it with gospel, classic country and oldies but goodies, the folks loved the eclectic mix.

I get a call from Lola. "Pastor Johnny, you better get down here, there's a guy talking crazy". When I walked into Jacob's Well, I noticed a young man dressed in a business suit sitting at a table. After I introduced myself he said, "Pastor, my father and I have been coming here for lunch for the last few days. We learned from Lola about your church and your mission here. We both like what we see. Pastor maybe you have noticed that just across the street we moved a house onto the vacant lot". I nodded yes. "Well I am here to donate that house and property to you as a gift to your ministry, if you can give us a tax receipt". I acknowledged that I could do that. In just a few months we signed the papers and the property was now ours. I eventually sold the house and put the money into our ministry funds. God is so good.

The lesson here is you reap what you sow! In social psychology, reciprocity is a social rule that says people ought to repay, in kind, what another person has provided for them; that is, people give back (reciprocate) the kind of treatment they have received from another. In the scripture God says;

"Those who are taught the word of God should provide for their teachers, sharing all good things with them. Don't be misled—you cannot mock the justice of God. You will always harvest what you plant. Those who live only to satisfy their own sinful nature will harvest decay and death from that sinful nature. But those who live to please the Spirit will harvest everlasting life from the Spirit. So, let's not get tired of doing what is good. At just

the right time we will reap a harvest of blessing if we don't give up. Therefore, whenever we have the opportunity, we should do good to everyone—especially to those in the family of faith." Galatians 6:6-10.

Folks please remember, you can never out give God!

Everything was going fine. The church was growing, our ministries were flourishing. Then I decided to accept an invitation to go to Wales, United Kingdom. I was asked to perform gospel music, but the problem is I would be away from my Judy and our church for almost two months. I should have reminded myself of the scripture;

"Take heed, therefore, to yourselves, and to all the flock, among which the Holy Spirit made you overseers, to feed the assembly of God that He acquired through His own blood, for I have known this, that there shall enter in, after my departing, grievous wolves unto you, not sparing the flock", Acts 20:28,29

Chapter 15

During the years of Harvest Chapel my life was filled with ministry. Not only at the Chapel and Jacob's Well, but there was so many extracurricular outreaches happening. God used the music and my testimony to open many doors in my life that would have otherwise remained closed. Revivals, churches, prisons, schools, radio and television. Conferences with organizations such as Gideon's International and the Full Gospel Business Men's Fellowship International, all opened by God's favor and my music and testimony. One such opportunity came to me one afternoon at Jacob's Well.

A Christian brother whom I had met while sharing my ministry, stopped by and invited me to Wales in Great Britain. He promised he would arrange for me to perform in colleges and schools. He said there would also be concerts in various auditoriums. He made it sound very inviting, so I decided to go, although, I had some reservation about leaving all my work at the Chapel with some of my church associates. So off to Great Britain I went. My leaving will be the first time since becoming a Christian that Judy and I would be separated for any length of time. This separation would turn out to be a costly decision. I don't know why I didn't take Judy with me, I should have. Maybe it was the memories of our experience while on our way to Alabama to preach our first revival. I may still have carried the memory of how overwhelming it was for me that I had put her and our children in harm's way, on the cold night we broke down on a lonely stretch of highway in the panhandle of Texas.

Maybe the weight of taking them away from their safe home and church threatened me, I don't know. Whatever it was, that separation would create a subtle rift in our relationship that lasted until now. She would never, except, for one occasion go on any mission trips with me. The lesson learned in hindsight, is I should have never gone anywhere or done anything unless she could be right there with me. We have always been better together.

It turns out that my time in Wales was not well organized and what was promised, most of it never happened. There were a couple of church services, and one city wide concert, there was one school, the rest were small group meeting which I had facetiously spoke of as tea parties.

Let me say this, after about three weeks the only place I wanted to be, was back home. But to God be all the glory. There were two very important occasions that despite my displeasure with the people who had invited me to Wales, God did amazing things.

The first happened at a very large main line orthodox church. The pastor was a stately man and seemed very interested in our discussions about the Holy Spirit. It would later be revealed to me that he had experienced the baptism of the Holy Spirit accompanied by the manifestation of unknown tongues, but he was fearful to inform his congregation. In this morning service at his church that secret would be uncovered.

The church platform was a large two-tiered stage. At the very top tier is where the pastor's pulpit was located and where he sat when he had a guest. For me, this setup placed me too far away from the congregation.

I moved myself down to the floor leaving this gentle clergyman sitting alone on his perch with his clergy collar circling his neck beneath his black suit, which it seemed he was comfortable to do.

I began my portion of the service as usual with a couple of songs to warm up the audience, but right in the middle of the second number I heard God say, "stop singing, I want you to call James forward". "Stop singing, call James"? I vacillated, and tried the Spirit, then God confirmed his word by repeating, "Stop singing, call James". Therefore, that's what I did, and there was no response. I waited, then God said again, "call James". So, I ask again for James to come forward. At this request a tall fellow with fiery red hair and a million freckles on his ruddy face stood up. When he got to me he put his hands on my shoulders and whispered in my ear, "I'm not James". "What", I exclaimed! "Then what are you doing here, God wants James"! Again, the young man takes my shoulders in his hands and whispers, "I think the pastor's name is James". With that said, I turned to the pastor sitting on his lofty perch, "Pastor what is your name"? Looking at me with this surprised look on his face, as if he'd been caught, he said, "my name is James", to which I said to him, "please, come down here"!

Then like a little windup marching toy soldier he marches down the steps and off the stage. When he stops he's standing between me and the redheaded man. Straightaway, the power of the Holy Spirit exploded on the scene as if scripted. Then right on cue, the pastor fell backwards under God's power into the arms of the redheaded man. From that moment, there would be wave after wave of God's anointing power washing over the people of God.

All to the glory of God, people were being healed, saved and humbled in God's Presence. After the meeting, the pastor invited the congregation to remain, so the people could ask questions if they wanted to know more about the Holy Spirit. During this afterglow the pastor revealed to his congregation that he had indeed received the baptism of power as promised in scripture but had been afraid to mention it because of church doctrine and their traditions against the baptism. Tonight, he said, "I have been set free from my fears". Please remember my friends, never quench the Holy Spirit or despise small beginnings. This would be my lesson I learn while in Wales.

I had grown bitter with all these "tea parties" and I couldn't wait to be finished with them...it finally came, the last one. My only thought throughout that meeting was, "let's get this over with so I can get back home". I hurried through my portion of the program, but now my hosts have decided to spend a time in prayer. That's when my next lesson would begin. As everyone was praying I felt a tug on my arm, when I turned to look, there standing behind me was a spindly man, probably no more than five feet in height. I looked over to the narrow-boned fellow just as he says, "Johnny could I talk to you outside". As far as I was concerned his invitation to get out of that house was welcomed. Once we were outside he says, "Johnny would you go with me to my boss's house, he has had a stroke, besides that, before he became my boss he like you was and international musician traveling with the international singer Roger Whittaker". Roger Whittaker was well-known for his baritone singing voice and his trademark whistling ability, he was indeed a very popular performer.

I told the man I would like to go with him, but I didn't want to get separated from the folks I had come with. The man whose name I learned as Bob said, "don't worry Johnny" we'll be back in plenty of time. So off we rode into the dusk of evening. The car was an old Austin/Morris, with the steering wheel on the right side. After traveling for some time through a maze of small English lanes, we finally arrive in front of a quaint English house. As we approached the screened in porch Bob rang the doorbell, that's when I noticed the silhouette figure of a man. On entering the home, there stood, the most impressive fellow I had ever seen. His physical presence was statuesque in both his demeanor and features. Bob introduced me to him in the most unexpected manner. "Nigel, this is Johnny, he's a musician like you and I brought him here to tell you how to get saved"! Bob's introduction caught me off guard, and his choice of words made the man stand taller as if to brace himself for whatever was coming next. When Bob spoke his name, even his name evoked masculinity, "Nigel" … this man was a man's man. As I sat down across from him, he gave me a welcoming smile as if to imply, "nice to meet you". But beneath his smile I sensed a tremendous heaviness. In his eyes I saw a void, which I would have described as hopelessness. He listened intently and without interruption as I gave a brief testimony, which I shortened by cutting to the chase and simply ask him, "Nigel... do you want to be saved"? He didn't hesitate but with a voice of forlorn, longingly and loud..." cried, "YES", as if begging, "please, please help me". Quickly I fell on my knees beside him, as Nigel knelt with me. There we were, this trio of men crying out before The Almighty and Gracious God to come and help Nigel. God responded!

Nigel gave his heart to The Lord that night. Then he told me his sad story. "Men" he said, "just before you arrived. I had arranged for my wife and children to go to her mother's. I had written my last words in a note to her and told her that I couldn't live with this paralysis in my body caused by this stroke any longer. I told myself I was doing this for her and the children. I wanted them to go on without me, they didn't need a cripple in their lives. The truth men, if I'm honest, it was my pride. I felt too proud to live this way. This was my mindset just before you rang my door. I had already loaded my revolver and was ready to pull the trigger, when I heard the ringing. Something or someone told me to wait and I'm so thankful I did. I know now my life still has purpose and that God has something for me".

After saying goodbye to both men that night, a day or so later, I was on the plane headed back to the states. While I sat there watching the plane ascend higher into the sky I repented to The Lord.

"Dear Lord forgive me of my poor conduct and attitude. Dear Father, I had come to Wales with a spirit of arrogance and pride and it blinded me as to what your will was for me and what You my God could do".

In my contrition God spoke to me sternly, *"John remember this and never forget it. No matter when or where I might lead you, never forget, I have my reasons. My son always be mindful that everything I do in your life has my purposes in mind".*

I made a covenant with The Lord on the plane that very day, to never forget this lesson, that nothing is too small or insignificant, when God is in it.

Later I would think of Nigel as one of those" Rocks" which God promised we would save that day at "The Tree" when he called me to preach.

Troublesome times awaited when I returned to Harvest Chapel. A few days after my return, my secretary Francis came to my office door, "Brother Johnny, you have to see this".

Though I was in a very melancholy mood concerning the state of things which I found after my return from Wales, I went with her. As we walked toward the preschool the unusual sound grew louder. What I saw were birds. Hundreds of what appeared to be sparrows, roosting in the branches of a big Oak tree behind the school. They were loud. I noticed Judy and the students standing on the back porch laughing, as some of the children had their hands cupped over their ears. These birds were noisy. As I took in this unusual scene, the words of Raymond came to mind, "Brother Johnny, keep your eyes on the sparrow". The words from the old Gospel hymn came to me as I returned to my office.

"Why should I feel discouraged, why should the shadows come?
Why should my heart be lonely and long for heaven and home?
When Jesus is my portion. My constant Friend is He:
His eye is on the sparrow, and I know He watches me;
His eye is on the sparrow, and I know He watches me.[lxvii]

Judy and I left our first love, Harvest Chapel, soon after that day. All that we had accomplished was in the rearview mirror. I left behind, and I never looked back.

I would have probably not had thought about leaving without a fight, had it not been for the invitation I received from a group of believers in Idaho. I had preached for this congregation sometime before, so we were not strangers. Their offer to be their pastor was more than I could resist which included a house and salary. I took this offer but not just for those reasons. I also saw it as my way out of the troubles taking place at Harvest Chapel. It was hard for me to do, for I had a great fondness for the people and what I had witness God do over the past three years. I didn't want to taint the memories of all that, so I walked away.

Soon Judy, the children and I found ourselves in Emmett, Idaho. We didn't arrive their alone, soon Francis, Lola, Jessie and Laura, and other families from Harvest Chapel followed. They too weren't ready to let go of the ministry we all had together at Harvest Chapel. The new congregation seemed a bit concerned about this entourage which arrived with me. Yet God did a quick work, through all of this. This church was not entirely the same group I had met before. This new church had just recently been formed around some very enthusiastic charismatic individuals. They had no permanent facilities but were holding meeting in The Moose Lodge. When I told them about my Jacob's Well ministry, they decided that was the model they wanted to pursue. We soon located a very large facility in the middle of Emmet. My Harvest Chapel team new the drill and they opened the doors to a first-class dining facility. The new Jacob's Well, had an ice cream parlor, poolroom, video game room, a log cabin play house in one corner for the toddlers. It had banquet rooms, full commercial kitchen, a beautiful dining area and a huge stage for live entertainment.

Our new Jacob's Well soon became the talk of the town and people came from as far away as Boise to dine and enjoy the weekly gospel entertainment. Everyone in the congregation was excited. On Sundays, we were closed and had our church services in the main dining room.

Our famous, "all you can eat biscuits and gravy", were still a big hit with all the working guys. It was at breakfast time that a local pastor introduced himself to me. He told me he had a congregation meeting in his garage at home. I ask him why don't we merge the two congregations and we could share the preaching. When he asked how would we handle the finances I told him we would take up the offering with, his instructions to have his congregation earmark their offerings. It worked out beautifully for months, then God spoke, "Idaho is not where I want you John, I want you to go back to Alabama and wait for my instructions". I made my plans, then told my congregation I was leaving and ask them if they would consider the other preacher to be their pastor. They all agreed to my instructions and from the two groups, one church was born. I purchased a school bus from a Baptist church, then took out all the seats except the front two rows. I built a bulk-head between the seats and the storage area and what furniture we didn't sell, we loaded in the bus and headed to Alabama.

My family in Alabama were, to say the least, surprised to see us. In just a few days my brother Ken and his wife Ernestine offered me a maintenance man's job in Huntsville, Alabama where my brother was stationed as an Alabama State trooper and where they were managing this apartment complex. There we were with a three-bedroom apartment and salary.

It was a little handyman work and painting. The rest of my time I spent studying, writing songs and waiting on a Word from The Lord.

The Lord finally spoke one day while I was writing a letter. My first intentions were to write to some friends and then I found myself writing to a Nation.

In the letter, I was imploring our countrymen to call their congressman and senators, demanding that they work diligently to overturn the 1973 Roe vs. Wade, a landmark decision by the United States Supreme Court on the issue of abortion. The Court had ruled 7–2 that a right to privacy under the Due Process Clause of the 14th Amendment extended to a woman's decision to have an abortion, but that this right must be balanced against the state's interests in regulating abortions: protecting women's health and protecting the potentiality of human life. In a nutshell, the law allowed the murder of the unborn human babies.[lxviii]

I had been studying this issue for some time and was strongly opposed. I petitioned all those who would read my letter to get actively involved in pushing back against this legalized murder. If you remember abortion was recommended at my birth, not in those specific terms, but when my mother's doctor told my dad he couldn't save us both.

I created a letterhead for my letter. I titled it NationaLight Ministries International. Though it wasn't a legal 501c3 non-profit corporation. I felt it was necessary to give the letter a larger perspective. NationaLight would later become a registered 501c3 non-profit corporation ministry in the State of Washington.

When I finished writing the letter God spoke to me, "I want you to share this letter to every major newspaper in the country and all the major magazines and periodicals". I did as God asked! I found their addresses in a publication registry from my local library and sent copies of the letter to more than four hundred editors. Then God said, "I want you to send a copy to your Senator and the preachers, James Robinson and Jimmy Swaggart". He then told me to hand carry a copy to the PTL Club in Charlotte, North Carolina which was the ministry headquarters of Jim and Tammy Bakker.

The first part was easy, but how to get to PTL was a different story. I was acquainted with some folks who had moved to North Carolina and worked at the PTL ministry. I called them and told them what The Lord had ask me to do. They invited me to come and stay with them and they would try to help me get an audience with Jim Bakker.

That same week, I told the pastor of the Antioch Baptist Church, where we had been attending of my plans. He asks me to share my story with the His church on Sunday. The congregation was moved by my sincerity and passion on the subject. After the service a gentleman approached me, he told me he was an underwater diver with NASA and that he helped to train the astronauts on how to move in a weightless environment, by doing tasks underwater. This is how they trained for weightlessness for outer space. He told me he also flew a private plane and would like to fly me at no charge to Charlotte and that is exactly what happened. The folks in Charlotte did as they promised. I didn't get an opportunity to talk to Jim Bakker, although I did get the letter to his right-hand man at the PTL Club ministry.

I had taken my guitar with me on the trip, and the folks ask me if I would perform for the young people that evening at their church. The hosts of the youth activity that evening were disc jockeys from a local radio station which by the way was owned by the Jimmy Swaggart Ministry, WAME radio. When they heard my reasons for being in the area, they invited me to be a guest on their ten o'clock morning talk show the following day.

As I shared my message the phone lines in the station lit up. After the program, there was a fellow who had been listening to my message and had called asking to meet me. His name, Alan Christenbury, a WWII Veteran of Pearl Harbor. In fact, both he and his wife, a nurse, were there on that day. President Franklin Roosevelt called the unprovoked attack on Pearl Harbor a "date which will live in infamy," in a famous address to the nation.

Alan ask if I would stay until the evening and be a guest on his program which aired at eight o'clock. I of course said yes, because my mission was to tell my story as often as I could to anyone who would listen. At the close of the program Alan turn to me and ask, "Johnny could you move to Charlotte and cohost my show"? Alan felt the program needed a spiritual element to it. I told him I must first discuss it with my wife and I would pray about it, and I would let him know.

The flight back to Judy and the children was a blessing. I had so much to share with her. After I told her about the invitation, she encouraged me to go and get things set up, then come back for her and the kids. I called Alan and told him I accepted his offer. I told my pilot friend and he flew me back once again, so Judy could have the car.

Our radio show was called "Let's Talk Common Sense America". Alan had borrowed the idea from a revolutionary war pamphlet named "Common Sense", written by Thomas Paine advocating independence from Great Britain to the people in the Thirteen Colonies. This was the beginning of the American Revolution. Our program, "Let's Talk Common Sense America", was encouraging our listeners to demand transparency in government and a return to constitutional law. [lxix]

However, our listeners were more enthusiastic than the radio managers, for after several weeks they finally pulled the plug on our program. They felt we were too political and our message was inviting a tax revolt. It was true I had been advocating that Americans stop filing their income tax statements and if for just one season we could have a national solidarity by prohibiting our employers from withholding our tax money from our checks we could pressure the government to hear our just cause and stop the killing of the unborn.

Of course, it was a complete failure, for the IRS were scaring companies and workers, that if they did anything of this sort, they would go to jail. It was just more than the radio station or the ministry behind them could support. They didn't want to be involved with this type of rhetoric. I understood.

Fortunately for me I had my family with me, and I had been working during the daytime at the same church where I had performed on my first visit to Charlotte. The pastor gave me the maintenance job at the church and Judy was teaching in the Christian school, so our children could attend tuition free. When the school year ended, Judy ask if we could return to California.

We had been gone for almost two years and she was missing her older sons Gary and Tracy. I was really enjoying the church. The pastor had given me an adult Sunday School which was growing in attendance. I was also playing in the worship band and doing some occasional preaching for the pastor. To add to this, I was having great fellowship with the men of the church. There were so many reasons for me wanting to stay. "Yes, I told her, we will go back". I decided it was Judy's turn to choose what we were going to do next.

So very soon we were back on the old Route 66/highway 40 to California.

All went well until we came to Needles, California. It was so hot that we were feeding our fair skin red headed baby girl, popsicles and cooling her down with ice packs. By the time we arrived into Barstow, we were exhausted. I had only enough money to get a motel which had a very inviting swimming pool, which we all took advantage of immediately. We had some hamburgers for dinner and I figured I had enough money for gas and food to get us to Sacramento where we would stay with our dear friends Jerry and Lana who had been members of Harvest Chapel.

As we were packing to leave the next morning, I noticed that the desert heat had caused the recaps on my front tires to bubble and they were tires waiting for a flat to happen. At the tire shop they said I needed a hundred bucks to replace them. I called my brother Joe who was now living and working in California to wire me the money. Soon we were on our way and safe in our friend's house. Francis my former secretary who had returned to California (along with all the other folks who had gone to Idaho with us) had arranged for me to preach in Stockton at the church where I bought the pews. While there, I learned that the old pastor Brother Reynolds was very ill with throat problems. His wife, Sister Reynolds ask me if I would come and be the pastor. I told her I would come, but I would not take the pastors position, but I would do the preaching and pastoral duties till He recovered, if they could find me a house.

They called the next day to tell me their churches neighbor, who was an elder at the Church of Christ, said his church owned a house across the street from their church and they would love to have a Christian family living there.

We lived in the house at 641 North Lillian Avenue for approximately six years. We also started a Christian School at Brother Ardley's church, Windsor Christian Academy. Judy taught K thru sixth grades. I taught seventh thru twelfth grades. We used a self-paced program and all our students performed exceptionally well on their annual national assessment exams, scoring higher than the national average. When summer came we had just closed school for our third year.

Judy had accepted the director's position at the West Lane Foursquare Church preschool. For some summer work, I started a lawn care and gardening company which I called "Mays and sons". Our business was blessed with the help of one of our student's parents who help me land the gardening contract with the American Savings Banks. It was a lucrative contract but almost more work than my boys and I could do. So, when Judy told her boss Pastor Curtis Holland who had ask her if I could do the lawns at his church. At first, I balked at the idea, but later relented when he agreed to find someone as soon as possible. One morning while attending the needs of the church, I noticed Pastor Curtis and his staff pulling into the parking lot.

Getting out of his car, he walked up to me and said, "your wife tells me you and your sons and daughter are musicians and you lead worship at your church, I was wondering if you would come and take over my worship service." I thought to myself, "there goes my wife letting the cat out of the bag again, first the lawns and now the music".

Again, I balked and gave him the excuse that I had visited his church and saw the kind of worship they had. I told him my boys and I had a style of our own when it came to worship ministry and it might not be enjoyable to his congregation. I told him it might be to different. In his church they had a grand piano and organ player with a robed church choir. My sons and I used piano, guitar, bass and drums, and that we probably wouldn't fit in. He asked if I would just give it a try. I told him I would do it for a few weeks and then he would need to find someone else. I spoke to the folks at our old church that we were discontinuing the school, that we were going to move from the house on Lillian, and I would be doing the worship at the church where Judy was working. They gave us their blessings and thanked us for our years of service. It was a sad parting because I loved and appreciated them so much. They had helped my family in so many ways.

I remembered later where I first met Pastor Curtis Holland, it was on a softball field. I was umpiring for the city of Stockton recreation league and there was to be a championship game for the fast pitch church league and they wanted me to umpire it. I hated to do it, but I had to toss the Foursquare teams catcher in the second inning for cursing. I had warned him in the first inning that I would not allow it and if it happened again he was gone. I remember the pastor apologizing for the players bad sportsmanship.

When he was asking me to come and do his music he must not have put two and two together. Anyway, as it turned out I stayed much longer than a month in fact I was there for three years and came on the staff as full-time associate, without the pastor ever officially hiring me.

What happened is I heard a word from the Lord that he wanted me in the church full time. I felt God lead me to make an offer to Pastor Curtis. Here's what I told him. "Pastor, I want to come on your staff for six months with no pay. All I ask for is an office, and if in six months you think I'm earning my way, then the church can start paying me". Well exactly six months later he walked into my office and laid a check on my desk. I got paid every week after that for two years plus a few months.

It was a great time for my family at West Lane and we made many lifelong friends, of course including Brother Curtis and his wife Lola. I still preach for him on occasion in their fellowship which is now in Bakersfield.

My leaving the Stockton church came as result of God leading me to have my own church. Pastor Curtis and I discussed this, and he had arranged that I meet with the district superintendent. At that time, Foursquare church was looking for church planters. My wife and I had visited her mother who had moved from Lake Tahoe to Gardnerville, Nevada to be close to her daughter Barbara and her family. Judy's oldest son Tracy had also bought a home there. In 1990 there was a real-estate boom and people were moving to that area from as far away as Los Angeles, to retire or find work in the construction of all these new homes. New businesses were also coming into town because of the population growth. We really liked the area. It was the high desert, sitting in view of the Sierra Nevada mountains with

Carson City the State Capitol only sixteen miles away and Reno with the international airport only thirty minutes from there. Perfect climate, perfect location.

When I sat down with the superintendent and as he was talking about all the places they were thinking of starting new churches, I was thinking about Gardnerville, so I ask him, "what do you think about Gardnerville"? He jumped up from his desk, pulled a paper from his brief case. Pointing to the top of his list, there was Gardnerville, Nevada. "I don't know why I didn't mention that right away", he said excitedly. I told him if the district would give me at least six months support I would go do it. Because I had great references from Pastor Curtis Holland and he like my resume, he agreed to financial support for a year, two thousand a month for the first six months and one thousand for the remaining six months.

So off we went. The first week we looked for a place to live which would also be large enough to hold meetings. We found a new ranch style home on Centerville Road. I opened the church office in a strip mall downtown on Highway 365. We put a sign in the front yard "Carson Valley Foursquare Church meets here". I put my picture and placed a press release with the local newspaper, with the headline, "Carson Valley Foursquare Church Announcing New Pastor", giving the appearance of an already established church. I was sure to include location and times of our services. The first Sunday we had twenty-eight people in the living room, the next week we had to use the foyer and by the third week the kitchen. We were using the master bedroom for children's church. Judy, Libby and I stayed in the back two bedrooms. During this time, all our boys were on their own.

Robert was working at the California Department of Corrections as a Correctional Officer. My son John who had come to live with us while we were on Lillian and had graduated from our Christian School was now a Marine. Christopher was working in the grocery store in Stockton and staying with his schoolmate Robert.

So here the three of us are back to work for Jesus and enjoying God's blessing. The new church was growing fast, when the letter from Douglas County came with news that I was in violation of a zoning law for having a church in a private residence. The letter instructed me to contact the Douglas County Planning Department, and if I continued to hold church meetings in the house I could face incarceration.

I went to the Planning Department and talked to a long-haired Berkeley graduate who was the head of planning. He repeated to me what he had written in the letter. I ask him to show me the zoning law which he claimed I was in violation of. As I read the law aloud, he listened. "If a residency is being used exclusively for religious purposes there must be an application for a use permit and then approved by the County Supervisors", or something to that effect. What caught my attention as I read was the word "exclusively". I ask the planner, "what does the word exclusively mean to you? He told me he was not in the position to define the meaning of words in the law. I said to him, "isn't this the zoning law that you say I'm violating, and yet you don't know the meaning of the words that make up this law and you a university graduate. Are you telling me you don't know what the word exclusively means"?

That's when he said he would have to consult with the District Attorney.

I said, "we'll tell him this is my opinion, "the word exclusively as best I can remember from my Bible College days means; when something is restricted or limited to say person or group, or area of concern like my having Bible studies and a gospel singing in my home". You see sir I don't live in a church, this residence is my home, and I invite friends of the Carson Valley Foursquare Church which has its business and pastor's office in a commercially zoned strip mall on highway 365. I'm sure you know the place. I tell you what, you have the District Attorney call me if he wants to talk about this issue any further, for as far as I am concerned I'm within my rights according to the wording of your own law".

When I got back to the office I prepared a press release and took it to the editor of the local paper. When the paper was published the headline read, "Douglas County playing hardball with the Carson Valley Foursquare Church".

Before the sun went down I got that call from the District Attorney wanting me to have a meeting with his office, planning and the fire chief. After that meeting, the County offered me a year to relocate my church, which I promptly agreed to, because little did they know that God had given me favor with the Washoe Indian Tribe.

One of my elders in the church, was Brother Delaney, the former Chief of the Washoe Tribe. God used this dear man to sort out the politics between the tribe and the church. With his influence we negotiated a lease for a beautiful and spacious lodge building on the reservation overlooking the Carson River. For the next two years the church grew spiritually and numerically.

Brother Dale and Randa Williams, who had been with me at the Foursquare Church in Stockton, brought their family to help me evangelize. Dale has always been like a son to me. My dear friend Pastor Earl Crouchley and his family drove for several weeks from Sacramento to help, they finally moved to Gardnerville. Many families from the town and the reservation began to attend. I couldn't have done this without them.

In the fall of 1992, while attending a ministerial luncheon with a preacher from the Church of Christ in Carson City, he told me he had just returned from Moscow, Russia. He said there was a great revival going on there and the opportunity to minister was wide open since Perestroika, a political movement for reformation within the Communist Party of the Soviet Union that had started in the 1980s.

This movement is widely associated with Soviet leader Mikhail Gorbachev the one and the same whom President Ronald Reagan called for; "Mr. Gorbachev tear down this wall". Not only had the wall which had divided West and East Berlin since 1961, but now the iron curtain had fallen off the nation to give open opportunity to preach the gospel.[lxx]

The preacher then connected me with a group of evangelists who were based in Branson, Missouri. I called them and ask them if I could join them in Russia. They were excited about me coming, especially when they learned I was a musician. After my first mission trip with them, I couldn't rid myself of the longing for Russia. I knew God was calling me to Russia. So, after a couple of months I went back to the country. After this second mission I knew I needed to make a choice.

Since the Carson Valley Foursquare Church was established and I felt it was in good hands, I decided in the middle of 1993, to resign my church. I had peace about leaving. I knew the mission God had given me to plant a church and to establish leaders had been accomplished. There were times later that I would feel I may have left to soon, but the burning in my heart for the Russian people had overwhelmed me.

For the next twelve years, I ministered with an "Apostolic Anointing", traveling from the far north of Russia to the Black Sea. I crusaded in St. Petersburg extensively. In schools, colleges, hospitals, orphanages. I preached in Russian prisons, and on the streets. I planted a church in Kolomna, Russia and ordained the pastor. My teams distributed tens of thousands of Bibles. So many were being saved and baptized. There were healing services and deliverances. During that twelve-year period, I made twenty-two mission trips to the former USSR. However, during that same period, not only was I preaching in Russia, but I was also doing preaching and evangelistic outreaches, around the world and across America.

I preached considerably in the Pacific Northwest. I went to visit my friend Neil Parks who was living in Richland, Washington at the time. He introduced me to a local disc jockey, Ed Daily, who also had a weekly television program on a Trinity Broadcast Network affiliate. I performed on his program. After the telecast the station manager ask me to lunch. Joining us was a pastor who was also the regional director of the Foursquare churches. Two things happened at that lunch. I was invited to start my own weekly television program and the pastor ask me to help him out in a Foursquare church in Baker, Oregon. I produced and recorded in six-month intervals, the TV program, which would take me two weeks in real time. I called it the "Homeward Bound Show". The program aired for two years bringing the gospel in music and preaching to the region.

The results of the Baker Foursquare church were bitter sweet. Bitter, I could not save the church from closing. Sweet, I made lifelong relationship that resulted in powerful and effective ministries. From that church came Paul and Diane Thorne who became partners with me in my missionary organization Nationalight Ministries International which is a State of Washington non-profit. They also provided personal support to me by opening doors and with generous financial support. Their daughter Nicole and her husband Juan are the creators of our website at (http://www.nationalight.net/).

Joining my Nationalight Ministries team from the Baker church, were two amazing musicians, Carla Bailey and George Rau. George and Carla are both ordained ministers with Nationalight. They have travelled with me to both Europe and Africa. George is now a pastor and Carla is an evangelist.

Ed Daily and his brother Ted, would eventually buy a radio station near Tacoma, Washington. They invited me to come and help them with the advertisement and support of the station. While I was with them my friend Ken Gaub ask me to visit him in Yakima, Washington. Ken has taught me so much about the unlimited possibilities of faith. During my visit with him he told me he had taken liberty to book me into several of the area churches. Two of those churches became great partners with me in my ministry.

The church in Thorp, Washington introduced me to two amazing couples; Jim and Ellen Breeze and Jim and Peggy Coble. The contributions these folks made to my ministry have been invaluable. They traveled the world with me, provided personal support and opened many doors. They too served on the board of NationaLight. Peggy serves as the Secretary/Treasurer. She and Randy Murieen, pioneered our Kenya outreaches. Every one of these folks have played an integral part in the ongoing ministries of our organization for which I am truly grateful.

The second church was in Everette, Washington. It was an Open Bible Church, pastored by David and Joanne Eggebratten. David is a talented musician and songwriter. He also owned a recording studio and printshop, both were in his home. They would invite me to stay with them and allowed me to record several gospel albums and print a gospel tract.

The travels in my lifetime gave me so many wonderful relationships with God's people, it had also taken me to thirty nations, islands and provinces and all fifty states of our great nation. Preaching and traveling entirely on faith and most of the time away from my Judy, which was the hardest part of all. There would be short periods of time when I would be home with her. During those times, I would find some odd job as I waited for the next mission door to open and it would. Then we would say our goodbyes and I would be off.

There was only one time when she came abroad, to be in London with me. I had planted a church in London among the Russian brethren I knew from my early ministry in Russia, whom had fled to England seeking asylum. Judy came and ministered with me, teaching the women how to organize a Sunday School, and how to teach children the Bible. Together we took a trip to Paris, which had always been a dream of hers. However, when it came time for our train to travel through what is known as the "Chunnel", she was having second thoughts. The Channel Tunnel is a rail tunnel linking London and Paris beneath the English Channel at the Strait of Dover.

We had a great time in Paris though the weather was cold and for me just being with her was a great joy. We also visited Ireland, where I introduced her to many of my friends. It saddened me when she returned to the states later and left me alone in London.

If I tried to tell you all I have witnessed, it would be impossible. But I will tell some of the most memorable works of the mercy and grace of God I encountered.[lxxi]

Chapter 16

After returning from London I had spent most of the that year traveling hundreds of miles performing evangelistic meetings from Corinth, New York in the east to Salem, Oregon in the west and many stops in between.

I wanted to share with you a miracle story that happened as I was traveling back to Gardnerville. It was a hot July day in northern Nevada as I traveled westbound on Highway 80 toward Lovelock. The drive home in my old Caddy had been very entertaining, watching the dirt devils dancing across the high desert floor like baby tornadoes. I loved my Cadillac, a gift from a dear brother in Christ, Joe Fry. If you remember after three years of ministry and planting the church in Gardnerville, God had led me to resign the church and go to the missionary field to Russia. However, the one challenge every missionary evangelist usually has, to be able to go into countries like Russia, is the funding. My method for fund raising was to go from church to church and tell the story of the work and vision, which God had given me. That is why I am on the highway today and in the Caddy at the time that this miracle takes place. After thousands of miles, the Caddy began showing some wear; in fact, it was on this hot summer's day that I could have used the air conditioning, but the air condition pump had stopped working. So here I am driving along with the windows down, enjoying the beauty of the high desert of Nevada, watching the winds do their acrobatics in the hot desert sand. Here is something I have learned about God. He is never late. Oh, I know you wonder sometimes if he is going to be there or not, and the challenge to your faith gets awful fierce. Yet I have found he always arrives just in time, neither too late nor too early. It is as the scripture says, God has a time and season for everything.

"To everything there is a season, a time for every purpose under heaven". Ecclesiastes 3: 1.

Suddenly, and to my surprise, the largest dirt devil I ever saw appears in the median dividing the highway's westbound traffic from the eastbound. As I watched, it appeared to be coming straight for the Caddy. I thought, "Oh no, all that dirt is going to blow right inside my car in a matter of just moments." So, I started to slow the Caddy to save it from what I thought was to be a terrible mess. "I hope that dirt devil turns and misses me". The next thing I saw was shocking. It was not the wind creating the twister but a car turning repeatedly over like a giant fumbled football, coming down the median, and suddenly, the car stopped. Then like a WWII war film, boom, a great mushroom of dirt and dust exploded, swallowing up the wreckage. I came quickly to a stop on the shoulder of the highway, paralyzed with surprise. Leaving the Caddy, I ran toward the mushroom only to meet a woman appearing out from the great ball of dust, screaming, "Help me, help me, and help my husband." I ran past her and into the cloud of dust, I gave no thought at all as to what I would find. There in the eye of the mushroom cloud, the vehicle sat cockeyed, broken, pointing in the opposite direction from which it had been coming. The fan under the hood was still running. As I came to the driver's side of the car, I saw the body, a male, the husband I assumed, hanging out of the window with one leg twisted like a hemp rope, snagged by the steering wheel, dangling along the tilted side of the car, his head near the ground. Moving entirely on reflex, I reached through the window and tried to pry his foot loose from the

271

bent steering wheel that had snagged his body. As I pulled and twisted, I could feel and hear the bones and tissue crackling, making a sickening sound. Then it happened; suddenly, he was free, but I was unprepared for the weight of his body as he slid down the side of the crumbled wreckage, and his body began to coil to the ground. Panicked, I dropped to my knees beside the man only to hear the screams of the wife who now had appeared in view again, screaming, "Help me, help my husband." As I looked back to the man, now beneath my hands, my heart sank, and I heard myself think, "Oh my God, he is a goner, he is dead." I thought, "Oh, my God, I hope she didn't hear me." I turned to look at the wife, her hands now holding her face, and I could see in her eyes she had drawn the same conclusion I had, her husband was dead!

Above me, looking over my shoulder and with shock on his face, a truck driver stood behind me. He had been following the car when it veered into the median. "Did you call for help?" I asked. "I tried to reach them on my radio, but nobody has answered," his eyes never leaving the scene of the dead man beneath my hands; his face confirming what I was witnessing as well. I turn to the dead man and I began to pray, "Lord, have mercy on his soul." The thought did occur to me to pray for a miracle, but my faith could only speak for mercy on his soul. I continued to pray over the man when I heard the voice of another. I looked up toward the voice, it was a second driver, saying, "I got hold of 911. Help will be here soon." He too stared at the broken body. As the trio watched me pray, the miracle happened. The man awoke. Like coming out of restful sleep, he woke, his eyes shining with life. The wound in his head stopped bleeding as he spoke in a foreign language. His wife, surprised by the sound of his voice, cried out with a strong insistence in her voice, "Speak English," she said. "Speak English." The next word I heard as the man looked up to me was, "Help me sit up." As he pushed himself from the ground, a painful grimace came across his face; then he fell back. "Help me up," he said. "I think you had better try just lying still, help is on its way," I told him. The second driver spoke, "I have some water and towels in the truck." As he turned to leave, I looked back at the man. "You have been in a bad accident. I think it's best if you do not try to move." But he insisted on sitting up, so I said, "Do whatever you think you can." While he sat, I felt the presence of yet another. The state troopers had arrived and immediately took charge. He asked a question or two of all who were present, and I told him my story and the drivers confirming everything from their perspective, the wife still too traumatized to speak. Then as quickly as it all happened, it seemed I was back in the Caddy, back on the road. I drove a mile or two and watched the ambulance speeding down the eastbound side of Highway 80 toward the scene of the accident. I began to relax as I thought about God's miracle power. The miracle was finished, and I began to praise the Lord for His perfect timing. Not a second too soon or too late, God was there at the right place, at the right time with the prayer of the righteous, with the prayer of faith. Amen!

I wanted to share with you how I came to Ireland. In the year of 1995, I was back home in Gardnerville, catching up on some much-needed rest. So here I am enjoying my home with Judy, it was just what the doctor ordered. It was also in that same year that I had received a Word from The Lord, "to go to Ireland".

The problem was I didn't know anyone from Ireland, so I was waiting for God's directions as to how I was to get into Ireland. In Proverbs chapter eighteen and verse sixteen the Bible reads; *"A man's gift makes room for him, and brings him before great men"*.

Too often this verse is misunderstood because people think of the word "gift" mentioned in the verse, as talent or special anointing. In fact, this word "gift" is referring to the thing which you are giving or presenting. The pulpit commentary says it this way, "the term gift" here signifies the present which duty or friendship offers to one whom one wishes to please. This paves a man's way to a great person's presence. Brings him before great men. The Oriental custom of offering suitable gifts to one in authority, when a favor or an audience is desired, is here alluded to; "So the Magi, brought gifts to the newborn King at Bethlehem".[lxxii]

You might ask then, "what great gift would I need to give, to always have God perfect direction and His perfect will"? The answer is, *"without faith it's impossible to please God"*. When you give your faith to God, this gift brings you before the King of kings. The action behind this giving of your faith is found here.

"And so, dear brothers and sisters, I plead with you to give your bodies to God because of all He has done for you. Let them be a living and holy sacrifice, the kind He will find acceptable. This is truly the way to worship Him. Don't copy the behavior and customs of this world, but let God transform you into a new person by changing the way you think. Then you will learn to know God's will for

you, which is good and pleasing and perfect". Romans 12:1-2 NLT.

There it is…! When you present your life by your faith as a gift to The Lord, He then in turn will takes charge of your life and give you directions. Your place is to remain before Him and the result is the knowledge of God's Will and all that is pleasing to The Lord will be known by you.

"My sheep listen to my voice; I know them, and they follow me". John10:27

With that said, one day my friend Steve stopped by my home and ask if I would take a ride with him to Fallon, Nevada. He mentioned to me he had some business with a man there. I said to him that it sounds great and that by the way, there was a fellow in Fallon that I needed to see and perhaps if Steve didn't mind taking the time, maybe we could drop by. "Who do you want to see Brother Johnny"? I told him, "his name is Mickey". Steve began to laugh, "you're kidding, that's the same man I'm going to see"! Immediately I knew that God was going to do something powerful that day.

We arrived at Mickey's house only to find he was not there. His wife however asks us to come in and wait for him. "Brother Johnny, please let me make you and Steve a cup of coffee, Mick will be right back. Then she excused herself saying, "I have a couple of ladies in the dining room, we're just finishing our Bible Study then we will join you".

As we drank our coffee I couldn't help but hear the ladies talking, and by the sound of their voices I knew one of them was Irish. You can spot the Irish lilt easily. When the ladies joined us, I said to the woman, "you're Irish aren't you"? She told me she was born and raised there and that she and her husband had come to Nevada to work in the mining industry. I mentioned to her that God had spoken to me about going to Ireland, but I didn't know a soul there. She then wrote down a number and gave me the name of her brother in law saying, "Give David a call, I know he'd be glad to help you".

When I came home I told Judy what had happened, then I immediately called Ireland. A man answered, and I asked;

"Hello, is this David Robinson?

David: "It is, who am I speaking with"

"My name is Johnny Mays, I ran into your sister in-law in Nevada and she gave me your number".

David: "Okay, what can I do for you"?

"Well, I don't really know, I'm just calling to tell you that God has told me to come to Ireland. I've never been there and you're the only Irishman I know, except your sister in law.

David: "Who are you coming with"?

"No one just myself".

David: "What organization are you with"?

"No, it's just me, I'm coming by myself". (there was a long pause) then God said to me, "tell David the Holy Ghost is sending you"!

"David...the Holy Ghost is sending me"!

David: "That's it, that's what we need in Ireland, The Holy Ghost" …he was almost shouting… "when will you be coming"?

"I don't know yet, but as soon as The Lord provides I will call you".

We chatted for a while then I hung up, praising God for the open door. Now I must wait for the rest of the miracle.

Within a few weeks I was back on the road and back in Salem, Oregon. I had just been in this area a couple months before. I booked a room and after a short nap, I was feeling a bit hungry. While pondering which fast food joint I wanted to dine at, I was reminded of a couple I had met in the church where I preached the last time I was here. I remembered the lady giving me their phone number and telling me, "Brother Johnny, if you're ever through here again call us and we will fix you a home cooked meal". I remembered I had put the slip of paper in my wallet. When I looked, to my amazement it was there. I called the number and the lady answered.

I found their ranch style home in the country, which I would describe as a modest house, nothing fancy. They welcomed me in and we dined. We must have remained sitting at the dinner table a couple hours as I gave testimonies to my travels and the mighty things that God had done. Realizing how late it was getting I ask to be excused and thanked them for the wonderful dinner and evening. It was at that moment that I noticed Lauralee give her husband Ben, a folded slip of paper. He then hands it to me and said, "Brother Johnny, we want to sow into your ministry". I thanked them for their generosity. Just as I was walking out the door Ben said, "by the way, you won't have any problem cashing that, just go to my bank".

Driving back to my hotel my curiosity got the best of me because of Ben's departing remark. I turned the interior light on and unfolded the check and to my amazement the amount written on the check was, ten thousand dollars. I couldn't believe my eyes. There must be a mistake. Back in my room I immediately called, and Ben answered. Still flabbergasted I said;

"I'm sorry to call so late Ben, but I just had too".

Ben: "What's wrong"?

"Listen Ben, I'm sure you've made a mistake on your check".

Ben: "What's the problem"?

"Do you realize that you made your check out for… Ben, it's for ten thousand dollars, I spoke, nervously...chuckling.

Ben: "No it's not a mistake Brother Johnny, that's what we felt led to give".

"Brother, I couldn't go to the bank with a personal check of ten thousand dollars, remember I'm from out of state, I just wouldn't be comfortable".

Ben: "Not a problem, I'll meet you there about ten o'clock and we'll get it all taken care of for you.

The next morning, I was waiting outside when Ben arrives. Once we are in the bank everyone begins to speak to Ben, it's good morning, nice day, how can we help you Ben. Ben

278

smiled, "I need you to help Johnny, to cash his check, I think it's good".

The teller looks it over, looks at Ben with a smile, then asks me to endorse it. "How would you like your money Mr. Mays"?

Still standing there numbed by this enormous blessing, I tried to remain calm, "maybe six thousand in traveler's checks…the rest in large bills"? "Not a problem, just have a seat, grab a coffee and I'll take care of this for you".

As we waited Ben asked, "what are you going to do with your money Brother Johnny"? I told him that thanks to you and your wife, when I get back home, I am going directly to the nearest travel agent and purchase a ticket to Belfast, Northern Ireland. I then told Ben the story of the calling God had given me for Ireland. As we leave the bank Ben invites me to visit his factory which was just a few blocks from the bank. I was very impressed with Ben's story of how he and Lauralee had started their plastic extruding business in their garage. Ben had built two extruders and in time they built their factory building, and employed several people, "God has truly blessed us", he said. Then Ben ask me, "Johnny, how do you feel about me going to Ireland with you"? I responded that would be awesome, I've got lots of money I'll buy you a ticket". He laughed and told me he would be buying his own ticket. On my first trip to Ireland, God gave me the call, a contact, the finances and now a partner in ministry. Remember, *"A man's gift makes room for him"*. Many doors were opened in Ireland over the next twenty plus years.

Two important stories I want to share. The first begins with Mrs. McGuigan whom I met in a "wee" church in the village of Bessbrook. She was a recent convert. I say that meaning that though she had been a Catholic all her life and still attends Mass at the Chapel, she gave me her testimony of having a "born again experience".

Mrs. McGuigan ask me if I would speak to her son Christy who was a musician. Christy and I met, and we hit it off immediately. He told me he had been playing and singing for over twenty years. He sang me some of his original songs, I was blown away, and I recognized he had considerable songwriting skills. He gave me a copy of his first album, "All Growed Up". In the album Christy's accomplished versatility is clear in his varied musical styles and instrumentation which always complimented the diversity of his lyrics and distinctive vocals. Christy and I prayed together and after would have an opportunity to minister together.

After that first meeting Mrs. McGuigan ask me if I would consider an offer to stay in her home, that she had a big house with plenty of room and I would have a lot more privacy. She knew at the time that I had been staying with a large family. I too, was beginning to feel that I should find other quarters, so I happily excepted her offer. If you remember I mentioned that Judy had been in England and we went to Paris together, well she also came to Ireland at that time and she stayed with me at Mrs. McGuigan. By the way both Judy and I have Irish DNA we are both quarter Irish. While I was staying in Mrs. McGuigan's home my daughter Libby Star gave birth to my granddaughter Taylor, which also happen to be her father David Gray's birthday May the 6th! Judy had made me aware by phone that the baby could come at any time, so Mrs. McGuigan and I were walking the floor and were elated when we got the news.

Today Taylor is a sophomore at the University of Alabama. A beautiful red head, blue eyes and has developed into an awesome guitar player and singer. A genuine Irish Lass.

This would not be the only time I would be out of country when a grandchild of mine was born. Taylor's brother Gabriel would be born when I was in London. That night I just happen to be visiting my friends Gennady and Olga along with their daughter Alexandria. It was Gennady's birthday, which also happens to be my brother Gary's birthday, August the 9th. Today Gabriel is a junior in high school, a wonderfully smart and spiritual boy and a tremendous athlete just like his Dad. In fact, news just came to me that David had bowled his twenty-seventh perfect game, I would say that's pretty good.

My last grandchild born while I was out of the country was Matthew Ryan, who was the third child of my son Christopher and his first wife Melissa. She was the daughter of Mike and Sue Chames who were part of my worship team at the Carson Valley Foursquare Church. When my Judy called she ask me to call the hospital right away. She told me that Matthew Ryan had passed away at birth. When I called Chris answered. Both Chris and Melissa were devastated at the loss of their baby. I returned to do the funeral for them. The loss of this baby was the catalyst which brought a lot of damage to this little family. They would finally divorce. Not long after that Melissa would get married to a fine fellow named Bill. They would go on to have more children and gave my grandchildren a wonderful home. Recovery for my son Christopher took longer. He struggled with alcohol, which brought a lot of heartaches in his life. He too is an awesome musician, a bass player. If you remember he learn to play in church and performed in my worship band. Watching him go through this painful chapter of his life brought back memories of my own addictions and struggles. However, I thank God for the power of prayer.

Chris was playin in a rock n roll band when he met May Ju. A beautiful Chinese woman. I had the privilege of performing their wedding. She has been an inspiration to Chris and helped him turn his life completely around. Now they have two sons, David and Cody. Thank you, Jesus.

Some years ago, I wrote a song for people like my Melissa and Christopher who have been through the trauma of losing a child. I believe every baby that has died either of natural causes or legalized murder called abortions, go straightaway to heaven to be with their Father God.

I wrote this song with Matthew Ryan in mind. I took his initials M.R., I titled it Mister;

"Hey Mister just thinking about you tonight,

No, everything is fine, I'm doing alright.

I just had you on my mind,

It happens every now and then.

Hey Mister, I just wondered, how in heaven have you been.

Hey Mister, I never got to hold you when you came,

or give you butterfly kisses

and count the little fingers on your hand.

But every time I look upward,

thoughts of you cross my mind,

And I wonder what Mister is doing in Heaven tonight.

Do you sing the songs of angels and dance with them among the stars?

Have you ridden a golden chariot?

and traveled to worlds afar?

Have you heard the saintly chorus?

and the new songs they sing to Him?

Hey Mister I just wondered

how in Heaven have you been."

Now I must tell you about the Barden family. On one of my many return trips to Ireland, I called Mrs. McGuigan, she informed me that she was going to be on holiday and she'd decided for me to stay with the Barden family. This was an amazing opportunity. Brendan Sr. and Christine Barden and their kids. Brendan their oldest son was off to America, but Patrick, Mark, John, Phillip, David and the "Irish Rose among the thorns", a wee lass, Michelle. Their ages twenty something to elementary age, all still living at home. A wonderfully gifted Christian family, who together operated Cloughreagh Nurseries, Camlough Road, Bessbrook in Newry, Armagh Northern Ireland. They loved to fellowship around their long dinner table. I was enjoying Christine's delicious home cooking, and her awesome apple tarts. They loved talking about God's Word, playing guitars and singing with my new friend John McPhelemy. Today I feel as though they are all my family. We have ministered together not only all over Ireland but also in America.

In the year 2000 Patrick ask me if I would consider driving a Volkswagen van his father had donated to a pastor in Albania. I told him I was happy to do it. So off we went. We drove from the Barden home to Wexford, Ireland where we crossed the Irish Sea on the ferry. Then continued across England to The Straights of Dover where we crossed the English Channel into France on a second ferry. Then our journey took us through Belgium, Germany and Austria where Patrick bought a camera. Then we drove into Switzerland where we ate our lunch under blues skies and the Swiss Alps. We finally arrived at Bari, Italy and crossed the Adriatic Sea to Tirana, Albania on our third ferry. Meeting with the pastor, his family and congregation we gave him his gifts and stayed for a few days enjoying their warm fellowship. I preached in several venues, which included a radio broadcast on an underground radio station. Then I was blessed to baptize a Muslim convert in a lake near Montenegro. Patrick and I would say goodbye then take the ferry back to Bari where we boarded a train to the ferry crossing near the island of Sicily. On that leg of the trip we were awakened in the middle of the night with fists pounding on our berth door, "polizia, polizia"! I open the door standing face to face with the Italian Police and their police dogs. They brought the dogs into our berth and thoroughly searched our luggage. I never knew if this was something they did randomly or had our joyful mannerisms alerted someone as suspicious. Remember in the book of Acts when the Holy Spirit empowered the Disciples in the Upper Room, they were accused by some people of appearing to be drunk.

The police of course found nothing, so we continued the train to Catania. In Catania we were met by my friends from the Foursquare Church in Stockton, California, where I had been the music pastor. Norman and Ramona Baker. Ramona was a beautiful soul and a talented singer who had sung with my music team. Norman a retired Marine Sergeant, was the fire chief at the Naval Base in Catania. When Sunday rolled around their pastor which had a store front church and a congregation of mostly American Naval personnel invited me to sing a few songs before their guest speaker preached. After the service, this beautifully dressed and gorgeous black woman came running up to me and ask if I ever go to Memphis. I told her all the time. When I'm visiting my Mother in Alabama I usually fly into Memphis. She told me her daddy was a pastor there and if I would take the time to call on him and perhaps visit with him, because he loves country music. I told Clarissa, that was her name, that I would. Sometime later I visited and met her parents, Bishop Roger and Dr. Laura Christopher of the Immanuel Baptist Church of Millington, Tennessee. We have become lifelong friends and I have ministered in their church on many occasions along with my Irish friends, Christy McGuigan who happened to be in Nashville on one occasion and came over to minister with me at their church Then also the Barden brothers Patrick and Brendan. Patrick had come to America to join me on a southern gospel tour. Patrick has many talents, but one of his out-standing gifts, he builds stringed instruments and his violins are highly sought after by orchestra musicians. Brendan is an engineer in St. Louis.

LONDON

In the early nineties, you may remember I was ministering all over Russia. I had spent several weeks with some new converts in the city of Zaraysk, a very old city. The religion of the city was predominantly Russian Orthodox. There are five churches in Zaraysk, the oldest of which is St. Nicholas Cathedral, consecrated in 1681.[lxxiii]

Two of the families whom I stayed with in Zaraysk, Alex Ilyin his wife Valentina and Dmitri Sorokin and his wife Nadya, have come to London to seek asylum. After they arrived they found a group of fellow asylum seekers meeting in the St. Luke Anglican Church. Dmitri had contacted me about coming to London and preaching to their group. When I arrived at Heathrow I was met by him and a driver named Nikolai Sergienko, who I would discover that both he and his wife Leah were classical pianist. Nick was leading a worship team for the Russian congregation. After being with them and meeting the Anglican priest, I found that the priest wasn't that fond of the idea that I was there to preach. He called me into his office along with his Russian associate who was a liaison between the church and the Russians. He warned me that I was prohibited from preaching, or performing any kind of healing or deliverance ministry. I would be restricted to singing a few songs

I was happy to comply and took no offense. I rehearsed with Nick and the music team. When it was my turn to perform, the Power of The Holy Spirit came upon my songs and the music. The Russian congregation was so moved by God's Presence that the priest was absolutely flabbergasted by what he was witnessing that he left the building.

You can handcuff and mussel old Brother Johnny, but no man can restrain the Power of God when He is determined to show Himself.

After this the Russians approached me about starting their own church. I told them we could if this was the desire of the majority. We began in Alex's home. Later we moved into a Presbyterian church who was kind enough to share their facilities. After several months, I came upon this small Chapel which appeared to be shuttered. The sign had a contact number. When I call the man, he agreed to meet me. Patrick Wright was his name and he came with his pastor a man named Paul. They were with the Apostolic Church of England. Doctrinally very like the Pentecostals in America. The organization had a colorful history This organization. had its roots in the Holy Ghost movement kindly called The Welsh Revival of 1904-1905.

When I told them that I represented a congregation of Russians looking for a building they immediately gave us access to the Chapel rent free. There had been services held in that facility for nearly a hundred years, and they were concerned that its use for the gospel had ended. So, when they discovered we wanted to have our church in the Chapel, they enthusiastically received us into their fellowship. The church remains there today with Dmitri as their pastor. It wasn't long after that a second church was formed by a musician I had met in Moscow, Russia named Oleg and his wife Tatiana. Tatiana was a marvelous preacher. This church too is still going strong and winning Russian people to The Lord.

Nick and his family would eventually immigrate to Vancouver, British Columbia and open a very high-level music school there.

All the teachers in the Amadeus Music Academy have Masters Degrees in music from Russian universities and are very familiar with the Russian piano school methodology. This technique is considered the most unique method for piano performance, establishing this distinctive approach to learning the Russian piano technique. Besides their music school, they were both on church staffs as music directors. The fruits of our work among Russians remains for over a decade of preaching in Russia and consequently ministries in London. I have two more short stories from Russia.[lxxiv]

I would return to visit Zaraysk to visit the parents of Dmitri and Alex. I had gifts for them and videos of their grandchildren. When my interpreter Hector and I arrived in the city we found the citizens celebrating the nine hundredth birthday of their town. There was music and food being offered throughout the city. Parades with floats were awesome, and the music from the marching bands could be heard everywhere, it was quite the celebration. Many people were pouring in from the countryside and neighboring communities.

I spent most of the day with the families and now Dmitri's mother has accompanied us back to the bus station. As we waited we watch bus after bus arrive and unload happy folks who had come to celebrate. While we waited for our bus, a woman in her forties I'm guessing, though she looked much older, stepped off the incoming bus. Her face was weathered by working outdoors. Her hands were calloused from very hard work on the farm. On a village farm, there are not many motorized implements. Most of the work is done entirely by hand. When she smiled her teeth, what few she had, were almost entirely of gold fillings. But her smile was infectious. As she came running toward me waving her hands, I looked to Hector for a sign, "what's she saying Hector"? Hector was laughing with joy as he says, "she is praising The Lord Brother Johnny," she is saying, God has blessed her today". When the woman gets to me she wraps me in this huge hug, begins kissing my cheeks and hands, while still talking away. When she turns to speak to Hector, he begins to interpret for me.

While she talks, she still holds tightly to my hands. I could feel her rough callouses and my heart was moved by her joy. Hector continues, "she's telling me she can't believe that when she left the village to come for the celebration that she would find "The Man of God", standing at the station. She said, a couple of years ago Brother Johnny came to her village and gave everyone a Bible and you preached the gospel. She said she got saved, went home and shared with her mother in law, and her drunken husband and they too received Christ".

I was emotionally overwhelmed. Tears of joy were now flooding my face as the farm woman and I stood together worshipping God. I thanked The Lord that He allowed me to witness His increase.

> *"It's not important who does the planting, or who does the watering. What's important is that God makes the seed grow". 1 Corinthians 3:7*

Near the city of Zaraysk is the city Kolomna, Russia, it too is very old being founded in around 1140 according to the latest archaeological surveys. As I have mentioned before while I was in the city of Kolomna holding services, I was introduced to a young Russian couple Arcadiy and Svetlana who had only just arrived into the city.

Kolomna's name may originate from the Old Russian term for "on the bend (in the river)", especially as the old city is located on a sharp bend in the Moscow River[lxxv]

Well, it was here at this ancient river bend that God led me to ordain Arcadiy and Svetlana and establish them as pastors. The first Sunday after their ordinations a congregation of about forty was born. While my team was with them, Arcadiy and Svetlana organized a service at his alma mater, the University in Kolomna and ask my team and I to minister there.

Along with me in those days was a well-known southern gospel baritone from South Carolina, Tom Taylor. Tom and I had put together a musical program of solos and duets. Just before our program was to start our interpreter told me that he would not be interpreting because all these students spoke English. He said preaching the gospel here will be difficult because as he put it, "They are very educated". Meaning they had all been educated as socialists, which probably meant they were either atheists, if not agnostics.

I learned that the students would be school teachers upon graduation. I prayed and ask God to help us all. As I approached the microphone God spoke to me. "Sing the Lennon/McCartney song "Yesterday".

Before I made any introductions, I simply strummed my guitar and began singing;

"Yesterday

All my troubles seemed so far away.

Now it seems, as though they're here to stay.

Oh, I believe in yesterday.

Suddenly, I'm not half the man I use to be.

There's a shadow hanging over me.

Oh, yesterday came suddenly.

When I got to the chorus, the entire audience began to sing along with me as I continued to play;

Why she had to go, I don't know, she wouldn't say.

I said something wrong, now I long for yesterday.

As we sang together we became friends. While we were singing God gave me a three-point devotional. One; We all have a yesterday. Two; We all hope for tomorrow. Three; We all have today and while it is today, we must seek wisdom. I encouraged them as future educators, if they were to be true to their calling, they could not afford to leave one stone unturned while they searched for knowledge, understanding and wisdom. They owed not only their students this benefit but also themselves. Tom and I continued with our musical program which we had prepared. I knew by their enthusiastic applause they truly enjoyed our music. We concluded by giving every student a Russian Bible. I had them open to the golden text John:316;

"For God so loved the world that he gave his one and only Son, that whoever believes in him shall not perish but have eternal life".

While we all prayed together with heads bowed, I knew in my heart that every person in the room had been touched by God's love. I challenge every one of you reading this to also consider this instruction, "You cannot afford to leave one stone unturned while you searched for knowledge, understanding and wisdom".

The Benefits of Wisdom

My child, listen to what I say, and treasure my commands.

Tune your ears to wisdom, and concentrate on understanding.

Cry out for insight, and ask for understanding.

Search for them as you would for silver; seek them like hidden treasures.

Then you will understand what it means to fear the Lord, and you will gain knowledge of God.

For the Lord grants wisdom!

From his mouth come knowledge and understanding.

He grants a treasure of common sense to the honest.

He is a shield to those who walk with integrity.

He guards the paths of the just and protects those who are faithful to him.

Proverbs 2: 1-9

One more story which I've previously published, but I believe it's worth repeating. I am not sure on which of the twenty-two journeys to Russia that this story occurred. I would love to share with you all the many powerful and amazing miracles that happened during those years, it would be impossible have chosen to share Luda's story with you.

The Woman in the Wheelchair

The city in which we were holding our meeting, I cannot remember; however, the hall I will never forget. It was one of the Stalin-designed theaters, spacious and gothic; its former glory was the cat's meow, but now, after all those years of socialist rule, its former glories were reduced by neglect and indifference to near rubble. The theater was filled with Russians. Why did they come? Were they seeking God, or maybe it was just curiosity as to what these Americans were doing in their town? I am not sure that they knew exactly why they were there or what they expected. Whatever the reasons, they were willing to brave the cold and travel a great distance to be in the meeting. The Word of God went forth that evening with not only powerful preaching but also anointed music and testimonies. The audience received our ministry and was open to the will of God. The invitation was given, and the Russians began to squeeze in around the prayer team at the foot of the stage. I recall vividly what happened next.

I was standing to the far side of the prayer line as a woman in a wheelchair rolled up to me, her face glowing with expectation. She spoke of course in Russian, and my interpreter, a young Russian woman, said, "Brother Johnny, she wants you to pray for her." Without hesitation, I reached my hands toward her and lay my hands on her head and began to pray. "What is going on here?" I thought. It was as if the words of my prayer were just falling to the floor. There was not any anointing at all. "Lord, what is it?" The Lord responded, "What are you doing? You have no clue for what you are praying." It suddenly dawned on me I had responded to the woman in the wheelchair like a pious robot with this cold, dead, religious, mechanical prayer. God was right; I had no clue what I was praying.

I stopped, humbled by my actions, and turned to my interpreter, and I asked, "Can you have her tell me her story and what she would like me to pray for?" The conversation became animated between the interpreter and the wheelchair woman. The woman did all the talking. Finally, the interpreter began to tell me the woman's story. A few years ago, she had an accident at the local train station. It was in the winter, and she had been standing for a long time in the cold waiting for the train. As the train began to approach the station, she told me she impatiently began to hurry toward the train. As she neared the train, suddenly she lost her footing on the icy platform, and off the platform she slid underneath the rolling train. It was terrible! The train rolled over her legs. The people standing by who witnessed this tragedy gathered her up and raced her to a nearby clinic. Unfortunately, there were no doctors on duty. In fact, by the time a doctor came, the chances of saving her legs were now impossible. The doctor had to amputate both of her legs. One leg he cut off below the knee and the other just above the knee. As the interpreter talked, I felt myself shyly peeking at her shoes and the wooden legs showing out from beneath her lap blanket. "Oh, my God," I thought. "Ask her what she wants from God." The interpreter spoke again to the woman and then looked back to me with a look of astonishment. "What did she say," I asked? "Brother Johnny, she wants God to give her legs." Paralyzed by the wheelchair woman's request and searching for any kind of faith that I might be able to muster, I cried, "Lord, help me to pray for her." I know it sounded like I was shouting to the interpreter when I said, "And if God gives her legs, what she going to do with those legs?" Words were exchanged between the two women as I continued to pray for my unbelief.

Then the interpreter said, "She said she has promised God if he gives her legs, she will walk everywhere, telling everyone what Jesus did for her."

I would later learn that her name was Luda. She was a mother. She and her son lived alone because after the accident, her husband had abandoned her and the boy. They lived in a high-rise apartment on the eighth floor in which she said, "The elevator seldom works." To get to her flat, she would have to crawl eight flights of stairs on her hands with her small son pulling her wheelchair up to the eighth floor. She was very poor, with only a small government check to feed the two of them. She told us, sometimes she would buy extra sugar and flour to bake cookies to sell to the townspeople for some additional money. It was a sad story, I tell you. Moved by the entire saga, I placed my hands forward, laying hands on her again; only this time humbled by her story and by God.

I prayed, "Lord; it is your choice, I can do nothing to help this woman". Then God spoke clearly, and to my amazement, these were His directions to me: "Tell her I have legs for her, and they are in America." "America, Lord, they may as well be on the moon," I thought to myself. The Lord continued, "Tell Sandy I am going to use her for the miracle." I looked back over my shoulder to see

Sandy, an American woman from California, who had joined the outreach team for this trip. Sandy was praying and did not see me turn to look at her. I turned back to Luda. "Madam," I said, "the Lord has given me a word for you." My interpreter spoke to the woman as I spoke. "God has legs for you," the interpreter paused. "Tell her what I said." She interpreted. "He also said they are in America."

Again, the interpreter paused as if to say, "Brother Johnny, what are you saying?" Again, I said, "Tell her." Looking at the expressions on the faces of everyone standing by, witnessing this amazing moment, I knew they were thinking, "What is happening here?" I explained the whole God thing again to the woman in the wheelchair as my interpreter shared. I could tell that the woman, Luda, understood, and she began to rejoice in the Lord, lighting up like a hundred-watt bulb.

Then I turned to Sandy, and I said, "Sandy, I have a word for you also." Sandy looked awkwardly surprised. "What do you mean?" she said. "God told me to tell you that he is going to use you for this miracle." At that point, Sandy was aghast with wonder, and I am sure doubts about my words. "Sandy, God is going to use you." "How?" she exclaimed. "I do not know," I said. Meanwhile, Luda was ecstatic, and her enthusiasm began to infect those standing by. "Brother Johnny, what am I going to do?" Sandy pleaded. "I do not know. I guess start by getting all the information you can about the woman and then let God lead you." With that said, I turned to leave, and nothing more was said to me about the incident. What more could I say?

A year later almost to the day, Sandy called my home. "Brother Johnny," she said, "Luda is on her way to America. God has worked His miracle." Sandy continued with her story. "When I got home, I began to pray about the "Word of Knowledge" you gave me, and the results are this. A prostheses company here in California has donated titanium legs valued at twenty thousand dollars and the therapy to teach Luda to walk on her new legs. The Russian airline Aeroflot has given her a round-trip ticket.

The Russian church at home is going to take care of her son while Luda is in America and gave her some traveling money. A church here in Sacramento is going to take care of her expenses while she is here. Brother Johnny, Luda arrives tomorrow at San Francisco Airport. Can you believe it? It is a miracle, and the TV news people are going to be there to cover her arrival." I saw Luda a few days after Sandy's call at Sandy's home; they were both overwhelmed by how God had put everything together. We rejoiced with great joy. Sandy told me that when Luda arrived at San Francisco, the Russian airline attendants, hand carried her off the plane. Then Sandy told me when Luda went home to Russia she walked on the plane on her miracle legs, telling everyone with great joy what Jesus had done for her. Her entire town witnessed a modern miracle of God. People have asked me, "Why didn't God just grow her some new legs?" I simply tell them, "I do not know. I am not in management, I am in sales."

"People of Israel, listen! God publicly endorsed Jesus the Nazarene by doing powerful miracles, wonders, and signs through Him, as you well know." Acts 2: 22, NLT

Chapter 17

It's 2004, I am now sixty years old and for the past twelve years I been away from home bringing the gospel to the world. It's time now for me to go home. I have no real leading as to what The Lord has in store, but I'm always confident that He is about ready to reveal His will for what He wants me to do. I know God will send someone to speak a word or the scripture will give me instructions.

God uses Pastor Glen Cole. I first met Pastor Glen Cole while Judy and I were still at Prison Ministries. Glen at that time was pastor of Bethel Temple, which later would change to the name of Capital Christian Center. I had great admiration for him for one very special reason. While Brother Cole was pastor of the largest church in Sacramento, he would take time to come for several weeks and hold a Bible study with a bunch of ex-cons in our Prison Ministries Chapel. When Pastor Cole encouraged me to consider ordination into the Assembly of God organization I took his counsel very seriously. Finally, in 2004 I began the long process of seeking ordination.
In 2005, I returned to the states to be ordain in August of that same year. Not long after my ordination I received a call from Brother Warren Parker, a dear friend who had partnered with me on several mission trips. Brother Parker wanted me to call the section presbyter Hugo Williams, so I did. During my chat with Brother Hugo he told me of a home missions church which needed a pastor and suggested I go look at it. The church was called Valley Christian Center located in the city of Dos Palos in the great San Joaquin Valley of central California. As Judy and I drove into the city limits, at the flashing signal light on highway 33, at Blossom Street we made a right turn and found the

church. The church was located directly across the street from a strip mall that had a grocery store, coffee shop and a liquor store. Left of the mall was a hamburger stand with a large ice cream cone shaped sign which read "Butch's" written across the cone. Next to the drive way entrance of the church was the barbershop. The church had a very nice-looking facility. We arrived just in time for Sunday school, were we met thirteen people, both middle age and elderly. They were very cordial. The minister that morning was a retired minister Reverend Melvin Crandall a man perhaps in his early eighties at the time. He was a wonderful preacher. The worship consisted of a Sister named Ann, who led the congregation without accompaniment. After a couple of choruses, I ask her if I could accompany her on the piano and she gladly said, "please do". We had a wonderful time that morning and after the service they all wanted to know if Judy and I were going to be the new pastors. I told them we were praying about it, but the decision was up to the presbytery. When I got the call from the Director of Home Missions, Dr. Sam Huddleston, I was preaching in Vancouver, British Columbia. Dr. Sam says, "If you and Judy want the church in Dos Palos it's yours. But I must tell you Brother Johnny, I originally had another couple in mind, but when they saw the town, they never even got out of their car, so you were our next choice". That evening after my chat with Dr. Sam, I had a dream and in the dream, I saw a tall marquee and on it were the words, "Dos Palos, God's Town". When I woke I knew God was leading me, so I called Dr. Sam I told him of the dream and I said, "Judy and I will take the church.

The following Sunday we had our first service, and just before service while talking to Sister Ann, I told her about my dream, which she quickly pointed out to me a tall reader board marquee standing by Blossom Street in the church yard. I don't know how I missed that, however, my first task was to climb up the tall sign and place on the marquee, the words which God had given me "Dos Palos, God's Town". It remains there today.

After our first church, a lady by the name of Mary Rose, who had been taking care of the churches business, showed us the parsonage located behind the church and gave us a key. Then she asks me did I want to see the church books sometime that week and that she would be happy to turn it all over to me. I ask her would she mind continuing to do what she was doing, she happily agreed she would.

After lunch Judy and I drove around the area and discovered there was more to the area than what we had realized. There was a downtown with shops and banks, a large farm implements, and tractors supply store, with a garage. We found the post office and city hall. There were several cafes, a pizza parlor, gas stations, convenience stores, churches, funeral home, elementary, middle, and high schools. We soon found out that the Dos Palos High School Bronco's sports teams had a trophy case of championships. For me, I knew that we were in the right place and at the right time.

Sister Ann, told me about the local radio station KDPT 102.9 a low power FM station, which had a broadcast radius covering Los Banos and part of Firebaugh. A governing board managed the station. Sister Ann told me she had a program on the station, and anyone could have a program with the board's approval.

I presented the board with a couple ideas. The first was a Sunday morning broadcast, with gospel music and preaching. The second was a morning drive show program format. Local news, music and talk. It would be a two-hour broadcast beginning at 6 am – 8am. The board approved them both. "The Big Valley Morning Show" was on the air, with Johnny and Paula. Paula was a wonderful lady whom I met, and she had talent for radio. We had a good chemistry and as a result, our morning show soon had a big following. The banter between Paula and I as we chatted about local issues, along with the musical line up of oldies, top forty country and the American standards was a perfect blend and entertaining. Later I would begin a daily Bible study program called, "Through the Bible Radio Class", airing Monday thru Friday at 8am.

During this time at city hall there was a political melt down developing between the sitting mayor/the city council, versus the city manager and the police chief. The issue was the Mayor and Council wanted the city manager to fire the police chief. The city manager refused to comply with their wishes, on the grounds he had only recently gave the Chief a glowing report. This issue created a major disturbance between the mayor/council and the citizens of Dos Palos. Paula and I began to cover the issue on our program. We made our position known. We were asking the city government to cease in their efforts to replace the police chief until after elections which was only three months away. The mayor and two council members were up for reelection. Our position was, that by waiting it would allow the new mayor and council to make the decision to this issue. If the present mayor and council win reelection this would give them a mandate from the people to do what they seemed intent on doing. They would not hear it. No matter how much the community protested the city governments relentless efforts finally had their way. First the mayor fired the long-standing city manager, then they hired an interim city manager and the new manager fired the Chief. This created pandemonium throughout the city. It was so bad the Mayor brought the County Sheriff into the city to take charge of the Dos Palos police department. This angered the citizens even more. The Sheriff called me and ask to speak on my radio show. He did, and it didn't go well for him.

He used the time to politic the idea that his departments could better serve our community than the Dos Palos police department. My argument with the Sheriff was that even though I was the new kid on the block, it seemed to me that the city had a huge historical pride in their community. I suggested that losing their police force would practically cause them to lose their place as a self-sufficient community and become just another wide place on a county road.

My argument seemed to give me favor with the citizens. The result of my advocacy many of the locals would ask me to run for city council, so I through my hat in the ring. I won that post on the council and held that seat for seven years as the mayor pro-Tem. In the eighth year I was elected unchallenged as the 26th Mayor of Dos Palos.

Our first order of business that first year was to undo what the previous Mayor had done. We removed the interim city manager, rehired the previous city manager, put our police chief back to work and sent the Sheriff and his deputies back to the county.

As a new council member, I was appointed as the representative to the Merced County Association of Government, an association of city and county governments, with members who meet to solve regional problems such as transportation, solid waste and air quality. The eleven-member MCAG Governing Board includes a supervisor from each of the five county districts and an elected official from each of the six incorporated cities located within the political boundary of Merced County which were Merced County; Cities of Atwater, Dos Palos, Gustine, Livingston, Los Banos and Merced. This governing board also served as the Transit Joint Powers Authority for Merced County and the Merced County Regional Waste Management Authority Board.[lxxvi]

I was also appointed to serve as a Commissioner on The Local Agency Formation Commission (LAFCo) which is an independent commission created by the State of California to promote the wise use of land resources while providing for the present and future needs of a community.

As one of the LAFCo Commissioners, I shared the responsibility to exercise my independent judgement while making decisions concerning appropriate local governmental boundaries and service providers. [lxxvii]

At one point in my eight years in Dos Palos I was not only Mayor, but Chairman of Merced County Association of Government, which included Chair of both the Transit Joint Powers Authority for Merced County and the Merced County Regional Waste Management Authority Board.

At the same time, I served for consecutive terms as Chairman of The Local Agency Formation Commission.

I heard the Merced County Supervisor for District 5 say to a group of men at a local coffee shop quote, "Pastor Johnny Mays is the most powerful political figure in Merced County. I was humbled at his remarks, because I knew that God had already told me that Dos Palos was God's town.

During our time in Dos Palos together with the mayor and council, and city departments the list of accomplishments in every area was amazing. The town had new businesses starting which meant more jobs, new police dispatch, new animal control buildings, new city hall, new city parks, we paid off our debts, and balanced our budgets.

At the same time, during this eight-year period my church grew as we had new folks coming and I had baptized many new converts. My musical team did concerts and outreaches. We had found favor in God's Town.

I had opened a new business a music store with a partner we called it "Johnny Adams Music". Sadly, Adam stayed only a short time and I bought back his part. The music shop became my office in the city. So, not only did we have a fantastic church, Judy had a wonderful Christian School in our church, I was a mayor, business owner, radio personality and sat on several boards. With all that progress, there was something my daughter Libby Star said, which gave me pause.

One day my daughter came to visit Judy and I at my business. On her visit she said something that scared me. "So, Dad with all that you are involved with I guess you're stuck in Dos Palos". I assured that her everything I was doing I had done as a witness for The Lord. Her remarks reminded me of a question ask me at an election debate the first time I ran for city council.

The question, "how does a preacher separate his religion from the policy decisions he must make as a council member". It was an easy question to answer. I said, "a person's faith cannot be separated from how that person reasons, it's like the ancient proverb, *'For as a man thinks in his heart, so is he'*.

I said, "I am no different than anyone else". We are what we believe we are, we make our choices based on a belief system. Regardless of one's religious beliefs even those who claim no religious believes, every man is a composite of his thinking, of his ideas, philosophy's, education and life's experiences, I am no different". "I told the audience if you elect me you will always get my honest opinions, I will not be lobbied or bribed".

I couldn't stop pondering what my daughter had said to me. I took her remarks before the Lord and I prayed;

"Lord my submission is to Your Lordship, nothing in my life owns me besides You O Mighty God. All that I am and all that I have is Yours, "I am not my own, you have bought me, I am Your servant first and always."

Within a few days, the Lord had me resign every position both church and political. I sold the business then said goodbye, to my church, my radio audience and to Dos Palos God's Town. With God's peace Judy and I moved on, even though we had no specific direction as to what the next chapter would hold in our lives.

Judy and I had witnessed God do so many wonderful things that we were excited to be going, yet sad to be leaving so many wonderful friends. There were tears from many, (perhaps a sigh of relief from some ;-)! I was humbled by the award plaques and commendations I received from every agency I had served, as well as the church and radio board. It was very humbling. I didn't need to look back as we drove out of town toward our new home in Stockton, because I left nothing undone. Judy and I chose Stockton because most of our children lived within the vicinity. Only my son John lived away in Colorado at the time.

Obviously by now though I haven't mentioned it, all our children are married with many beautiful children. My oldest granddaughters, Robbyn and Kristina, both have children, so now we are great grandparents.

While in Stockton I was asked to start a Bible study in my daughter's home. Many of our friends we had known from the Foursquare church attended. At the same time, I was preaching around in several churches. I had also been approached by Foursquare about starting a new church for them in Stockton but that would mean I would have to break ties with the Assemblies of God. Though both organizations are truly Godly and share similar doctrines I wasn't ready to leave the AG. A former pastor friend of mine and his wife from Dos Palos, Paul and Judy Steinhauer called me. Paul had left the United Methodist organization and had recently come into the Assemblies of God and were seeking a pastorate at the Full Gospel Church in Las Lomas a small rural community in Monterey County. Paul asked me if I would come along and lead a worship service for him while he preached. I did this a couple of times for him. The church decided Paul was not their man. Paul would just weeks later become pastor of The Sanctuary Church and Salinas Christian School. This was a very prominent and renown Church/School, a much better fit for Paul and Judy than the Las Lomas church.

As it turned out the folks at the Full Gospel Church ask me to come back and preach for them. So, for about a month I preached every Sunday. Judy and I would drive down, stay in a hotel. After a month, they quit calling.

Just weeks later while in Stockton my old friends from Branson, Missouri contacted me and ask me to join them on a mission's trip to Moldova, an Eastern European country and former Soviet republic. It was an exciting opportunity to minister to that part of the world again. Near my second week in Moldova I received a text from Judy telling me the church board from Las Lomas called and wanted to know if Judy and I would consider the opportunity to pastor their church. I text Judy back and told her I would pray about it and we would come and talk to them about it. We did, I came down and preached for them again. After service, the church board of three individuals invited us to lunch. It was there that the board proposed the question, "Brother Johnny do you think you could come and be our pastor on an interim basis". I was shocked at the question because I understood it be a full time permanent pastors position.

Before I could give them my answer, Judy says, "No he wouldn't…listen, if you don't know who Brother Johnny is by now and you're not convinced by now that he's the pastor God is calling to your church, then another year is not going to make a bit of difference". Again, I was shocked, but now it was my wife that had me smiling. I had never seen this side of her. She spoke with confidence and boldness. The board looked at her with the same surprised looked that I had. Then I said, "Judy's right, if you want us to come on as the new full-time pastors, we will come, otherwise the answer is no".

Quickly they responded, "Okay, well…we want you for sure. We must announce our decision before the congregation for two Sundays, then they will vote. It takes two thirds vote, and if they say yes would you be willing to live in the smaller parsonage and settle for "X" amount of dollars. Both Judy and I agreed. Three Sundays later I preached my first sermon as the pastor of the Full Gospel Church of las Lomas, California.

The Full Gospel Church has been in the Las Lomas Community for more than sixty-five years and for fifty-eight of those years Reverend James Whertly was their pastor. When Judy and I came to the church, Pastor Whertly had been retired for about four years. During those four years the church had no pastoral authority operating in the church. So, when we came, many things were out of order. The church was divided. Half of the congregation was meeting in the sanctuary and the other half were meeting in the fellowship hall. About the only time they came together was at a potluck. The church board had complete control over the financial affairs and the congregation was completely in the dark about the finances or how the business of the church was being handled. During that four-year period, they would bring in interim ministers or special speakers, who all would soon leave because of the disconnect between the congregation and church board. There were many problems but with Pastor Whertly out of the picture, it had gotten to the point of chaos. I'm not sure if the board even understood why they were choosing Judy and I as their pastors.

The first thing I had to do was suspend the group meeting in the fellowship hall. They were told they must gather with the congregation in the sanctuary.

I ask the board for complete transparency in the finances and the reporting. I had everyone who desired to work in youth ministries or Sunday school, to be finger printed and backgrounds checked. We organized an office for Judy and me and began putting on the face of pastoral authority and order. I started a Friday night prayer meeting and began to pray that God would take back control of the church and its ministries. To add to all that, it would come to light, that the church board had a deep sinful moral problem. Within just months after our coming the entire church board resigned. God gave me a new board.

Unfortunately, the group which had segregated themselves from the sanctuary decide to all leave rather than to submit to God's authority. In the last four years the church has been healing and growing in the Word and Spirit. The numbers are growing slowly.

In my opinion, the model of ministry they were following doesn't fit the community's demographics of today. When the church first began the community was predominantly white, the style of worship was typical early Pentecostal. But now they were stuck in a rut, with no vision to go forward. They are wonderful, God fearing people who love the Lord. In fact, they suffered from a modern church problem.

The churches at large in Amcrica have lost their community relationship. Church is a body of believers. One miss conception that people have is that the church is this global body of people. That point is true, but that is only true from the context that the church is Christ's Body from every nation, tribe and tongue. The Kingdom of God does not grow from that perspective.

The Kingdom of God enlarges at a local level from the perspective that each community of believers adds to their numbers by sharing their faith and the gospel with their families, friends and neighbors.

With this perspective the local church community from its resources sends out ministries and missionaries to evangelize the world to support indigenous churches to also build communities of believers.

The church had lost its understanding of community and therefore had no vision for The Kingdom of God. We aren't out of the woods yet, but our Father is God and we know He holds our tomorrows.

"I don't know about tomorrow, I just live for day to day. I don't borrow from the sunshine, for its skies may turn to gray. I don't worry o'er the future. For I know what Jesus said. And today I'll walk beside Him, for He knows what lies ahead. Many things about tomorrow I don't seem to understand; But I know who holds tomorrow, and I know who holds my hand".[lxxviii]

Before I close I want to give thanks for the love and support of so many people in my life which have made this journey possible.

Hundreds of people have contributed to this life of mine. I could never say what I truly feel concerning their love and generosity which they have shown to me and mine.

"Our God will not forget how hard you have worked for him and how you have shown your love to him by caring for other believers, as you still do. Our great desire is that you will keep on loving others if life lasts, to make certain that what you hope for will come true. Then you will not become spiritually dull and indifferent. Instead, you will follow the example of those who are going to inherit God's promises because of their faith and endurance".

Hebrews 6:10-12 NLT

Leaving Woods Creek was my gateway to a priceless discovery of the grace of God, faith for the impossible, and mercy to endure through the fellowship of Christ's victory through suffering. Only the Lord knows the end of the journey.

I leave you with my prayers.

Chapter 18

Day One

Spring up O Well, Thou Fountain of my youth, from Your Cool Spring does my soul drink. Only in Thee O God, is my soul satisfied, for You alone quench my heart's thirst with The Waters of Life.

My Father, by Your Word, you invited me to Your Table and You sat me with those who have overcome. You clothed me in white apparel and You donned me with Your rich things, with the onyx and pearl, rubies and jade. You adorned me with Your finest silks and covered my head with expensive fragrances.

Your peace encamped about me as You gave me to drink a Cup of the Pure Water of Life. I lifted my cup to Your honor and glory and as it cooled my parched tongue, out of my mouth came songs of praise, gushing forth like a great geyser of worship, going up, up, up to all Your Heavens.

While I worshiped I heard the voices of the Redeemed and to my joy, all of Heaven joined me in singing. With new songs, we sang with one voice unto Thee and without end, our voices declared the everlasting chorus, "there is no God compared to You my Lord, for You Alone are God and there is none other."

As we celebrated In Thy Presence I found rest with Your Only Begotten Son, then down from Your Throne the Sweet Dove of Heaven flew and poured precious oils over me, with Your Own Right Hand, you anointed my head with the Oil of Gladness. Your tender Voice filled my ears with whispers of love, joy and sweet comfort.

Hear me, all Ye earth, for I will sing with my whole heart and I will tell of His excellent greatness. I will shout O my Soul and extol His Eternal Beauty, for who shall come before Him the Lord Most High, and who is worthy of His kindnesses? Only they who drink from Your Well the Water of Life my Lord, in Jesus Name. Amen

Day Two

Behold how mighty are Thy Works O God. For mine eyes behold the glories of Thy heavens and my ears listen to the sweet songs of Thy waters. It is by Your own hands Sovereign Lord, that the paths of the winds are established, and the coasts of the great lands are determined. You breathed fire from beneath the oceans and formed the islands as they sparkle like diamonds on the seas. The earth which You formed lifted its hands to praise You and the mountains stood up and still today they cast their shadows over us declaring Your Majestic Name.

There is no God like You. There is no other who can match Your vast wisdoms. There are none who can know Your secret plans unless You reveal it to them. With every passing moment O God of all Creation, Your Life is moving to and for in the earth, both the visible and the invisible. Eternity is Your dwelling place.

I shall recall Thy Word: "what are mere mortals that you should think about them, human beings that you should care for them"?

As I muse on this question my thoughts are left to wonder of how great are your kindnesses. It was Your Determination My Lord, to form him from the dust of the earth. You created him in Your image and gave him breath.

Alas O Merciful God, when in our sins we were lost, You O Lamb of God, redeemed him with a divine sacrifice, buy Your Own Blood You purchased him, you bought him with a price, and You declared him holy and hid him in The Cleft of The Rock.

When You clothed him in Your Righteousness, like a proud Father, you revealed Your Redeemed before the Mighty Hosts and exalted him in the Heavens. You endowed him with power and authority by Thine Own Holy Spirit and gave him a new name, Your Name.

For these acts of Your love, for every gesture of Your kindness and because of Your great mercies You have shown, I appeal to my dear brothers and sisters.

I plead with you to give your bodies to God because of all He has done for you. Let them be a living and holy sacrifice the kind He will find acceptable. This is truly the way to worship Him. In Jesus Name. Amen

Day Three

Gracious Father and Most High, "You O God remain the same forever! Your throne continues from generation to generation."

I beseech Thee therefore, O Lord do not forget us, do not abandon this Nation. It is true we are guilty of allowing the killing of the innocent and we have failed to repent against the injustice and corruption that permeates this country. Sin and blasphemies abound in every city, town and villages. Violence rages in our streets. The altars of our churches go unattended. Many have forsaken our assemblies. My Lord Only You can help us, so I must intercede and ask for Your mercies.

Restore us, O Lord, and bring us back to You again! Give us back the joys we once knew and let the Anointing of the Holy Spirit fall on us like summer rains. Thy Church needs healing and renewal. Too many have left their callings and entangled themselves in worldly affairs, they have forgotten that their sins have been forgiven. As for me O Lord, help Thy Servant Lord, strengthen my resolve that I may stand in these last days.

My Lord please tarry no longer, bring revival to Christian America so our Light will shine for all the world to see. In Jesus Name. Amen

Day Four

Dearest Father, Merciful Savior, Your Word declares that You O God, "have made from one blood every nation of men to dwell on all the face of the earth, and You have determined their pre-appointed times and the boundaries of their dwellings so that they should seek the Lord"

Father by Your own decrees You have chosen and appointed this Nation and every American for this time and place. Furthermore, Father by Your own divine grace the boundaries were set from before the beginning of time that we might seek and find the Lord!

By Apostolic authority and the inspiration of Your Spirit You herald all believers to intercede,

"Therefore, I exhort first that supplications, prayers, intercessions, and giving of thanks be made for all men, for kings and all who are in authority, that we may lead a quiet and peaceable life in all godliness and reverence. For this is good and acceptable in the sight of God our Savior, who desires all men to be saved and to come to the knowledge of the truth."

Almighty Father lead Your people by Your Spirit, for never in our history has the need been so great and Your intervention so desired. Father America needs divine intervention urgently we need revival in our churches and forgiveness of our sins. Father we need to confess as a nation that Jesus is Lord. We need Wisdom not political rhetoric, we need insight by Your Spirit not indignation from the flesh. Father prepare our hearts to choose wisely and humble ourselves before You. Dearest Lord above all, may Thy Will be done, in Jesus Name Amen.

Day Five

How shall I praise Thee O God of All Creation. What words shall I use to describe Your Glory and Majesty. Anoint Thy Servant Lord so with my words I will honor You with praise worthy of Your Name.

"Open up, ancient gates! Open, ancient doors, and let the King of glory enter. Who is the King of glory? The Lord, strong and Mighty the Lord, invincible in battle."

My Father my prayer is that within me shall flow a river of worship and praise. May my voice sing the songs like the ancient voices of Moses and Miriam, David and Joshua. O that this Temple would forever be adorned with Thy Presence, joining the Host of The Lord in everlasting choruses.

Has the LORD redeemed you? Then speak out! Tell others He has redeemed you from your enemies. Rejoice and again I say rejoice. For the Lord Thy God during Thee is Mighty to save. In Jesus Name, I pray. Amen

Day Six

Dearest Heavenly Father how magnificent are Your intentions for my life and for all whom You love. You are The Lord our Shepherd and by Your own strength You garrison Your Flock. No weapon formed against them shall prosper. Thy Word gives divine instructions and comfort to all whom believe.

My Dearest Lord You have given me a strong warning not to think like everyone else does. You have said, *"Don't call everything a conspiracy like the fearful do and don't live in dread of what frightens them"*. I will obey Thee my Father and take heed to Thy WORD. Gracious Lord of Hosts You are Holy in my life, for You only are the One I shall fear. If I must fear I will tremble only of Your Mighty Power, I will fear no other.

Hear me my Lord while the heathen rages my thoughts are only on Thee. You are the custodian of my life and have numbered my days. You orchestrate my days and set before me Your perfect Will for my life. In Thee I find sanctuary and rest. In Jesus Name I pray. Amen

Day Seven

Mystery of mysteries is Your Greatness O Mighty God. Who can know Your thoughts or speak of Your intent with understanding? My Lord forgive me and discern my heart, for my questions are not meant to bring any indictment against You or suggest that I should question Your determined will. Yet, if I may, I will only remind You of that which is written;

"Unless the LORD builds a house, the work of the builders is wasted. Unless the LORD protects a city, guarding it with sentries will do no good."

"O Lord of Heaven's Armies, you test those who are righteous, and You examine the deepest thoughts and secrets."

O my Father to whom shall I turn to for it is written in Thy Word that the everlasting results are in Your hands. So, it is true my Father, without Your interventions all my efforts are vanity, they are meaningless beatings of the wind.

Let thy servant ask of Thee O Royal Head and Exalted God. Dearest Lord by Thy Grace Father, would You rise from Your Holy Place and stretch forth Your Mighty Arm so to awaken my faith within me.

Would You help my unbelief and help me Father to carry out the calling You have given me and assist me in doing Your work while my time remains?

My Lord, my convictions for this request are met with strong merit, for I know that without Your Presence in my fight, my battles will be lost, and I will have failed.

Serve me O Faithful One with Thy Anointing and Power. Fill my mind with Your Wisdom.

Direct my paths and spend my days at Your leisure. Finish in me Your strongest desires.

It is You O God who redeemed me and gave me sanctuary from all my enemies. You only are The One who healed me of all my diseases and delivered me from the snares of my reproach. Stand with me my Shield and let me abide in Thy Shadow so that I might finish the race You have ask me to run. In Jesus Name. Amen

Day Eight

Hear this all Ye Earth, The Lord of Heaven reigns and His Name is exalted above all names. Indeed, my Lord Your Presence and Power fills the earth and the noise of the heavens declare Your majesty. Even the hidden and invisible worlds declare Your Wisdom. O Father, arise from Your Golden Throne, let the Seraphim's express to the Righteous which stand before Thee of Your glorious intent. Fill the earth in this day my Lord with holy terror and the creation shall tremble at Thy Word when You declare it.

"LORD, remind me how brief my time on earth will be. Remind me that my days are numbered–how fleeting my life is.

Lord how long shall the nation's mock Thy servants who bear Thy Name. Let their testimonials be published and this Gospel be known throughout the lands. Arise O Mighty God and send forth the Refiners Fire, purge the hearts of the lost and save them by Thy grace. Turn this disgraced nation to repentance and save us. In Jesus Name, I pray. Amen

Day Nine

Oh, my Dearest and Loving Father in a time of continuous anguish and sorrow, oh how I long for Your Word to manifest this promise.

"On that day, a fountain will be opened for the house of David and for the people of Jerusalem, a fountain to cleanse them from all their sins and impurity."

My Lord I continue to pray for Your Church. I will intervene for Israel and for all who will harken to the call of grace. By Your Spirit O Holy One, pour out Your Power and Presence. May the knowledge of the Gospel saturate the earth as the waters cover the seas. Do a quick work, for how long my Father Shall You tarry, while everyone who has eyes can see that the night is quickly approaching, and many remain lost. My Lord as it was in the days of Thy servant Noah, when he had prepared the Ark and it was ready, it was You O Gracious Lord, who by Your Spirit called for both the clean and the unclean to come aboard. They came, from every realm of Your creation and then You closed the door.

My FATHER, hear my prayer… if the sparrow and the otter received Your mercy and the Lion and the Lamb came forth by Your own hand, how much more will You do in these last days for them who are created in Your image, all for whom Your Son Died.

Let Thy Grace abound my Lord and save us from this corruption and revive us in Jesus Name I pray. Amen

Day Ten

"Lord, there is no one like You! For You are great, and Your Name is full of power. Who would not fear You, O King of nations? That title belongs to You alone! Among all the wise people of the earth and in all the kingdoms of the world, there is no one like You."

Dearest Heavenly Father there is no question concerning Your Preeminence, there is no one who saves the soul from death. Greater love has no man than He who lays down His life for His enemies.

Oh, Great God during this time of remembrance, receive my adoration my Lord, how be it my vocabulary cannot describe, nor can my voice express the feelings I desire to convey.

Dearest Savior, you know my heart and You discern my intentions, receive my worship and my gratitude for all that You have done for me. To Thee Christ Jesus is my life given it is all that I have and the beginning of my worship. Your Life, Your Death and Your Resurrection are the pillars of my hope. Thank You for all Your answers to my prayers, in Jesus Name. Amen

"God sent His son, they called Him, Jesus;
He came to love, heal and forgive;
He lived and died to buy my pardon,
An empty grave is there to prove my Savior lives!

Because He lives, I can face tomorrow,
Because He lives, all fear is gone,
Because I know He holds the future,
And life is worth the living,
Just because He lives!"

Day Eleven

Sing aloud O Ye Heavens, burst forth with praise all Ye Lands for The Lord, The King of Glory sits among the Seraphim and His Holy Presence fills the Temple. Who shall be exalted above The Lord, for The Lord God Almighty Reigns Supreme.

At the earliest hour of the day my heart is filled with the knowledge of Your Presence. O my Father what shall I say more of Your Beauty and Your Grace. When I think of all Your Goodness toward Your servant, who am I that You are mindful of me.

You my Lord are The Glory and The Lifter of my head. You garrison about me without measure, you pour forth Your boundless blessings toward Your children. When I am asked who is this God whom I serve. Without hesitation and with resounding joy I speak of the Everlasting One, The Bright and The Morning Star, the God of Abraham, Isaac and Jacob.

You O Mighty Deliverer gave all who believe salvation through Your Only Begotten Son, our Lord Jesus. His Life ransomed us from despair and futility. Our sins had consumed us, death had bound us all, but You rescued us.

Hallelujah my Lord! You did not forsake me, but delivered me from all my iniquities. My life is now joined to You for I am now accepted in The Beloved. Thank You Sweet Lord, for saving me by Your Grace, in Jesus Perfect Name. Amen

Day Twelve

Dearest Heavenly Father, Precious Lord God Almighty, let me kneel before Thee, humbling my heart before Your Holy Presence.

My Lord when I consider Your Power, I must ask myself why must I fear? Why am I anxious by the threats of my enemies? For it is You who would say to the mountains, move, and they must obey. It is You, which by Your own breath the heavens were formed and after ages have past, they remain in their places and testify of Your Greatness.

Yes, Father I know these things, yet fear, worry and trepidation gather about me like raging enemies. O Lord help me, help my unbelief and strengthen my faith. Let me echo the words of Thy prophet, for he declared;

> *"For I am with you, and I will take care of you. I, the Lord, have spoken!"*

My Lord receive my prayer, forgive my doubts and fears and strengthen my resolve to trust You with all my heart and lean not on my own understanding. In Jesus Name. Amen.

This is my worship…

Blessed assurance, Jesus is mine! Oh, what a foretaste of glory divine!
Heir of salvation, purchase of God, Born of His Spirit, washed in His blood.

This is my story, this is my song, praising my Savior all day long;
This is my story, this is my song, praising my Savior all day long

Day Thirteen

Dearest Lord, my Jesus, tender and kind is the stewardship You have shown over my life. You lead me with loving mercies and Your patience with me is matchless.

Truly it as written, *"there is now no condemnation in Christ Jesus."* You never pressure me into situations or cause me to feel anxious. With You my Lord, it is never about winning or losing, but always about our togetherness.

O Father my sight is fixed on Your Son. I need no other compass. I have learned that He goes before me in every situation and is steadfast in every adverse circumstance. Knowing this my Father, I have learned to rest in You and my determination is to remain yoked with My Beloved Savior, Your Son.

Tomorrow is not a term with which I am any longer concerned. I understand my life and my peace are in the moment and all my hopes are confirmed in His Promises and by His Presence. The seasons of the earth are established by Your Will, and every appointment You have made concerning my time shall come to pass. Calendars are created by men to simply count the days, the turning of months and years tend only to remind me of the haste in which our lives are spent.

Today I look to Him and expect only His best. My faith is sure for I am convinced He hears me and sees all things concerning my journey. Thank You Lord Jesus for all our eternity is found in You. In Jesus Name. Amen

Day Fourteen

Dearest Father, Your Name is the Lord of Heaven's Armies. It is by Your Grace that You have put Your Words in my mouth and hidden me safely in Your hand.

You My Lord have established my goings. Even though I stumbled in my journey, you would not abandon me, for You have determined my success and declared my victory. There is none like You, O Gracious and Merciful Father.

Lord Jesus by Your perfect obedience and honor to Your Father, you have opened a Door to every spiritual blessing. You have kept nothing from Your Servants, but by The Holy Spirit have endowed Your beloved with every good thing.

By Your Strength I shall continue to exalt Your Name. I shall boast of Your Greatness in every song and testimony. By Your Continued Anointing I shall open Thy WORD with understanding and tell all which have ears of Your Glorious Promises. Many shall hear and be glad. They shall shout of Your Salvation and Healing. In Jesus Name. Amen

Day Fifteen

Dearest Most Magnificent Father in Thy Presence I have fulness of joy. My petitions are like treasures to me, for I know You honor them and give great value to all my prayers which I bring before You.

You O Sovereign Lord You have commanded me to pray without ceasing. You have directed me to always be prepared, to be instant in every season. O Father let me not fail You, for my deepest desire and my greatest determination is to honor You with my whole life and be obedient to Your call.

Loving God while the world about me slumbers my eyes cannot find sleep. All my thoughts are aroused by Your Presence. With every quiet moment, I await Your voice. I open the Holy Bible to feast upon Your Word. I desire to quench my thirsting soul with the knowledge of Your greatness.

As it is written: *"Open, "O heavens, and pour out your righteousness. Let the earth open wide so salvation and righteousness can sprout up together. I, the Lord, created them."*

Yes, indeed my Gracious Father You are doing a Work which no one can deny. You are anointing Your servants for such a time as this. Let the joyful sounds of victory begin My Lord. Let the Lord of Heavens Armies stand among His bounties and Glory among His People. Let all Thy benefits manifest, and The People of Your Pasture be completely healed. In Jesus Name. Amen

Day Sixteen

Dearest Heavenly Father You O Lord remain my eternal companion, my forever friend, giving me courage and hope for my journey.

How often O Lord has my foot stumbled, yet You would not let me fall. In all my weaknesses, you steadied my steps and kept me standing.

As David declared, *"Yea though I walk through The Valley of Death" I shall fear no evil, for Thou art with me."* You my Sweet Lord, remain along side of me when my doubts arise and my fears dismay. You always help my unbelief.

Gracious Majesty I will join the Prophets and *"Say to those with fearful hearts, "Be strong, and do not fear, for your God is coming to destroy your enemies. He is coming to save you."*

Today my Father I pray heal us, comfort us and deliver us from all our pains, sorrows and fears. Anoint Thy servants with the Oil of Gladness and receive our worship. Our songs will tell of Thy faithfulness and declare Thy excellent mercies. In Jesus Name. Amen

Day Seventeen

Our Gracious Lord how lofty are Your ways. Only by Your Grace have You revealed Your ultimate intentions. Now through Christ we have access to the Mind of God, where in are all mysteries revealed by the Spirit.

The wisdom we speak of is the mystery of God...Your plan that was previously hidden, even though You made it for our ultimate glory before the world began.

From the beginning of creation, it was Your Will O Mighty God to have a one-on-one relationship with Your Creation. We discovered Your divine-creation purpose cradled in an eternal desire for intimate and spiritual relationship with humankind as Jesus said; *"Love the Lord your God with all your heart, with all your soul, and with all your mind"*.

In a moment so determined that nothing will deter Your appearing, every eye will see what many have refused to believe. Your Glory will not be hidden, for the Knowledge of The Lord will fill the earth. Thank You. In Jesus Name. Amen

Day Eighteen

My Father and Lord of Glory how wonderful is Your kindness and gentleness. Insight and understanding are revealed by The Holy Spirit.

"Jesus went a little farther and fell on His face, and prayed, saying, "O My Father, if it is possible, let this cup pass from Me; nevertheless, not as I will, but as You will.

My Dearest Father I am reminded that in my weakness— the strength of God is manifested. My Lord on The Cross, you chose to weaken Yourself to Death. In Your willing weakness, Your Strength manifested so to redeem Your most coveted creation, humankind. This was the hope of the Father and by Your trustworthiness, His faith in You is confirmed by Your obedience.

By Your Wisdom Father I understand too, that to be vulnerable to another's choice was only known by You once before in Eden, but now, yet once again, because of Your Nature of Love and longing to share that love… You O God, like all who must believe, you will take the quantum leap of faith and adjoin Yourself to Your Own creation. Because of the incarnation of Jesus Christ, you will await The Choice of Thy Son. You O Father of All will place Your trust in Christ as all believers must…

Jesus did not disappoint You. He overcame and joined You on The Throne of Glory and now all whom believe in Him, may join You there. In Jesus Name. Amen

Day Nineteen

Dearest of All Heaven and Lord of All, hear my prayer my Gracious Father and hear how Thy Children suffer. Many are they which need healing. Miracles my Father are unique only to You. The stars hold their places because of Your Authority. The seas and the mountains bow to none other. Our lives O Great Shepherd of Our Souls are in Your caress. Listen to the lament of The Redeemed for we cry for Your Mercies. Heal the sick Father. Deliver the oppressed. Lift the downcast. Gather the lost sheep. Bring home the wanderer. Unto Thee only can we be saved. In Jesus Name. Amen

Day Twenty

Dearest Heavenly Father as it is written: "Your words are what sustain me; they are food to my hungry soul. They bring joy to my sorrowing heart and delight me. How proud I am to bear Your Name, O Lord"

Dearest One, on the day You separated me from the darkness of my sin, you have not failed to keep me in Your Presence. You are my sustenance. You quench my soul from thirst and satisfy my hunger. For this I cannot speak enough of Your mercies and grace. Bless You my Lord.

On this eve, I come before You with many requests for Your children. They desire Your intervention and long for Your provisions. Honor Thy Children with Your great and powerful anointing to lift us up.

Our Redeemer is our Advocate to whom we make our requests known to You O Mighty God. Let the answers to our prayers give Testimony to You and Your Son. Holy Spirit undergird The Sons and Daughters of God, make them more the conquerors but over-comers. In Jesus Name. Amen

Day Twenty-one

Father in Heaven how we adore Your promises. Your Word reminds us that if two or three will agree on anything on earth it shall be done in heaven. You O God are the Genesis of all our Blessings. You have promised every blessing to us as an inheritance.

My Lord and my Dearest Father how great are the undeserved privileges which You have bestowed upon Your Children. We all with boldness greet You with our worship and praise. You have delivered a great victory for all who believe.

He, *"Who knew no sin became sin for us, that we might be made righteous,"* Your Righteousness, bestowed upon us and by that same grace we received a promise of healing and recovery.

Day Twenty-two

Dearest Lord my Heavenly Father this is The Day which You have made and as it is written; *"God has come to save me. I will trust in Him and not be afraid."*

My Lord, you are the Music and the Words of my songs. My praise is of Your Magnificent Victory. You My King, have given me joy unspeakable filled with glory. I drink deeply from the fountain of Your salvation! I shall never thirst again. Hear my songs all of you when I sing, "Thank You Lord! Praise His name!"

Let every Overcomer with grateful heart speak to the nations. Proclamations should be declared and published of all that our Gracious Lord has done. Quoting from Dr. King Jr. "let it ring from every village and every hamlet, from every state and every city," indeed...for where The Spirit of The Lord is we discover, True Freedom. So...with great boldness let the world know how mighty He is!

Praise the Name of Jesus! With new songs sing to the Lord, for He has done excellent things. Make known His praise around the world. Let all the people shout His praise with joy! For great is the Holy One. In Jesus Name. Amen

Day Twenty-three

Dearest Heavenly Father in the quiet of the morning I wait for You. My days have slowed to each moment as patience accompanies my stillness. Why do I tarry and what do I seek? I seek You only, for You O Mighty God, you are my great desire. It is for Your Wisdom for which I am tethered to You. I shall not look for another, for only You have the Words of Life. I have no desire to count my days or seek them further. For they are all vanity without Your Presence. I cannot be satisfied with yesterday's musings, they are as stale bread and rancid oil. Let this Day, the Day You have made bring fresh Manna for Thy servant my Lord. Let it fill my soul with understanding for this is my greatest desire.

Dearest Lord I am content with my prayers, for I understand You are Faithful. I am pleased that for every petition You have given the answer. I am comforted by this thought that Your Perfect Will is all sufficient and all my needs are provided by Your Generosity.

Thank You Lord for loving me, caring for me and teaching me. In Jesus Name. Amen

Day Twenty-four

Dearest Heavenly Father my Dearest Lord of Glory, how wonderful is our fellowship. How I wait in Your silence as I come before You Lord. Your anointing abounds in the stillness of Your Presence and in Your hush, you reveal understanding. You need not speak as a man for Your WORD is Spirit.

My Lord, you are my advocate! You continue to contend for Your servant! Not only have You redeemed my life, but You have seen the wrongs done to me and protect me from the vengeful plots laid against me. All Your Judgements are righteous, and no charge spoken against Your servants shall prevail. You only Justify the Redeemed and declare them acceptable in Thy sight.

My Lord today, because I stand in Your favor, you welcome my boldness. Though it is only by Your grace granted that I speak before You, still it is Your will for Your children to ask of Thee all their hearts desires. My Lion of Judah, you hold nothing back of which You determine as pertinent to my needs. You take great joy in blessing me. Thank You my Father for the confidence You have instilled within my heart, I shall not fear. In Jesus Name. Amen

Day Twenty-five

Dearest Heavenly Father Thy Word speaks of those whose eyes see clearly. It tells of the message of them who heard the Words of God, and have knowledge from the Highest and who sees a vision from the Almighty, who bows down with eyes wide open. My Father Your Bible is replete with instances where You communicated with the Saints in this manner.

Today my Gracious Father I am more convinced than ever that You communicate with us however You choose. Nevertheless, Lord I believe it is wisdom for us when we have a decision to make, that our first stop should always be the Bible, not a standalone dream or vision.

Still and even with that said my Lord, when there is a dream or vision of which I believe is from You, I should not fear it, but confirm its worthiness because I have the inspired Word of God, The Bible. My Lord because You never change, and You are the same, yesterday, today and forevermore. I am confident Thy Word will make viable the vision or dream You have given me as it correlates with The Written Word of God.

So, hear my instructions Dearest Saints, don't be afraid to dream big and ask for visions. Then after your prayers allow our Father to substantiate His directions for you with understanding not only from your Bible but also in the mouth of two or three witnesses, whom will agree with you, then after it is tested, let His Will be established.

Let this be our prayer;

Dearest God of Wisdom and Grace help my unbelief and give me faith to trust You in me. Not only on the days when I am doing great and winning and nothing seems impossible, but also in those days when I doubt if I have courage, insight or stamina to believe. Don't let me quit, not ever.

My Father as I learn to trust in Your Word, help me to seek my dreams and follow my visions. Help me keep faith in Your Word so not to deceive myself. Yet when it is confirmed that my new direction is from You, let me not be deterred from following my dreams and fulfill the visions You have given me.

No matter how many people discourage me, doubt me, laugh at me, warn me, think me a fool, don't let me listen. Let me hear Your voice only telling me, "You can do it, and you will!" In Jesus Name. Amen

Day Twenty-six

Dearest Father not only by Your Word, but in dreams and visions, your children are seeing the insidious results of a world gone mad and what the end shall be.

While societies of all nations have turned from the innate morality given to them by the hand of God and abandoned themselves to unlawful and godless living, making their sins far greater than Sodom and Gomorrah, more devious than the leaven of the Pharisees, you my Father tarry Your coming. You continue to suffer with Your Patience because Your Love is great. People ask, why do You wait Your coming?

For You, O Mighty God Gracious and Merciful, you are not willing for any to perish, but for all who will believe to come to salvation.

Even so, while You my Lord prolong Your appearing, The Holy Spirit prompts us to new sense of urgency. For we The Church have a grave responsibility and must understand the fiery judgments that wait those who neglect so great a Gospel. We cannot forget that You O God are the Judge of the Living and the Dead and that all nations and peoples must come before You.

"Because we understand our fearful responsibility to the Lord, we work hard to persuade others. God knows we are sincere, and I hope you know this, too."

Partner with us O God, for The Battle belongs to the Lord. Anoint our heads with Divine Wisdom that we may preach with clarity and urgency, so they with ears to hear may hear. In Jesus Name. Amen

Day Twenty-seven

Dearest Father, You O Lord are the Glory and The Lifter of my head. You are The Wisdom of the Ages, The Ancient of Days. You my Lord redeemed Your first man Adam by covering his sins. You gave Noah Your plans and saved him from Your Judgements. For Your friend Abraham You declared a covenant that would bless all nations. You veiled Your face from Moses in The Burning Bush and Israel witnessed You going the journey with them as the Cloud by day and The Pillar of Fire by night. Again, and again, whether a fiery furnace, a den of lions or the anointing of a shepherd boy with great courage to make him a King, you presented Yourself among those whom You love.

Oh, how generous are Your Blessings. You withhold nothing from Your Servants. When You determined the time was right, you presented again Your Presence among us. The shepherds quaked at Your entrance. And learned men searched for You, as all who are wise do, they still seek You. You were found in a stable, clothed in the flesh of a child. You placed Yourself in the arms of a virgin girl and guarded by her love even though tens of thousands of Angels stood near.

O Great and Magnificent God, the rational mind cannot imagine Your Will, yet and still, My Father You my Lord, waiver not with Your intervention for mankind. At Calvary You delivered on Your Promise that Jesus would save Your people from their sins.

Oh, what great hope we gain when we celebrate Your Life. You my Lord established Your victory over the grave and death became Your footstool. Now my Lord how well Heaven celebrates Your Coronation, when You took Your Rightful Place at the Throne of Your Father. Today while we rejoiced at the birth of Emmanuel, all is prepared, nothing hinders. Now we wait for You to raise the final curtain. Our expectations of great joy reverberate over this world You named Earth. We long for our returning King to unveil His Glory before our human eyes. I pray even so, let it be, come quickly Lord. In Jesus Name. Amen

Day Twenty-eight

Dearest Lord my Heavenly Father, you my Lord have joined me to a great inheritance. By Your Grace eternity has begun and Thy Glory has filled my soul. Your perfect love casts out fear.

Father I pray for those whom are bound in fear. They have no peace. They cannot trust, no.... not even The Lord. This is a suffering for which there is no medical help. Only You my Father have power over fear.

Today I pray for Your mercy and grace towards all whom hide from their own darkness. Let the Glory of Your Presence light their lives. Let the Wisdom from Above incarcerate their fears, for they cannot overcome in their own strength.

"For the wise are mightier than the strong, and those with knowledge grow stronger and stronger." Thank You O Mighty God in the Name of Jesus. Amen

Day Twenty-nine

Dearest Father, You O Lord are the Glory and The Lifter of my head. You are The Wisdom of the Ages, The Ancient of Days. You my Lord redeemed Your first man Adam by covering his sins. You gave Noah Your plans and saved him from Your Judgements. For Your friend Abraham, you declared a covenant that would bless all nations. You veiled Your face from Moses in The Burning Bush and Israel witnessed You going the journey with them as the Cloud by day and The Pillar of Fire by night. Again, and again, whether a fiery furnace, a den of lions or the anointing of a shepherd boy with great courage to make him a King, you presented Yourself among those whom You love.

Oh, how generous are Your Blessings. You withhold nothing from Your Servants. When You determined the time was right, you presented again Your Presence among us. The shepherds quaked at Your entrance. And learned men searched for You, as all who are wise do, they still seek You. You were found in a stable, clothed in the flesh of a child. You placed Yourself in the arms of virgin girl and guarded by her love even though tens of thousands of Angels stood near.

O Great and Magnificent God, the rational mind cannot imagine Your Will, yet and still, You my Lord, waiver not with Your intervention for mankind. At Calvary, you delivered on Your Promise that Jesus would save Your people from their sins.

Oh, what great hope we gain when we celebrate Your Life. You my Lord established Your victory over the grave and death became Your footstool.

Now my Lord how well Heaven celebrates Your Coronation, when You took Your Rightful Place at the Throne of Your Father.

Today while we rejoiced at the birth of Emmanuel, all is prepared, nothing hinders. Now we wait for You to raise the final curtain. Our expectations of great joy reverberate over this world You named Earth. We long for our returning King to unveil His Glory before our human eyes. I pray even so, let it be, come quickly Lord Jesus. In Jesus Name. Amen

Day Thirty

Dearest Heavenly Father Lord of all Glory. Today my thoughts are upon Thy Glorious Son. When I consider His Glorious Victory, my heart cannot well express my gratitude.

While the enemies of His Cross hid in the shadows of evil, defiantly lurking and deviously waiting for any opportunity to engage with vigor against The Root of Jesse, The Lord of Heaven, Jesus would not bend to temptation but endured with Gallantry and Divine Poise.

When the Accuser of the Brethren with viper tongue waged slanderous charges against The Advocate of The Redeemed, Jesus waivered not, yet forever making intercession for us before the Judge of the Living and the Dead.

O how Great Art Thou my Dearest Lord Jesus. You came among us humbling Yourself to the flesh of a man and with mortal body You manifested The Glory of The Father and The Truth of The Highest.

My Lord for the joy that was set before You, you endured the Cross, you defeated him who had the power of death and bound the demon hoards to the eternal darkness of the damned. Overcoming, death, hell and the grave You took Your rightful place at The Right Hand of The Father. O how Great are You Lord.

Dearest Lord today we are celebrating more than Your Birth, yes Lord we are Glorifying Your unimaginable victory. Because of Your Grace and Your Mercy, we shall abide with You forever.

In Jesus Name, I pray. Amen

Day Thirty-one

Gracious Father Your generosity is renown. How awesome are the results of Your Amazing Grace? You have opened the treasures of Heaven to bless all whom seek You. To as many as have received Your Son, you have joined them to His inheritance.

Father Thy Goodness shall be spoken of in the courts of kings. Your Wonders shall be told by the village fathers. The sons and daughters of the faithful from every hamlet, town and city shall declare Your glory. All will see You at Your appearing will bow in adoration and confess You are The Lord of All. His Name Shall be Acclaimed as The Only Savior.

In this Season of Glad Tidings and Peace on earth may every person esteem their fellows with kindness and gentleness. May our words be filled with peace and wellness. Let our thoughts be as those of peacemakers, and may patience have its complete work in every life.

My Father there are no restraints on how much love can be offered. May it abound from house to house, and let every poet, musician and singer lift their words and songs with healing. May every thought and word be meant to bond us all as one family on earth. May every child born have an opportunity for peace? In Jesus Name. Amen

Thank You for Joining Me in Prayer.

OUR PHOTO GALLERY

Johnny and Judy Mays

Pa and Mama Mays

Mother and Dad

Robert, Gary, Tracey, Christopher, John Oliver

Libby Star

Judy and Johnny (2013)

Johnny Mays, Danny Hart,
Bob Ubanks, Merle Haggard

In Memorial

Bunny "Rest in Peace"

ENDNOTES

[i] http://radiostratosphere.com

[ii] Jackson's Military Road from Wikipedia, the free encyclopedia

[iii] Bob Wills song, "Roly Poly, daddy's little fatty, bet he's gonna be a man someday."

[iv] https://www.scribd.com/doc/251701141/country-history

[v] C-ration from Wikipedia, the free encyclopedia

[vi] https://www.bing.com/images/search?q=rabbit+tobacco+and+kudzu&qpvt=+Rabbit+Tobacco+and+Kudzu

[vii] http://www.cyberhymnal.org/htm/j/u/justasam.htm

[viii] http://all-that-is-interesting.com/hippie-communes

[ix] Dixie (song) from Wikipedia, the free encyclopedia

[x] https://www.letssingit.com/tom-t.-hall-lyrics-old-dogs-children-and-watermelon-wine-ht51wbk#axzz4uRv4GZBX

[xi] http://www.huffingtonpost.com/entry/all-about-mason-jars_us_55fc11dbe4b00310edf6a2a7

[xii] http://www.bamabirds.com/birdinfo/birdlist.htm

[xiii] Hank Williams from Wikipedia, the free encyclopedia

[xiv] https://www.azlyrics.com/lyrics/hankwilliams/imsolonesomeicouldcry.html

[xv] Alabama Hall of Fame is long with scores of actors, musicians, athletes, politicians and on and on it goes

[xvi] John of Gaunt from Wikipedia, the free encyclopedia

[xvii] Alabama Fever from Wikipedia, the free encyclopedia

[xviii] https://www.quora.com/How-is-Ancestry-com-affiliated-with-the-Mormon-Church

[xix] Paul Winchell from Wikipedia, the free encyclopedia

[xx] https://www.verywell.com/signs-you-are-an-introvert-2795427

[xxi] http://fiftiesweb.com/pop/prices-1953/

[xxii] http://teacher.scholastic.com/rosa/sittingdown.htm

[xxiii] Lion Oil from Wikipedia,

[xxiv] http://www.songfacts.com/detail.php?id=27680

[xxv] https://www.revolvy.com/topic/Western%20Flyer%20(bicycle)

[xxvi] https://en.wikipedia.org/wiki/Adrian_and_Blissfield_Rail_Road

[xxvii] https://en.wikipedia.org/wiki/Roy_Rogers

xxviii https://en.wikipedia.org/wiki/Champion_the_Wonder_Horse

xxix http://www.lingerandlook.com/Names/Cowboys.htm

xxx https://www.pinterest.com/pin/170010954656344028/?lp=true

xxxi https://en.wikipedia.org/wiki/Sun_Studio

xxxii https://en.wikipedia.org/wiki/RCA_Records

xxxiii https://en.wikipedia.org/wiki/History_of_radio

xxxiv https://en.wikipedia.org/wiki/White_Anglo-Saxon_Protestant

xxxv https://en.wikipedia.org/wiki/Sharecropping

xxxvi http://www.metrolyrics.com/busted-lyrics-ray-charles.html

xxxvii
https://answers.yahoo.com/question/index?qid=20140903222034AAY
VrRv

xxxviii https://en.wikipedia.org/wiki/Oral_Roberts

xxxix
https://www.revolvy.com/topic/Carling%20Brewing%20Company&ite
m_type=topic

xl http://www.allposters.com/-st/World-War-II-Propaganda-Vintage-
Art-Posters_c50710_.htm

xli https://en.wikipedia.org/wiki/Keesler_Air_Force_Base

xlii https://en.wikipedia.org/wiki/Route_66_(song)

xliii https://en.wikipedia.org/wiki/John_Gillespie_Magee_Jr.

xliv http://www.historynet.com/battle-of-wake-island

xlv
https://en.wikipedia.org/wiki/The_Teahouse_of_the_August_Moon_(
film)

xlvi https://en.wikipedia.org/wiki/California_Girls

xlvii http://www.nationalmuseum.af.mil/Visit/Museum-Exhibits/Fact-
Sheets/Display/Article/196058/lockheed-ec-121d-constellation/

xlviii http://www.songfacts.com/detail.php?lyrics=6361

xlix https://en.wikipedia.org/wiki/It_Is_No_Secret

l https://en.wikipedia.org/wiki/Stuart_Hamblen

li https://en.wikipedia.org/wiki/First_sergeant

lii http://lyrics.wikia.com/wiki/Elvis_Presley:Wooden_Heart

liii https://www.ptsd.va.gov/public/ptsd-overview/basics/what-is-
ptsd.asp

liv
http://www.usmilitariaforum.com/forums/index.php?/topic/256636-
a-vietnam-war-era-552nd-aew-c-big-eye-task-force-patch/

lv https://www.vocabulary.com/dictionary/platonic

lvi https://en.wikipedia.org/wiki/Beatnik

[lvii] https://en.wikipedia.org/wiki/Bad_Moon_Rising_(song)
[lviii] https://ryman.com/history/
[lix] https://en.wikipedia.org/wiki/Del_Reeves
[lx] http://www.allmusic.com/artist/don-chapel-mn0000144976
[lxi] https://en.wikipedia.org/wiki/Tie_A_Yellow_Ribbon_(Dawn_album)
[lxii]

https://en.wikipedia.org/wiki/Jesus_Is_Coming_Soon_(R._E._Winsett_song)
[lxiii] https://en.wikipedia.org/wiki/Jimmy_Snyder_(musician)
[lxiv] http://gaither.com/news/family-god-story-behind-song
[lxv] https://originofsongs.blogspot.com/2012/07/lighthouse.html
[lxvi] https://en.wikipedia.org/wiki/Paul_Westmoreland
[lxvii]

http://library.timelesstruths.org/music/His_Eye_Is_on_the_Sparrow/
[lxviii]

https://www.pbs.org/wnet/supremecourt/rights/landmark_roe.html
[lxix] https://en.wikipedia.org/wiki/Common_Sense_(pamphlet)
[lxx] https://en.wikipedia.org/wiki/Perestroika
[lxxi] https://en.wikipedia.org/wiki/Channel_Tunnel
[lxxii] http://biblehub.com/proverbs/18-16.htm
[lxxiii] https://en.wikipedia.org/wiki/Zaraysk_Kremlin
[lxxiv] http://amadeusacademy.ca/en/teaching-methodology-en/
[lxxv] https://en.wikipedia.org/wiki/Kolomna
[lxxvi] http://www.mcagov.org/
[lxxvii] http://www.lafcomerced.org/
[lxxviii]

https://www.musicnotes.com/sheetmusic/mtd.asp?ppn=MN0055287_U5

Made in the USA
San Bernardino, CA
12 December 2017